Hans G. Hoffmann

Lebendiges Englisch 1

Ein moderner Sprachkurs
für Schule, Beruf und Weiterbildung

Max Hueber Verlag

Hans G. Hoffmann

LEBENDIGES ENGLISCH 1

Ein moderner Sprachkurs für Schule, Beruf und Weiterbildung

Materialbeschaffung und Recherchen: Brigitte Hoffmann
Sprachliche Durchsicht und Beratung: John Curtis, Iris Owen, Adrian G. Phillips
Phonetische Durchsicht und Beratung: Graham Pascoe
Verlagsredaktion: Gernot Häublein
Umschlagentwurf und Layout: Karl Schaumann
Projektleitung: Roland Schäpers

Redaktionsschluß der 1. Auflage: Mai 1976

Dieses Lehrwerk berücksichtigt in Zielsetzung, Methodik und Aufbau die Grundlagenarbeiten des Deutschen Volkshochschul-Verbands ("VHS-Zertifikat Englisch 1") und des Europarats ("Threshold Level English") sowie die einschlägigen geltenden Lehrpläne der Länder-Kultusministerien.

2. Auflage

3. 2. 1.	Die letzten Ziffern
1988 87 86 85 84	bezeichnen Zahl und Jahr des Druckes.

Alle Drucke dieser Auflage können, da unverändert, nebeneinander benutzt werden.

Gesamtherstellung: Druckerei Ludwig Auer, Donauwörth · Printed in Germany
ISBN 3-19-002191-0

INHALTSVERZEICHNIS

Der Verlag dankt den folgenden Personen, Institutionen und Unternehmen für ihre freundliche Genehmigung zum Abdruck von Copyright-Material:

Amerikanische Botschaft (Bonn-Bad Godesberg): Foto S. 71_2
British Airways: Signets und Fahrpläne S. 54–55, Foto S. 56_2
British Broadcasting Corporation: Programmausschnitt aus "Radio Times" S. 19, Fotos S. 82 und 108_1
British Rail: Foto, Signets, Fahrpläne S. 34–37
British Tourist Authority: Fotos S. 6, 14_1, 14_2, 18, 26_1, 78_1, 78_2
Camera Press (London): Fotos S. 94_1 (Ethan A. Pussell), 94_2 (Linda McCartney), 108_2 (Karsh)
Deutsche Presse-Agentur: Foto S. 73
Ellefsen Photographe (Montreal): Foto S. 71_3
F. J. B. Hotels (Bournemouth): Karte S. 15
Michael Friedel (München): Umschlagfoto
Manfred Glück (München): Foto S. 74
Gernot Häublein (Riedmoos): Fotos S. 22_1, 26_2, 38_1, 51
Hans G. Hoffmann (Windeck): Fotos S. 10, 11, 14_3, 17, 19, 22_2, 23, 29, 30, 38_2, 42, 43, 50, 56_1, 59, 71_4, 75, 78_3, 79, 83, 86, 87, 88_2, 91, 94_3, 95, 98, 99, 106, 107, 112, 114, 115, 119, 122, 123
John James (City of Portland Photographer): Foto S. 71_1
Keystone Pressedienst: Foto S. 7
Northern Songs / ATV Music (Brighton): Liedtext S. 107 (John Lennon / Paul McCartney)
Newsweek: Foto S. 118 (Fred Leavitt); Texte S. 118 (verändert), 122 (die Geschichte 30A beruht in ihrem Hauptteil auf einer Kolumne von Stewart Alsop, *Newsweek*, 1969)
Philips (Hamburg): Foto Elektrorasierer S. 66
Picturepoint (London): Foto S. 110
Punch / Werner Lüning (Lübeck): Punch-Zeichnungen S. 21, 69, 76, 81, 90, 93, 102, 105, 113, 124, 125 (den meisten dieser Cartoons wurden entsprechend den methodischen Erfordernissen des Lehrbuchs andere als die Originaltexte unterlegt)
Ronson Products (Leatherhead): Foto elektr. Zahnbürste S. 66
Rotel Tours (Tittling): Foto S. 120
Sharp Electronics Europe (Hamburg): Foto Recorder S. 66
Süddeutscher Verlag Bilderdienst: Foto S. 88_1
Syndication International (London): Foto S. 96
The Daily Telegraph: Foto S. 46; Text S. 78 (verändert)
The New Inn (Winchelsea): Speisekarte S. 21
The Post Office (London): Realien S. 39, 41
The Samaritans: Abbildungen S. 62–64
The Star of India (London): Speisekarte S. 19
Westdeutscher Rundfunk: Foto S. 84

Die Zeichnungen S. 6, 7, 13, 26, 35, 52, 60, 67, 70, 72 wurden von Herbert Horn (München) angefertigt.

VORWORT

Das Lehrwerk **Lebendiges Englisch** ist für Jugendliche und Erwachsene geschrieben, die in überschaubarer Zeit und mit Vergnügen praktisch anwendbares Englisch lernen wollen.
Um diesen Anspruch zu erfüllen, geht dieser Sprachkurs in vieler Hinsicht neue Wege:

■ Er führt mit nur zwei Bänden zum Kenntnisstand des Mittleren Schulabschlusses bzw. des gleichwertigen Volkshochschul-Zertifikats Englisch 1. Je nach Intensität des Sprachunterrichts kann dieses anspruchsvolle Lernziel in 2–4 Jahren erreicht werden.

■ **Lebendiges Englisch** stellt das aktive, interessante und zunehmend "freier" werdende Gespräch zwischen den Lernenden (und dem Lehrer) in den Mittelpunkt. Dies wird durch Lektionsthemen und Übungsformen erreicht, die zur Meinungsäußerung in der Fremdsprache anregen und sie in reizvoller Vielfalt ermöglichen. Im Inhalt dieses Lehrwerks spiegelt sich die private und berufliche Umwelt des modernen Menschen mit ihren erfreulichen wie problematischen Seiten. Immer wieder werden die Lebensumstände deutschsprachiger und englischsprachiger Menschen zueinander in Beziehung gesetzt.

■ Dieser unmittelbar interessierenden Thematik entspricht beim Lernen ein schneller Wechsel von einer sprachlichen Aktivität zur anderen: Hören, Sprechen, Lesen, Schreiben; Fragen, Antworten, Zustimmen, Widersprechen, auf Texte / Bilder / Daten reagieren usw.

■ Dem Inhalt entspricht die realitätsnahe, abwechslungsreiche und durchgehend farbige Gestaltung, die dieses Lehrwerk vom Erscheinungsbild herkömmlicher Sprachlehrbücher wesentlich unterscheidet.

Lebendiges Englisch ist für den Klassenunterricht bestimmt, eignet sich mit Hilfe der Begleitmaterialien *Arbeitsbuch* und *Arbeitsbuch-Cassetten* aber auch besonders für begleitendes Lernen zu Hause und für das Selbststudium.

Im Text des Buches werden Symbole benutzt, die für die Arbeitstechnik wichtig sind:

ꝏ bedeutet: Zum entsprechenden Lektionsabschnitt liegen Tonaufnahmen vor, deren Einsatz vom Lehrer bzw. vom *Arbeitsbuch* gesteuert wird.

→ **6K** bedeutet: Vergleichen und lesen Sie Lektionsabschnitt 6K.

→ GI19 bedeutet: Vergleichen Sie im Arbeitsbuch Grammatikübersicht I, Abschnitt 19.

1

1A At the hotel

A Good morning, my name is Turner. Is there a letter for me?
B Mrs Mary Turner from Leeds?
A That's right.
B Yes, here's a letter for you, madam.
A Thank you.

1B What's your name?

A What's your name, please, sir?
B My name is Egli.
A And your first name, Mr Egli?
B My first name is Hans.
A Are you German, Mr Egli?
B No, I'm Swiss. I'm from Bern in Switzerland.
A Thank you, sir. Here's your ticket.

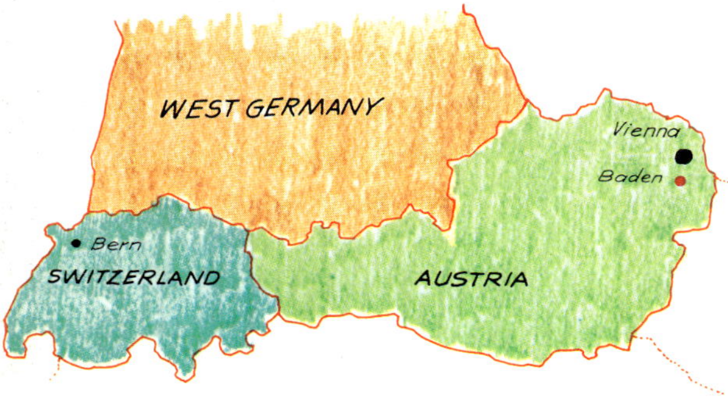

1C Where are you from?

A Where are you from, Miss Bauer?
B I'm from Baden.
A Baden? Where's that? In Germany?
B No, it's in Austria. It's a town near Vienna.
A Are you Austrian, Miss Bauer?
B Yes, I am. Baden is my home town.

1D How d'you do

A Mr Hill, this is my friend Rolf Schmidt.
B How d'you do.
C How d'you do.
B Are you from Germany, Mr Schmidt?
C Yes, I'm from Bamberg. That's a town in Bavaria.
B Is this your first visit to London?
C Yes, it is. I'm here on holiday.
B How nice. Have a good time here in London.
C Thank you.

1E Hello and good-bye

S Hello, Janet! What a surprise!
J Hello, Sandra! Nice to see you. How are you?
S Oh, fine, thanks. And you?
J I'm very well too, thank you. But how's your father? Is he still in hospital?
S No, he isn't. He's quite well again. His leg is much better. But he's alone at the moment. My mother is in Ireland with her sister.
J Oh, is she? – Well, I'm glad your father is all right. Please give him my regards. – There's my bus at last. Good-bye for now!
S Bye, Janet! All the best!

1 F **Fürwörter (Pronomen)** (→ GI19–20)

What is **your** name? *Wie ist Ihr Name?* Where are **you** from? *Wo sind Sie her?*	**My** name is Schmidt. *Mein Name ist S.* **I** am from Bamberg. *Ich bin aus B.*
His name is Egli. *Sein Name ist E.* **He** is from Bern. *Er ist aus Bern.*	**Her** name is Turner. *Ihr Name ist T.* **She** is from Leeds. *Sie ist aus Leeds.*

Put in: your, you, my, I, his, he, her, she.
a. Are ..... German, Miss Bauer? – No, ... am Austrian. b. Is there a letter for me? ..... name is Turner. c. Mr Egli is Swiss. ..... is from Bern in Switzerland. d. Where is your mother? – ..... is in Ireland with ..... sister. e. Is this ..... first visit to London? – Yes, ... am here on holiday. f. Is Mr Schmidt from Bamberg? – Yes, Bamberg is ..... home town.

1 G **Kurzformen** (→ GI18)

He's (= He is) quite well again. **She's** (= She is) in Ireland. **It's** (= It is) in Austria. **That's** (= That is) right. **What's** (= What is) your name?	**Here's** (= Here is) a letter for you. **There's** (= There is) my bus. **Where's** (= Where is) that? **How's** (= How is) your father? She **isn't** (= is not) here at the moment.
I'm (= I am) from Bern.	How **d'you** (= do you) do.

Use the short forms.
a. *Here is* your ticket, madam. – No, *that is* not my ticket. b. *What is* this? – *It is* a bus ticket. c. Are you Austrian? – No, *I am* Swiss. d. *Where is* your father? – *He is* in hospital. e. *There is* a letter for you, sir. f. *How is* your mother? – *She is* very well, thank you.

1 H **Please answer.**

Is Mrs Turner from Leeds? – Yes, she is.

a. Is Miss Bauer from Baden? b. Is Mr Egli Swiss? c. Is Bern in Switzerland? d. Is Sandra's father alone at the moment? e. Is Sandra's mother in Ireland? f. Is Baden near Vienna?

1 I **Please answer.** ꝏ

Is Miss Bauer German? – No, she isn't. She's Austrian.

a. Is Mrs Turner from Vienna? b. Is Bern in Austria? c. Is Mr Schmidt Swiss? d. Is Mr Egli's first name Rolf?

1 J **Put in: am, are, is.**

(→ GI9–10)

..... you from Switzerland, Miss Bauer?
No, I ..... from Austria.
Where in Austria ..... you from?
I ..... from Baden.
..... that near Vienna?
Yes, it ..... near Vienna.

1 K **Put in: at, from, in, near, on, to.**

a. Where are you ....., Mrs Turner? b. Are you here ..... holiday? c. Is this your first visit ..... London? d. Your ticket is ..... the hotel. e. Bamberg is a town ..... Bavaria. f. Baden is a town ..... Vienna. g. My mother is ..... hospital. h. My father is alone ..... the moment.

1 L **Questions on 1A–1E.**

a. What is Mrs Turner's first name? b. Where is Mrs Turner from? c. Is Mr Egli Swiss? d. Where is Bern? e. Where is Baden? f. Is Baden Miss Bauer's home town? g. Is Bamberg in Austria? h. Is Sandra's father still in hospital? i. Why is Sandra's father alone at the moment?

1 M **Questions in the classroom.**

What's your name?
And your first name?
Are you German?
Where are you from?
Is this your first English lesson?

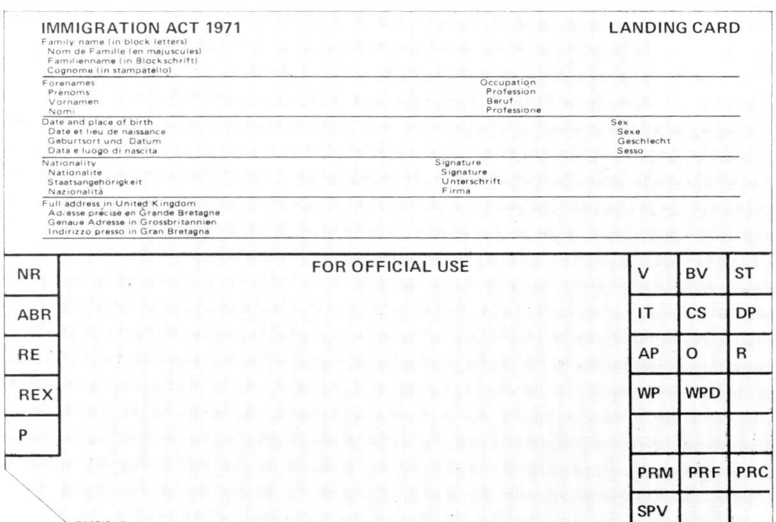

IMMIGRATION ACT 1971 LANDING CARD

Family name (in block letters)
Nom de Famille (en majuscules)
Familienname (in Blockschrift)
Cognome (in stampatello)

Forenames / Prénoms / Vornamen / Nomi
Occupation / Profession / Beruf / Professione

Date and place of birth / Date et lieu de naissance / Geburtsort und Datum / Data e luogo di nascita
Sex / Sexe / Geschlecht / Sesso

Nationality / Nationalite / Staatsangehörigkeit / Nazionalità
Signature / Signature / Unterschrift / Firma

Full address in United Kingdom / Adresse précise en Grande Bretagne / Genaue Adresse in Grossbritannien / Indirizzo presso in Gran Bretagna

FOR OFFICIAL USE

NR ABR RE REX P

V	BV	ST
IT	CS	DP
AP	O	R
WP	WPD	
PRM	PRF	PRC
SPV		

T112(3rd)

A letter from New York

2

2A

July 7, 1975

Dear Rita and Mark,

We are now in New York. It is very hot in the streets between the skyscrapers. But our hotel room is nice and cool - it is air-conditioned.

There are fine museums, bridges, and parks in New York. Central Park with its lakes and meadows and trees is a wonderful place to relax.

There are always surprises in New York - like the "Little Church Around the Corner" right in the middle of a lot of very tall buildings.

At the moment, many people are out of work here. There is too much crime. The streets are not only unsafe - they are dirty, too, because the dustmen are on strike. New York is a city full of problems.

With best wishes,
Yours,

Gabi and Carsten

New York:
streets between skyscrapers

A fine museum:
the Guggenheim Museum
on the edge of Central Park

2 B **Fürwörter (Pronomen)** (→ GI19–20)

Where are **you** at the moment? *Wo seid ihr im Augenblick?*
We are in New York. *Wir sind in New York.*

Is **your** hotel room air-conditioned? *Ist euer Hotelzimmer klimatisiert?*
Yes, **our** room is nice and cool. *Ja, unser Zimmer ist schön kühl.*

Where are Gabi and Carsten? *Wo sind Gabi und Carsten?*
They are in **their** room at the hotel. *Sie sind in ihrem Zimmer im Hotel.*

2 C **Put in: you, your, we, our, they, their. Write down the complete letter.**

Dear Rita and Mark,
Carsten and I are in New York at the moment.
New York in July is a very hot place, but ..... hotel room is nice and cool because it is air-conditioned.
The streets between the skyscrapers are very hot. ..... are dirty, too, because the dustmen are on strike.
The parks with ..... meadows and trees are very nice. ..... are often in Central Park.
Thank you for ..... letter from Austria. We are glad ..... are all well.
Yours,

Gabi and Carsten

Central Park: a wonderful place to relax

The dustmen are on strike

Brooklyn Bridge in New York

Right in the middle of a lot of very tall buildings: the "Little Church Around the Corner"

2D Plural der Substantive (→ GI1)

-s = [z]	-s = [s]	-es = [iz]
hotel – hotels *Hotels*	lake – lakes *Seen*	bus – buses *Busse*
meadow – meadows *Wiesen*	park – parks *Parks*	church – churches *Kirchen*
museum – museums *Museen*	street – streets *Straßen*	bridge – bridges *Brücken*
problem – problems *Probleme*	ticket – tickets *Karten*	place – places *Orte*
tree – trees *Bäume*	visit – visits *Besuche*	wish – wishes *Wünsche*

2E Talk about New York.

There are	(a lot of) (many)	good nice fine wonderful	?	in New York. in Central Park.

2F Please complete.

Gabi and Carsten ..... in New York.
In July ..... is very hot in New York, ... the hotels ..... nice and cool because ..... are air-conditioned.
..... are fine lakes and meadows and trees in Central Park.
The "Little Church Around the Corner" is ..... in the middle of a lot of very tall .....
At the moment, the streets are ..... because the dustmen are on .....

2G Please answer.

> Are Gabi and Carsten in New York? – Yes, they are.
> Is it very hot in the streets? – Yes, it is.
> Are there fine museums in New York? – Yes, there are.

a. Are the hotel rooms air-conditioned? b. Is Central Park a wonderful place to relax? c. Are there lakes and meadows in Central Park? d. Are the dustmen on strike? e. Are the streets dirty? f. Are many people out of work at the moment? g. Is New York a city full of problems? h. Are there always surprises in New York?

2H **Questions on 2A.**

a. Where are Gabi and Carsten?
b. Is it nice and cool in the streets between the skyscrapers?
c. Why is the hotel room nice and cool?
d. What is there in Central Park? – There are . . .
e. Why is the "Little Church Around the Corner" a surprise?
f. Why are the streets dirty?

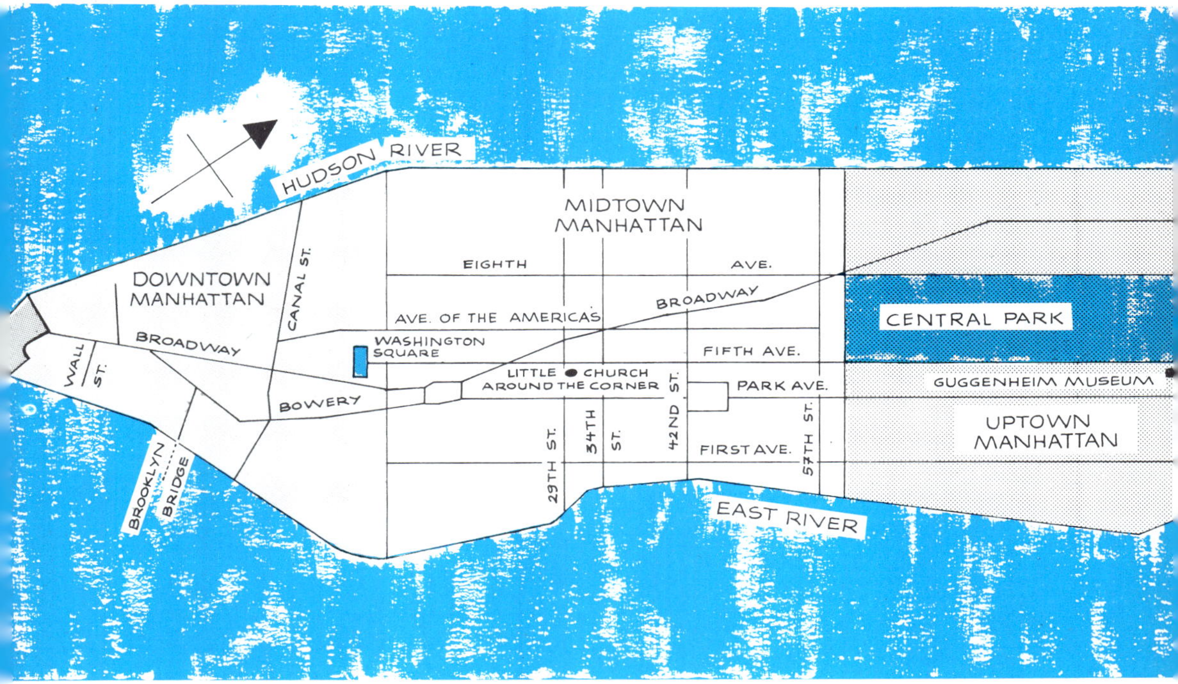

2I **Put in: at, between, from, of, on, out of.**

a. Is this their first letter ..... New York? b. The streets are so hot because they are ..... skyscrapers. c. The "Little Church Around the Corner" is right in the middle ..... a lot of very tall buildings. d. ..... the moment, many people are ..... work. e. The streets are dirty because the dustmen are ..... strike. f. New York is a city full ..... problems.

Calling from the seaside 3

3A

A Hello, Gerry. Ron here.

B Hello, Ron. Are you back at home at last?

A No, we're still in Swanage. It's just wonderful down here – we've got sunshine all day, the sea is nice and warm . . .

B Good hotel?

A Yes, very pleasant, and not too expensive. It has everything – a heated swimming pool, flower gardens, playgrounds for the children. And the food is good too.

B I'm glad you're all happy. What about tennis?

A The hotel has two tennis courts, but there are also lots of other things: table tennis, mini golf . . . they even have a motorboat for their guests.

B Have you got a pleasant room?

A Yes, it's large and quiet and it's got a balcony. It hasn't got a TV, thank goodness. The children are so busy they have no time for television anyway. – But how are you, Gerry?

B I've got a lot to do at the office. Everybody else is on holiday, you know . . .

3B **Questions on 3A.**

a. Where are Ron and his family?
b. Is the hotel good?
c. Is it expensive?
d. What has the hotel got for its guests?
e. What's the weather like in Swanage?
f. What's the sea like?
g. What's the food like?
h. What's their room like?
i. Is there a TV in the room?
j. Why have the children got no time for television?
k. Is Gerry on holiday too?

3C **Kurzformen** (→ GI18)

We're (= We are) still in Swanage. *Wir sind immer noch in Swanage.*
I'm glad **you're** (= you are) all happy. *Ich freue mich, daß ihr alle glücklich seid.*

We've (= We have) got sunshine all day. *Wir haben den ganzen Tag Sonnenschein.*
I've (= I have) got a lot to do at the office. *Ich habe im Büro viel zu tun.*

It **hasn't** (= has not) got a TV. *Es hat keinen Fernseher.*

's kann je nach Zusammenhang für *is* oder *has* stehen:

It's (= It is) just wonderful down here. *Es ist hier unten einfach herrlich.*
It's (= It has) got a balcony. *Es hat einen Balkon.*

Use the short forms.
a. *I am* glad *you are* all right. b. The sea *is not* very warm at the moment, but the hotel has a heated swimming pool. c. The hotel *has not* got a flower garden, but *it has* got a playground for the children. d. *They have* even got a motorboat for their guests. e. *We have* got a very nice room. f. It *has not* got a balcony, but *it is* large and quiet. g. *We are* so busy *we have* got no time for television. h. *You have* got a fine flower garden.

3D **Die Kurzform aren't** [ɑːnt]

The streets **aren't** (= are not) dirty.

Please answer.

Are the children busy? – No, they aren't. Are there skyscrapers in Swanage? – No, there aren't.

a. Are the streets in Swanage dirty? b. Are there many hotels in Swanage? c. Are the dustmen on strike in Swanage? d. Are there many people out of work? e. Are the rooms at the hotel air-conditioned? f. Are there many Germans at the hotel? g. Are the hotels very expensive there?

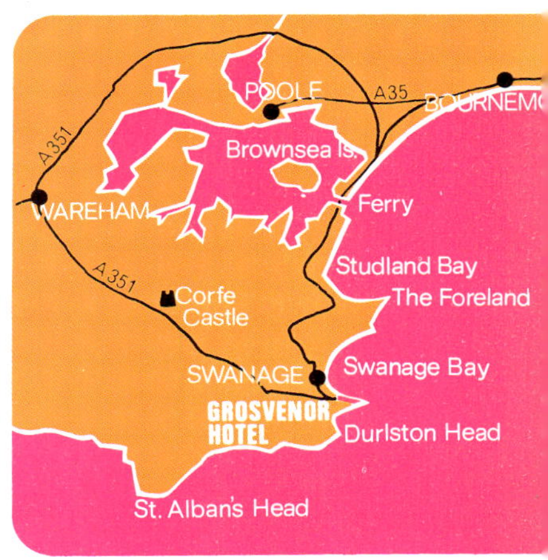

3E **Die Kurzform haven't** ['hævnt] ꝏ

We **haven't** (= have not) got a swimming pool. *Wir haben kein Schwimmbad.*

Please answer.

> Have you got a swimming pool? – No, we haven't.
> Have the Turners got a swimming pool? – No, they haven't.

a. Have you got a playground for children at this hotel? b. Have they got a motorboat for their guests? c. Have you got the flowers, Sandra? d. Have you got a letter for me? e. Have the children got their tickets?

3F **Have – has** (→ GI11)

Beachten Sie den Unterschied zwischen *have* und *has*:

I you we they	**have**	a nice room	he (= Ron) she (= Sandra) it (= the hotel)	**has**	a flower garden

Has steht bei *he/she/it* und bei Wörtern, die durch *he/she/it* ersetzt werden können.

Put in: have, has.
a. We ..... a very nice room. b. It ..... a balcony. c. We ..... sunshine all day. d. The hotel ..... a heated swimming pool and playgrounds for the children. e. They even ..... a motorboat for their guests. f. The children ..... no time for television. g. Gerry ..... a lot to do at the office. h. I ..... no problems.

3G **Have (got) / has (got)** (→ GI11–13)

Statt *have/has* wird umgangssprachlich auch häufig *have got / has got* gebraucht:

We have We've got (= We have got)	sunshine all day.	*Wir haben den ganzen Tag Sonnenschein.*
It has It's got (= It has got)	a balcony.	*Es hat einen Balkon.*

In Verneinung und Frage wird die Form mit *got* bevorzugt:

It **hasn't got** a TV. *Es hat keinen Fernseher.*
Have you **got** a nice room? *Habt ihr ein schönes Zimmer?*

3H Talk about your holiday in Swanage.

I	has got	a nice room.
We	's got	sunshine all day.
The hotel	hasn't got	no time for television.
Our room	have got	a balcony.
It	've got	a flower garden.
The children	haven't got	a heated swimming pool.
They		two tennis courts.

3I Please answer.

Have they got a motorboat?
Yes, they have.

a. Have they got sunshine all day? b. Have they got a nice room? c. Has the room got a balcony? d. Is the sea nice and warm? e. Is the hotel good? f. Has it got a swimming pool? g. Is the food good? h. Are the children busy all day?

3J Please answer.

Has the hotel got a golf course?
No, it hasn't.

a. Has it got a private beach? b. Has it got a cocktail bar? c. Is it expensive? d. Is there a tennis court? e. Have they got boats for their guests? f. Have the rooms got air conditioning? g. Have all the rooms got balconies? h. Has Ron got a TV in his room?

3K Everything or everybody?

Everything is wonderful here. *Hier ist alles herrlich.*
Everybody is happy here. *Hier ist jeder glücklich.*

Put in: everything, everybody.
a. ..... is busy at the moment. b. ..... is expensive in New York. c. I haven't got time for ..... d. Have you got ....., Ron? e. Has ..... got his ticket? f. This swimming pool is not for ..... – it's only for our guests.

4

4A Booking a room

A Have you got a double room for three nights?

B We have one twin-bedded room left, sir. It's on the ground floor.

A Oh, a twin-bedded room is all right. Has it got a bath?

B Yes, it has a bath, sir. And it's nice and quiet. It's at the back.

A That's fine. How much is it?

B It's eight pounds fifty, sir.

A What about breakfast? Is that included?

B Yes, of course, sir. A full English breakfast is included in the price.

4B A reservation letter

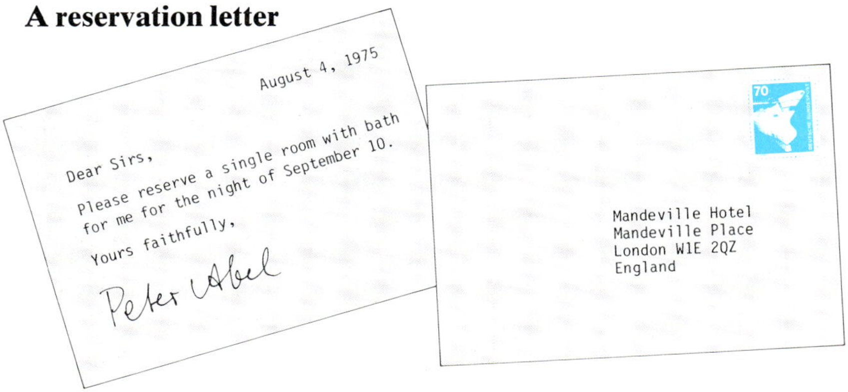

August 4, 1975

Dear Sirs,

Please reserve a single room with bath for me for the night of September 10.

Yours faithfully,

Peter Abel

Mandeville Hotel
Mandeville Place
London W1E 2QZ
England

4C Plans for the evening

Wife What shall we do tonight?

Husband We can watch television.

Wife We can't watch television every evening.

Husband What about a drink at the White Horse, then? I always have a lot of fun there.

Wife And what about me? How can I have fun in a pub? You can go there when I'm at my dressmaking class. Can't we go to a Chinese or Indian restaurant and have a good meal?

Husband Yes, that's a good idea. We can have dinner at the Star of India and watch the Midnight Movie on television afterwards.

SOUPS:	p
Dal Soup	15
Mulligatawny Soup	20

KEBABS:	
Seekh Kebab	60
Shamee Kebab	60
Nargis Kebab each	60
Reshmee Kebab	60
Tas Kebab	60
Turkish Kebab	75

FISH:	
Prawn Curry	85
Bhuna Prawn	90
Prawn Patia	90
Prawn Spinach	90
Madras Prawn	90
Shrimp Patia	90
Shrimp Curry	85
Scampi Curry	£1.00

CURRIES (Meat Dishes):	
Chicken Curry	85
Chicken Bhuna	90
Chicken Korma	90
Chicken Madras	90
Ceylon Chicken	90
Chicken Dhansak	£1.20

SWEETS:	p
Rasugolla	25
Gulabjam	25
Barfi	25
Jalebi	25
Mixed Sweet	35
Dahi (sweet or plain)	20

FRUITS:	
Pineapple	30
Lychees	30
Mango	30
Papaya	30
Guava	30
Fruit Salad	40
Ice Cream	20

HOT DRINKS:	
Coffee	20

ENGLISH DISHES:	
Roast Chicken, Chips & Peas (*Half Poussin*)	90

SPECIAL SERVICE FOR TAKE-AWAY FOOD

SATURDAY tv

BBC2

8.55 pm
2nd House 2nd Run
Introduced by **Melvyn Bragg**
Knots
To stop YOU *giving me a pain in the neck I protect my neck by tightening my neck muscles, which gives me the pain in the neck you are.*
A typical example of what psychiatrist **R. D. Laing** calls a 'knot.' His book was used as the basis for a stage play performed by the Actors Company.
DR LAING – his other books include *The Divided Self* and *The Politics of the Family* – wrote *Knots* in 1970. Since it is a very simple text, many people were puzzled as to what they should make of this one.
Laing says: 'I have always tried to write literature, regardless of what people thought I was doing, several people have said that they found it a relief to see something they recognised in their lives. It turns some of the agony into humour.'
The original stage adaptation was written by EDWARD PETHERBRIDGE. The film we are showing tonight was made by the ACTORS COMPANY and directed by DAVID I. MUNRO.
Cast:
CAROLINE BLACKISTON
PAOLA DIONISOTTI, SHARON DRUCE
ROBERT EDDISON, ROBIN ELLIS

10.55-1.30 am
Midnight Movie Fantastic
Caligari to Quatermass
The Cabinet of Dr Caligari
starring Werner Krauss

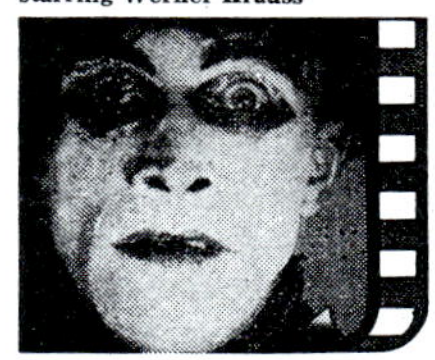

Conrad Veidt
The *Midnight Movie Fantastic* season begins with one of the most famous and influential films of all time, a haunting story of madness and murder. BBCtv's special presentation reproduces the highly atmospheric colour tinting of the original version.

Dr Caligari..........WERNER KRAUSS
Cesare....................CONRAD VEIDT
Francis................FRIEDRICH FEHER
Jane........................LIL DAGOVER
Alan.HANS HEINZ VON TWARDOWSKI
Dr Olson...........RUDOLF LETTINGER

4D Going to the theatre

A Where are the tickets?

B Haven't you got them?

A No, I haven't. But wait a moment. Perhaps they're in my other suit. – Yes, here they are.

B Let's get a move on. Mike is waiting for us.

4E **Kurzformen** (→ G I 18) ꝏ

We **can't** (= cannot) watch television.
They're (= They are) in my other suit.
Let's (= Let us) get a move on.

Use the short forms.
a. *We have* got two twin-bedded rooms left. b. *They are* on the ground floor. c. *Let us* book a double room for three nights. d. You *cannot* go to your dressmaking class tonight. e. *Let us* watch television tonight. f. *That is* a very good idea. g. We *cannot* have dinner here.

4F **Use the form with got.** ꝏ

We have one room left.
– **We've got** one room left.
It has a bath. – **It's got** a bath.

a. *I have* a letter for you.
b. *You have* a nice garden.
c. *He has* a lot of problems.
d. *She has* a surprise for you.
e. *It has* a bath and a balcony.
f. *We have* sunshine all day.
g. *They have* a heated swimming pool.
h. *She has* a TV in her room.

4G **Information about a hotel room**

One student is a guest (A); another student is the clerk (B).

A	Has it got Is it	a balcony / a bath / a TV? a double room? a twin-bedded room? air-conditioned? at the back / quiet? on the ground floor?

B	Yes, (of course) No,	it has. it hasn't. it is. it isn't.

4H **What about . . .?** ꝏ

What about a drink at the pub?
Yes, that's a good idea. Let's have a drink at the pub.

a. (a good meal at a Chinese restaurant) b. (a cocktail in the bar) c. (a swim in the sea) d. (a holiday at the seaside) e. (a game of chess) f. (breakfast in bed)

4I **Make plans for the evening.**

(watch TV)
A Shall we watch TV?
B No, we can't always watch TV.
A Why can't we watch TV?

a. (have dinner at a restaurant) b. (have a drink with the Turners) c. (go to the White Horse) d. (go to the theatre) e. (watch the Midnight Movie)

4J Breakfast at the hotel.

BREAKFAST MENU

Fruit Juice · Fresh Grapefruit
Corn Flakes · Porridge

Grilled Bacon, Sausage and Tomato
Grilled Bacon, Sausage and Fried Egg

Toast with Marmalade or Jam
Tea · Coffee

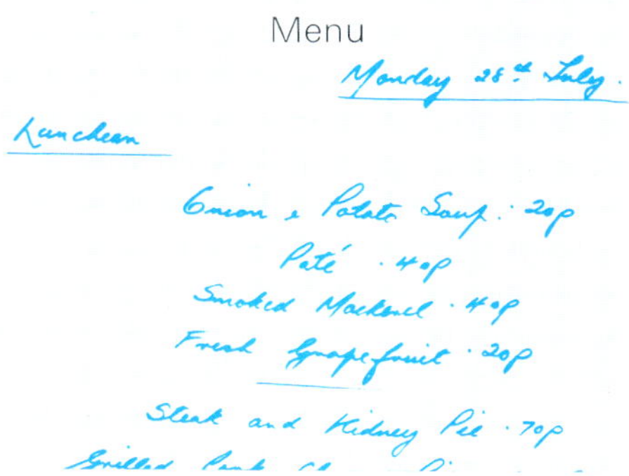

Order from the breakfast menu.

What will you have, madam/sir?
I'll (= I will) have . . .

4K Please complete.

What we do in the evening
We often ..... to the park to ..... there.
Sometimes we have a ..... at the White Horse.
We always ..... a lot of fun at the pub.
Or we ..... to a restaurant and ..... a good meal.
Or we have a ..... of chess.
Sometimes we ..... the Midnight Movie on .....

A good meal at a restaurant . . .

4L **Wortstellung** (→ GII42–43)

Zeit- od. Orts-bestimmung	Subjekt	Verb	Objekt	Ortsbestimmung	Zeitbestimmung
	We	have	sunshine		all day.
At the moment,	I	have	a lot to do	at the office.	
At the hotel	we	can('t) watch	television		every evening.
	We	can('t) have	dinner	at a restaurant	tonight.
	We	can watch	the movie	on television	afterwards.

Please translate.
a. Wir können heute abend in ein chinesisches Restaurant gehen. b. Danach können wir uns den späten Film im Fernsehen anschauen. c. Im Hotel haben sie in jedem Zimmer einen Fernseher. d. Wir können nicht jeden Abend fernsehen.

"I'm ringing from a phone box in Piccadilly."

"I'm staying at a hotel near Oxford Street."

5

5A In London

H Hello, Susan, this is Helga. I'm in London.
S You're in London? What a surprise! Where are you ringing from?
H From a phone box in Piccadilly. I'm staying at a hotel near Oxford Street.
S What are you doing here in London? Are you working or just having a holiday?
H I'm taking an English course at a language school in Oxford Street. They're running one of those intensive courses, you know – business English, very advanced stuff . . .
S I see. Then you must be pretty busy. But all the same, you must come and see us soon. Can you come round to dinner tomorrow evening?
H Oh, that's a lovely idea. At what time?
S Any time after six. Is that all right?
H Yes, fine. Good-bye, Susan!
S Bye for now! See you tomorrow.

5B Questions on 5A. One student asks another.

a. Where is Helga?
b. Who is she ringing?
c. Where is she ringing from?
d. Where is she staying?
e. What is she doing in London?
f. Where are they running intensive courses?

5C Talking about Helga

Susan Oh, by the way, my German friend Helga is here in London at the moment.
Brian Oh, is she? What's she doing here?
Susan She's taking a course at the Ashley School of English in Oxford Street. It's an intensive course.
Brian An intensive course? How many hours is that?
Susan Between 15 and 30 a week.
Brian Good heavens! That's hard work. Is English that important to her?
Susan Oh yes, it is. After all, she's got a top job with an American company in Germany. Her English has to be very good.
Brian Where's she staying?
Susan At a hotel not far from the school. It isn't cheap, but her company is paying for everything.

5D **Questions on 5C. One student asks another.**

a. Where is Helga taking an English course?
b. Why is it hard work?
c. Why is English very important to her?
d. Who is paying for the hotel and English course?

5E **Please answer.**

What's Helga doing here? (take an English course) She's taking an English course.

a. What's Susan doing? (wait for Mike) b. What's Ron doing in Swanage? (just have a holiday) c. What are the children doing? (watch television) d. What are you doing? (talk about our English course) e. What's Gerry doing at the White Horse? (have a drink with Ron) f. What are Gabi and Carsten doing? (relax in the park)

London: Oxford Street

5F **Verlaufsform** (→ GII28)

I'm staying at a hotel near Oxford Street.
Ich wohne ("bin wohnend") in einem Hotel in der Nähe der Oxford Street.

I'm taking an English course at a language school in Oxford Street.
Ich besuche ("bin besuchend") einen Englischkurs an einer Sprachschule . . .

What **are** you **doing** here in London?
Was machst du ("bist du machend") hier in London?

Durch die Verlaufsform wird der vorübergehende Charakter einer Handlung hervorgehoben. Das Geschehen "läuft gerade ab". Ähnlich in einigen deutschen Mundarten: *Er ist (gerade) am/beim Arbeiten. (= He is working.)*

5G **Please answer.**

Where are you ringing from? (from a phone box in Piccadilly)
I'm ringing from a phone box in Piccadilly.

a. Where are you staying? (at a hotel near Oxford Street) b. Where are they running an intensive course? (at the Ashley School of English) c. Where's he waiting? (in the bar) d. Where's she working? (in her office) e. Where are they having dinner? (at the Star of India) f. What are you talking about? (hotels in New York) g. What are the children watching? (the Midnight Movie) h. What is the company paying for? (the hotel and the English course) i. Who's Janet ringing? (her mother in Leeds)

5H **A oder an?**

a [ə]	**an** [ən]
a company, **a** Swiss company	**an** American company
a course, **a** language course	**an** English course
a holiday course	**an** intensive course
a nice office, **a** large office	**an** office
a pleasant surprise	**an** unpleasant surprise

A steht vor Wörtern, deren gesprochene Form mit einem Mitlaut beginnt.
An steht vor Wörtern, deren gesprochene Form mit einem Selbstlaut (*a, e, i, o, u*) beginnt.

Put in: a, an.

a. English is ..... important language, ... very important language. b. Sandra is taking ..... evening course in German at ..... language school in Oxford Street. c. Is Baden ..... Swiss town or ..... Austrian town? d. Have you got ..... quiet room with ..... bath? e. Can you come round for ..... hour or two? f. Shall we go to ..... Chinese restaurant? – No, let's go to ..... Indian restaurant. g. They are staying at ..... expensive hotel near Piccadilly.

5I [ðə] **oder** [ði]?

the = [ðə]	**the** = [ði]
the school	**the** Ashley School of English
the language	**the** English language
the holiday course	**the** intensive course
the Piccadilly Hotel	**the** Oxford Hotel
the London office	**the** office
the happy children	**the** unhappy children

Vor Wörtern, deren gesprochene Form mit einem **Mitlaut** beginnt, wird *the* normalerweise [ðə] gesprochen.
Vor Wörtern, deren gesprochene Form mit einem **Selbstlaut** (*a, e, i, o, u*) beginnt, wird *the* normalerweise [ði] gesprochen.

Read these sentences aloud. QO

a. Where's *the* Ashley School of English? b. It's not far from *the* hotel. c. Is Helga taking *the* intensive course? d. What's *the* company paying for? e. Are you taking *the* cheap or *the* expensive room? f. Can we have *the* twin-bedded room at *the* back? g. *The* other room is air-conditioned. h. What are your plans for *the* evening? i. Let's have a drink at *the* White Horse. j. *The* Indian restaurant around *the* corner is very good. k. Shall we watch *the* Midnight Movie tonight?

5J **Personalpronomen: Objektfall** (→ GI19)

This is	for **me.**	*mich*
	for **you.**	*dich/Sie/euch*
	for **him.**	*ihn*
	for **her** (= Rita).	*sie (Rita)*
	for **us.**	*uns*
	for **them** (= Kay & Ron).	*sie (Kay & Ron)*

Put in: me, you, him, her, us, them.

a. Are you still out of work? I've got a job for ..... b. She's got a job with an American company, so English is very important to ..... c. Where are the tickets? Have you got .....? d. I must have a room for three nights. Can you book one for .....? e. We must get a move on. Mike is waiting for ..... f. I'm glad your father is quite well again. Please give ..... my regards. g. We're always at home. You must come and see ..... soon.

6

6A Eating out

Waiter Can I take your order, sir?

Customer Yes . . . I think I'll have a tomato soup to start with.

Waiter One tomato soup, yes, sir.

Customer And then I'd like a fillet steak . . .

Waiter Large or medium, sir?

Customer Medium, please. And I'd like it well done.

Waiter Very well, sir.

Customer What do you serve with the steak?

Waiter We serve all grills with lettuce and grilled tomatoes, sir.

Customer Oh, then that's fine. Can I have some chips as well?

Waiter Certainly, sir. Would you like anything to drink?

Customer What kind of beer do you have?

Waiter We've got lager and bitter, sir.

Customer Then I'll have a half of bitter, please.

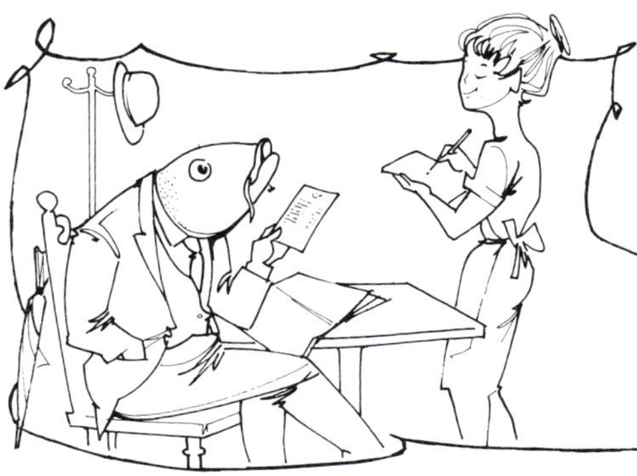

6B A misunderstanding?

Customer Do you serve fish here?

Waitress Yes, we do. – We serve everyone.

6C Sorry, no cream

Waitress What will you have, sir?

Customer Bring me a cup of coffee and a cheese sandwich, please. – Oh and I'd like the coffee without cream, please.

Waitress I'm sorry, sir, we haven't got any cream. But I can give you coffee without milk.

6D Lunch in a restaurant

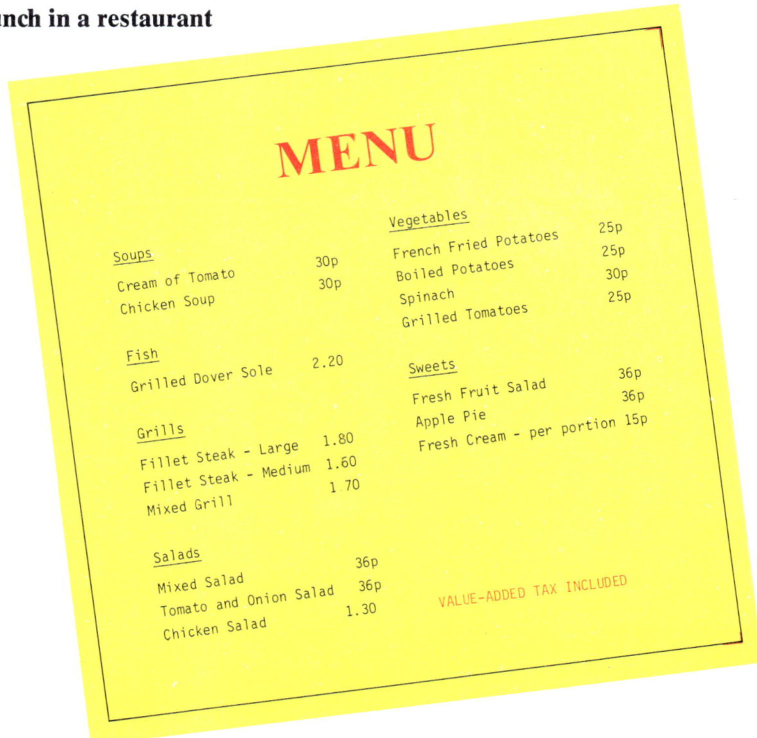

MENU

Soups
Cream of Tomato 30p
Chicken Soup 30p

Fish
Grilled Dover Sole 2.20

Grills
Fillet Steak - Large 1.80
Fillet Steak - Medium 1.60
Mixed Grill 1 70

Salads
Mixed Salad 36p
Tomato and Onion Salad 36p
Chicken Salad 1.30

Vegetables
French Fried Potatoes 25p
Boiled Potatoes 25p
Spinach 30p
Grilled Tomatoes 25p

Sweets
Fresh Fruit Salad 36p
Apple Pie 36p
Fresh Cream - per portion 15p

VALUE-ADDED TAX INCLUDED

One student is the waiter or waitress, another the customer.

What will you have, What would you like to have, Can I take your order,	madam? sir?	(Yes,)	(I think)	I'll have I'll take I'd like	a(n) . . . the . . .

6E Geldbeträge

15p fifteen p(ence)	£1.30 one pound thirty / one pound (and) thirty p(ence)
30p thirty p(ence)	£1.60 one pound sixty / one pound (and) sixty p(ence)
25p twenty-five p(ence)	£1.70 one pound seventy / one pound (and) seventy p(ence)
36p thirty-six p(ence)	£1.80 one pound eighty / one pound (and) eighty p(ence)
	£2.20 two pounds twenty / two pounds (and) twenty p(ence)

Ask the prices of the dishes on the menu (→ 6D).

How much is the chicken soup? – It's thirty p(ence), madam / sir.
How much are the chips? – They're twenty-five p(ence), madam / sir.

6F One student is the waiter or waitress, another the customer.

bacon / sausages
Would you like some bacon?
Yes, please. And can I have some sausages as well?

a. potatoes / tomatoes
b. chips / spinach
c. fruit salad / cream
d. coffee / apple pie
e. toast / jam

6G Grundzahlen

1 one	11 eleven	21 twenty-one
2 two	12 twelve	30 thirty
3 three	13 thirteen	35 thirty-five
4 four	14 fourteen	40 forty
5 five	15 fifteen	48 forty-eight
6 six	16 sixteen	50 fifty
7 seven	17 seventeen	60 sixty
8 eight	18 eighteen	70 seventy
9 nine	19 nineteen	80 eighty
10 ten	20 twenty	90 ninety

Please answer.

How many rooms do you need? (5)
I need five.

a. How many eggs do you want? (12)
b. How many tickets have you got? (10)
c. How many children have they got? (4)
d. How many courses are there? (16)
e. How many people are there in your class? (22)
f. How much is this room? (£7)
g. At what time can I come? (3)
h. What's the house number? (89)
i. What's your room number? (51)

6H At a hotel

Tourist What time do you serve meals?

Clerk Well, breakfast is from seven to ten thirty, lunch is from twelve to three, and dinner is from six to nine thirty.

Tourist There's not much time for sightseeing, is there?

6I

Meals are served at the following times

Breakfast	7.30 a.m.	-	10.00 a.m.
Sunday	8.15 a.m.	-	10.30 a.m.
Lunch	12.30 p.m.	-	2.30 p.m.
Sunday	12.30 p.m.	-	2.00 p.m.
Dinner	6.30 p.m.	-	9.30 p.m.
Sunday	7.00 p.m.	-	9.00 p.m.

You are a hotel guest, another student is the clerk. Ask questions and give answers like the following.

Guest: What time do you serve breakfast?
Clerk: From seven thirty to ten, madam/sir.
Guest: And on Sundays?
Clerk: From eight fifteen to ten thirty.

6J Fragesätze mit do (→ GI7)

What **do you serve** with the steak? *Was servieren Sie ("tun Sie servieren") ...?* What kind of beer **do you have**? *Was für Bier haben Sie ("tun Sie haben")?*	What **can I have** with the steak? **Would you like** some bacon? How much **is the chicken soup**? What kind of beer **have you got**?

Normalerweise wird die Frageform mit *do* gebildet (→ 7F, 7H).

Bei *am, are, is, can, must, shall, will, would* und bei *have got* wird nicht mit *do* umschrieben.

6K Practise questions and answers with do.

Do	you they	drink have run serve want	a cheese sandwich? a lot to do at the office? enough time for sightseeing? intensive courses? the steak with grilled tomatoes? your coffee with milk? your steak well done?	Yes,	I we they	do.

Shopping 7

7A

(A = Assistant, C = Customer)

A Good morning, madam. Can I help you?

C Yes, please. I'm looking for a book about London.

A Do you want a guide of some sort? This little red book here is one of the best. Everybody uses it – even policemen and taxi drivers.

C Yes, I know it's very good – I've already got it. You see, I don't actually want a guide. I'm looking for a book with photos to give my husband when I get back to Germany.

A I see. – Then have a look at this book here. It shows all the London sights in colour, and the texts are not only in English but in German and French as well.

C Oh, the pictures are really splendid – I think I'll take it. – But there's something else. You know, I'm interested in ghosts and such things. Do you have any books about . . . er . . . haunted houses . . . er . . . a kind of guide to haunted houses here in London?

A Haunted houses? Well, there must be hundreds of them in this city. But I don't think we have a book on the subject . . . Oh yes, we do! – This paperback here tells you a lot about ghosts and haunted places. The author is President of the Ghost Club, so he knows his stuff.

C How much does it cost?

A Sixty p, madam.

7B **Questions on 7A. One student asks another.**

a. What is the customer looking for? b. Is the customer a man or a woman? c. Does she want a guide? d. Which is one of the best guides to London? e. Do only tourists use the little red guide? f. How does the customer know that Nicholson's guide is very good? g. Who does she want a book with photos for? h. The assistant shows the customer a book about London. What is good about this book? i. What else is the customer interested in? j. What is the title of the paperback? k. Why does the assistant say the author "knows his stuff"? l. How much does *Haunted London* cost?

7C **Die -s-Form des Verbs** (→ GI3)

Ohne **-s**			Mit **-s**		
I you we they (= taxi drivers)	**use**	it	he (= the taxi driver) she (= the waitress) it (= the hotel) everybody	**uses**	it

Die *-s*-Form steht bei *he/she/it* und bei Wörtern, die durch *he/she/it* ersetzt werden können. (→ 3F)

7D **Aussprache der -s-Form**

-s = [z]	answers, brings, comes, gives, knows, pays, reads, reserves, rings, runs, sees, serves, shows, stays, tells
-s = [s]	completes, costs, gets, helps, likes, looks, makes, puts, takes, talks, thinks, translates, waits, wants
-es = [iz]	practises, relaxes, uses, watches

7E **Add a sentence with too.**

> I use the little red guide. (my wife)
> My wife uses it too.

a. I know the President of the Ghost Club. (Gerry) b. I like their children. (my wife) c. They come here every Sunday. (Janet's sister) d. I drink whisky. (my friend) e. The book costs a lot of money. (the course) f. I often watch television. (my father) g. I want a quiet room. (Mr Turner) h. We have a lot of problems. (the Ashley School)

7F **Die -s-Form von do** (→ 6J)

How much does [dəz] this book here cost? (sixty p)
It costs sixty p.

Please answer.
a. What does he want? (a fillet steak) b. What does this picture show? (a London museum) c. What does she drink? (lager) d. How much does he know? (everything) e. What does he read? (books about ghosts) f. Where does she stay when she is in London? (at the Mandeville Hotel) g. What does the company pay for? (the course and the hotel room)

7G **One student asks a question, another student answers.**

a. What's one of the best guides to London? b. Who's President of the Ghost Club? c. What's *Haunted London*? d. Where's Swanage? e. What's the name of an interesting church in New York? f. What's the name of a very large park in New York? g. Where's the White House? h. Who's President of the United States? i. What's the President's first name?

7H **Verneinte Sätze mit don't** (→ GI8)

I **don't** want a guide.
Ich will keinen ("tue nicht wollen einen") Führer.

I **don't** think we have a book on the subject.
Ich glaube nicht ("tue nicht glauben"), daß . . .

Normalerweise wird die verneinte Form mit *don't* (= *do not*) gebildet (→ 6J).

There**'s not** / There **isn't** much time.
We **can't** watch TV every evening.
We **haven't** got any cream.

Bei *am, are, is, can, must, shall, will, would* und bei *have got* wird die verneinte Form nicht mit *don't* gebildet.

7I Please answer.

> Do you want a guide of some sort? – No, I don't.
> Can you do it at the office? – No, I can't.
> Have you got the text in English? – No, I haven't.
> Are you looking for a taxi? – No, I'm not.

a. Do you know this book? b. Do you have any books about haunted houses? c. Do you often watch TV? d. Do you like the school? e. Can you translate this for me? f. Can you give me five pounds? g. Have you got the tickets? h. Have you got a picture of the Little Church Around the Corner? i. Are you interested in ghosts? j. Are you very busy at the moment?

7J One student asks a question, another student answers.

> What are you looking for? (a book about London)
> I'm looking for a book about London.

a. What's the company paying for? (the hotel room and the English course) b. Where are you ringing from? (a phone box in Piccadilly) c. What are you interested in? (ghosts and such things) d. Who's this boat for? (the children) e. Who's Mike waiting for? (his wife) f. Who are you booking the room for? (Mr Ronald Taylor from Leeds)

7K One student asks a question, another student answers.

Where do you live?	I live in . . .
Do you work in . . . too?	Yes, I do. / No, I don't. I work in . . .
How do you travel to work?	I go to work by bus / by tram / by car / by train / by underground / on foot.
When do you start work in the morning?	I start work at seven / seven thirty / eight / eight thirty . . .
Do you have lunch at work?	Yes, I do. / No, I don't. I have lunch at home / at a restaurant . . .
When do you stop work in the afternoon?	I stop work at four thirty / five / five thirty . . .
When do you get home?	I get home at . . .
What do you do in the evening?	I watch television / go to my English class / read a book / read a newspaper / listen to music / go for a walk / go to the pub . . .
What are you interested in?	I'm interested in sport / gardening / politics / languages / music / foreign countries . . .

8 Calling passenger inquiries

8A

A Passenger inquiries. May I help you?

B Yes, please. What time is there a train to Swanage in Dorset tomorrow?

A Well, you can't go to Swanage direct by train, sir, but if you hold on a moment, I'll tell you the best way to get there.

B Yes, thank you.

A . . . What you do, sir, is you go to Wareham, and Swanage is eleven miles from Wareham. From Wareham station it's a journey of thirty-six minutes by bus . . .

London and Southampton to Bournemouth and Weymouth

London Waterloo	10 30		11 30			12 30		13 30	
Southampton	11 42	12 26	12 42			13 42	14 26	14 42	
Bournemouth	12 16	13 03	13 16			14 16	15 03	15 16	
Branksome	12 21		13 21			14 21		15 21	
Parkstone			13 24					15 24	
Poole	12 27	13 13	13 28			14 27	15 13	15 28	
Hamworthy			13 33					15 33	
Holton Heath									
Wareham	12 38		13 40			14 38		15 40	
Wool	12 46		13 48			14 46		15 48	
Moreton			13 56					15 56	
Dorchester South	13 00		14 04	14k39		15 00		16 04	16 20
Upwey & Broadwey				14 47					16 28
Radipole				14 50					16 32
Weymouth	13 11		14 15	14 53		15 11		16 15	16 35

Mondays to Fridays

B I see.

A . . . and the buses go about every one to two hours.

B Yes . . .?

A So, shall I give you the times to Wareham?

B Yes, please do.

A Tomorrow, what time, sir?

B Around lunchtime.

A If you leave at eleven thirty from Waterloo, you'll arrive in Wareham at one forty.

B Anything a little later?

A If you leave at twelve thirty, you'll get to Wareham at two thirty-eight.

B That'll do very nicely. Thank you very much for your help.

A Not at all, sir. Good-bye.

B Good-bye.

8B

Passenger Excuse me, when's the next train to Oxford, please?
Railway official Fourteen oh five, sir.
Passenger What, isn't there one before that?
Railway official No, sir, we never run one before the next one.

8C

Passenger Excuse me, how long do we stop at York?
Railway official From two to two two.

8D **Questions on 8A. One student asks another.**

a. Where does the passenger want to go?
b. Where is Swanage?
c. Can you go to Swanage direct by train?
d. Where do you go from London to get to Swanage?
e. How far is it from Wareham to Swanage?
f. How do you travel from Wareham to Swanage?
g. How long does it take to travel from Wareham to Swanage by bus?
h. How often do the buses go?
i. When will you arrive in Wareham if you leave at eleven thirty from Waterloo?
j. What is Waterloo?
k. When will you get to Wareham if you leave at twelve thirty?

8E **Die Kurzform 'll** (→ GI18)

I'll (= I will) tell you the best train. *Ich werde Ihnen den besten Zug sagen.*
You'll (= You will) arrive at one forty. *Sie werden um dreizehn Uhr vierzig ankommen.*
That'll (= That will) do very nicely. *Das genügt mir vollkommen.*

Use the short forms.
a. I think *I will* take the later train. b. *You will* get lunch on the train. c. Ask the official. *He will* help you. d. *She will* arrive at two minutes to two. e. *It will* be thirty minutes by bus. f. *We will* leave at two twenty from Waterloo. g. *They will* take the bus from Wareham station. h. *That will* cost a lot of money. i. *What will* you do without a car?

8F

DEPARTURES				
Time 15 08	Time 15 10	Time 15 14	Time 15 19	Time 15 36
Platform 1	Platform 2	Platform 3	Platform 4	Platform 5
DARTFORD	SANDWICH	GRAVESEND	SEVENOAKS	RAMSGATE
Via Greenwich	Via Folkestone	Via Bexleyheath	Via Orpington	Via Chatham
Calling at London Bridge	Not calling at London Bridge	Calling at London Bridge	Calling at London Bridge	Calling at London Bridge
All trains call at Waterloo				

Charing Cross Station in London. One student is a passenger, another a railway official.

A What time does the train for Dartford leave?
B Fifteen oh eight.
A At eight minutes past three? I see. – Which platform, please?
B Platform one.
A Does the train go via Greenwich?
B Yes, it does.
A Does it stop at London Bridge?
B Yes, it does.

Now you go on with the trains for Sandwich, Gravesend, Sevenoaks, and Ramsgate.

8G **At various times during the English lesson, students ask one another:**
What time is it, please?
It's . . .

6.00	6:00	06 00	It's six o'clock.
6.01	6:01	06 01	It's one minute past six.
6.05	6:05	06 05	It's five (minutes) past six.
6.10	6:10	06 10	It's ten (minutes) past six.
6.15	6:15	06 15	It's (a) quarter past six.
6.30	6:30	06 30	It's half past six.
6.42	6:42	06 42	It's eighteen minutes to seven.
6.45	6:45	06 45	It's (a) quarter to seven.
6.50	6:50	06 50	It's ten (minutes) to seven.
6.55	6:55	06 55	It's five (minutes) to seven.

8H

St. Pancras	Nottingham	
00.05	03.11	MO B
06.50	09.29	B
07.50	**10.07**	A
09.05	**11.12**	✕ ☕
09.35	**12.19**	
10.05	12.19	B ✕ ☕
11.05	**13.00**	✕ ☕
11.30	**14.09**	
12.05	14.09	B A
13.05	**15.00**	A
13.30	**16.09**	
14.05	16.09	B A
15.05	**17.00**	A
15.30	**18.17**	
16.05	18.17	B A
16.50	**18.45**	☕
17.05	19.21	B A
17.57	**19.56**	✕ ☕
18.50	**20.55**	✕ ☕
19.30	**22.18**	
20.05	**22.00**	FO

St. Pancras		Nottingham	
21.00	E	**23.45**	
22.20		**00.41**	
23.20		**01.28**	SO
23.55		**02.13**	SX

Heavy type denotes through train

✕ Restaurant car ⎫ whole
☕ Buffet car ⎭ or part journey

MO Mondays only
FO Fridays only
SO Saturdays only
SX Saturdays excepted

A ✕ SX ☕ SO
B Change at Leicester
C Change at Derby
E Euston
G ✕ SX

A British Rail timetable

St Pancras Station in London.
One student is a passenger, another a railway official.

twenty past ten (a.m.)

A Excuse me, what time is it, please?
B It's twenty past ten.
A Twenty past ten? – What time is the next train to Nottingham, please?
B At eleven oh five.
A Is it a through train?
B Yes, it is, madam / sir.
A What time does it get to Nottingham?
B At one o'clock.
A Is there a restaurant car on the train?
B Yes, there is.

Now you ask the questions and give the answers.

a. ten to nine (a.m.) b. ten to six (p.m.) c. twenty past nine (a.m.) d. ten past eleven (a.m.) e. twenty past one (p.m.) f. ten past seven (p.m.) g. twenty to five (p.m.) h. five to ten (a.m.)

8I Bedingungssätze

If you hold on a moment, *Wenn Sie einen Moment am Apparat bleiben.*	I'll tell you the best way to get there. *(dann) sage ich Ihnen . . .*
If you leave at 11.30 from Waterloo, *Wenn Sie um 11.30 Uhr von W. abfahren,*	you'll arrive in Wareham at 13.40. *kommen Sie um 13.40 Uhr in Wareham an.*

Make sentences of this type.

If	you we there	are is go have pay ring	by train, for the tickets, dinner at the Ritz, interested in ghosts, no cream, no train, Passenger Inquiries, to the White Horse,	I'll you'll we'll they'll	be there in two hours. go by bus. have a lot of fun. have my coffee with milk. like this book here. pay a lot of money. pay for the drinks. tell you the best train to get there.

9

Telephone boxes in London . . .

. . . and in New York's Chinatown.

9A

What the phone can do for you

You can get a lot out of your phone – if you know the right number. In London, for example, you can hear tourist information in German if you dial 246 8045.
Or you may dial 836 2872 to listen to poets reading their own poems.
If you don't know what to cook for dinner, dial 246 8071 for the recipe of the day.
And your children can hear a bedtime story if they dial 246 8000.
For information on almost anything under the sun you can ring 353 4242. That's the number of the Daily Telegraph Information Service.
Do you have problems so big that you think you can't go on? You'll find understanding, help, and advice if you call "The Samaritans" at 626 2277.
You want to meet other people, make a friend, or perhaps find a wife or husband? Why not ring 359 6321 then?
If you do, you'll hear men and women talking on tape. They, too, are looking for a friend or partner.

9B **Questions on 9A. One student asks another.**

a. What number do you dial for tourist information in German?
b. What number do you dial if you want to hear a poet reading his own poems?
c. What can you do if you don't know what to cook for dinner?
d. What number can your children dial if they want to hear a story at bedtime?
e. What will the Daily Telegraph Information Service do for you?
f. What is the number of the Daily Telegraph?
g. What do The Samaritans do?
h. What is the phone number of The Samaritans in London?
i. What number can you ring if you want to make a friend or find a partner?
j. What will you hear if you dial 359 6321?

To make a Call

Have money ready 2p  **or 10p** 

Lift receiver

Listen for continuous purring

Dial number or code and number

When you hear rapid pips, press in a coin

To continue a dialled call put in more money during conversation or when you hear rapid pips again

Dialling Codes

To call a **London** all-figure number, that is one beginning **01-**, dial only the last seven figures, those after the hyphen eg for 01-992 4321 dial 992 4321

To call any other all-figure number dial all the figures eg 021-643 2107.

To call a number on an exchange in the following list, first dial the code shown and then the number

	code
Aberdeen	0224
Accrington	0254
Airdrie	023 66
Aldershot	0252
Aldridge	0922
Amersham	024 03
Andover	0264
Ardrossan	0294
Ascot *Berks*	0990
Ashford *Middx*	69
Ashtead	27
Ashton-in-Makerfield	0942
Atherton	052 34
Avonmouth	027 52
Aylesbury	0296
Ayr	0292
Badgers Mount	095 97
Banbury	0295
Bangor *Co Down*	0247
Bangor *N Wales*	0248
Barnsley *Yorks*	0226
Barnstaple	0271

	code
Bournemouth	0202
Bowmansgreen	
(4 fig nos)	265
(5 fig nos)	61
Bracknell	0344
Bradford *Yorks*	0274
Bridgend *Glam*	0656
Bridgewater	0278
Bridlington	0262
Brighouse	048 47
Brighton	0273
Bristol	0272
Broadstone	020 124
Bromsgrove	073 93
Brookwood *Surrey*	048 67
Brownhills	054 33
Burgess Hill	044 46
Burgh Heath	25
Burnham *Bucks*	062 86
Burnley	0282
Burntwood	054 36
Burton-on-Trent	0283
Burwarton	074 633

	code
Chorley *Lancs*	025 72
Chorleywood	260
Christchurch *Hants*	020 15
Clacton-on-Sea	0255
Cleckheaton	097 62
Cleethorpes	0472
Clevedon	027 57
Cleveleys	039 14
Coatbridge	0236
Cobham *Surrey*	266
Colchester	0206
Colnbrook	964
Colwyn Bay	0492
Congleton	026 02
Copthorne	034 25
Corby Northants	053 66
Cosham *Hants*	070 18
Coventry	0203
Cranleigh *Surrey*	048 66
Crawley *Sussex*	0293
Crayford	29
Crewe	0270
Crowborough	089 26

The Dialling Instruction Booklet (inside the A-D Directory) gives additional codes, charges, services and information about STD

Call the operator if the exchange you want is not shown in the list above or in the Dialling Instruction Booklet, or if you need help in obtaining a call

For the operator dial 100

Directory Enquiries
(from phones on 01-exchanges only)

Dial 142
if the number you want is in **London**
(addresses with London postal district codes)
eg. Southwark Bridge Road, LONDON, SE1 9BA
City Road, LONDON, EC1V 1JT

Dial 192
if the number you want is elsewhere in the United Kingdom or Irish Republic
eg. Pelham Road, BEXLEYHEATH, Kent, DA7 4LZ
Hope Street, EDINBURGH, EH2 4EN

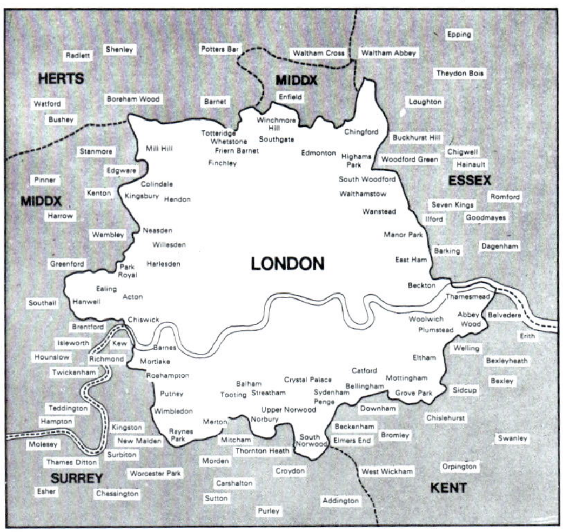

For other enquiries dial 191

CO 200 B (London) Issue No. 2 Special

9C **Telefonnummern**

170	one-seven-oh
999	nine-nine-nine
246 8045	two-four-six eight-oh-four-five
9600	nine-six-double-oh
743 3111	seven-four-three three-one-double-one
928 5000	nine-two-eight five-oh-double-oh

One student asks, another student answers.

What number are you calling from? What's your number? Your number, please?	391 4591 620 3810 805 4900	900 4823 433 6600 827 6009	Ladybank 209 Otterburn 261 Cardiff 33022
My number is . . .	277 2261	629 9000	Darlington 720319

9D

TELEPHONE SERVICES (LONDON)

Bedtime story 246 8000 · Dial a poem 836 2872
Directory enquiries (London) 142 · Emergencies (fire, police, ambulance) 999
Pop music 160 · Recipe of the day 246 8071
Telegrams (inland) 190 · Time: Speaking Clock 123
Tourist information (English) 246 8041 · Weather forecast (London area) 246 8091

What number must I ring?	If you want to	find out hear know report send	a bedtime story, a fire, a phone number, a poem, a telegram, an accident, pop music, the recipe of the day, the weather forecast, tourist information, what time it is,	you must	call . . . dial . . . phone . . . ring . . .

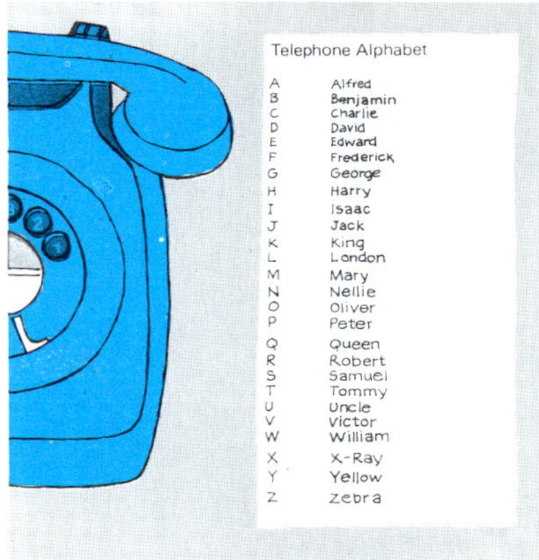

9E **One student asks a question, another student answers.**

a. Do you have a phone? If so, what's your number?
b. What number is the Speaking Clock in this country?
c. What number do you ring if you want to send a telegram in this country?
d. What number do you dial for the emergency services (fire, police, ambulance) in this country?
e. Can you get recipes by phone in this country? If so, what number do you dial?
f. What number do you phone for the weather forecast in this country?
g. You want to phone a friend, but you don't know his number. What do you do?
h. Can you dial a poem, pop music, or a bedtime story in this country?

9F **One student asks a question, another student answers.**

a. What time do you get up in the morning?
b. What time do you leave for the office?
c. What time do you start work?
d. What time do you have lunch?
e. What time do you stop work in the afternoon?
f. What time do you get home?
g. What time do you have your evening meal?
h. What time do you go to bed?

9G **Wortstellung** (→ 4L, GII43)

Fragewort	Hilfsverb	Subjekt	Hauptverb	Objekt	Adverb usw.
	Do	you	want	a fillet steak?	
What	do	you	serve		with the steak?
	Can	I	have	some chips	as well?
	Would	you	like	anything to drink?	
What	will	you	have		for dinner?
What	have	you	got		for me?

Please translate.

a. Was würden Sie gern trinken? b. Wollen Sie den Kaffee mit Sahne? c. Haben Sie auch Bitter? d. Um welche Zeit servieren Sie (das) Abendessen? e. Können Sie morgen zum Dinner kommen? f. Wollen wir in ein indisches Restaurant gehen? g. Veranstalten diese Schulen Intensivkurse?

10A

10 The Milkman

Jack Dixon is a milkman. But that doesn't mean he just puts milk bottles on people's doorsteps. Apart from milk, the modern milkman sells all sorts of other things as well: eggs, bread and potatoes, sausages and bacon, even tights.

Jack also wakes people up in the morning so they can get to work on time. Some of his customers even give him their front-door keys so he can get in and put the milk in the fridge while they are out at work.

He is up at five in the morning and sometimes doesn't get home until six or seven in the evening. But he doesn't mind that. What he doesn't like is having to work on Bank Holidays when everyone else is enjoying a day off.

He has about 450 customers, and a lot of them do not pay on time. Sometimes unpaid bills run to as much as £300. That's a lot of money.

"Milkmen are born, not made," says Jack, and it is clear he likes his job. But for his two children he has better things in mind. He is taking evening courses in English and maths so he can help them with their homework. He hopes they will make it to the university one day.

10B **Questions on 10A. One student asks another.**

a. What's Jack Dixon's job?
b. What does he sell, apart from milk?
c. What other things does he do for his customers?
d. When does he get up in the morning?
e. What time does he get home in the evening?
f. Does he mind the long working hours?
g. How does he feel about Bank Holidays?
h. Do all of his customers pay on time?
i. How much do his customers sometimes owe him?
j. How much is £300 in German marks / Austrian schillings / Swiss francs?
k. Does Jack like his job?

10 C **Why . . .? – Because . . .** **One student asks another.**

a. Why does the milkman sell other things apart from milk? b. Why do some customers give him their front-door keys? c. Why does he have to work on Bank Holidays? d. Why is he taking evening courses? e. Why does he hope his children will go to the university?

10 D **Mr and Mrs Average**

The average Briton	eats about four and a half eggs drinks about four and a half pints of milk drinks about five pints of beer smokes about 68 cigarettes works about 42 hours watches television for about 17 hours	a week.

One student asks a question, another student answers.

a. How many eggs do you eat each week?
b. How much milk do you drink?
c. How much beer do you drink?
d. How many cigarettes do you smoke?
e. How many hours do you work?
f. How many hours do you watch TV?

10 E **The police**

Policemen keep order. They protect people and property. They help people in emergencies. They give information to strangers. They arrest criminals. American policemen carry guns. British policemen don't carry guns.

Now you say what a policeman does: He keeps order. He protects . . . He . . .

Talk about the policemen in the pictures. What are they doing?

Policemen in London . . .

. . . and in New York.

10F **Berufsbezeichnungen** (→ GII6)

Im Gegensatz zum Deutschen steht hier der unbestimmte Artikel (*a/an*):

Frank is **a** policeman. *Frank ist Polizist.*
Tony is **a** taxi driver. *Tony ist Taxifahrer.*

Bei Berufen bzw. Ämtern, die es nur einmal gibt, steht dagegen kein *a/an*:

The author is President of the Ghost Club.
Der Verfasser ist Vorsitzender des Ghost Club.

Talk about what people do. QO

Her husband writes poems. He's a poet.

These are the jobs: milkman, railway official, shop assistant, student, taxi driver, waitress.

a. Jack Dixon sells milk. b. Mary Wade works in a restaurant. c. Bill drives a taxi. d. Lucy Butler works in a shop. e. Mike Bennett is at the university. f. My father has a job with British Rail.

10G **Verneinte Sätze mit doesn't** (→ 7H, 7F, 6J, GI8)

That **doesn't mean** he just puts milk bottles on people's doorsteps.
Das bedeutet nicht . . .

He **doesn't get home** until six or seven in the evening.
Er kommt nicht nach Hause vor . . . / Er kommt erst um . . . nach Hause.

What he **doesn't like** is having to work on Bank Holidays.
Was ihm nicht gefällt, ist, daß er an Feiertagen arbeiten muß.

One student asks a question, another student answers. QO

Does he drink whisky? (beer) No, he doesn't drink whisky, but I think he drinks beer.

a. Does he know her phone number? (address) b. Does she want a salad? (a sweet) c. Does he speak English? (French) d. Can he go there by train? (by bus) e. Does the train stop at Waterloo? (London Bridge) f. Does the hotel have a swimming pool? (a tennis court) g. Has the hotel got a playground for the children? (a private beach) h. Does she like Indian food? (Chinese food) i. Does the company pay for the course? (for the hotel room)

10H **So = damit**

Jack wakes people up **so** they get to work on time.
Jack weckt die Leute, damit sie pünktlich zur Arbeit kommen.

Make sentences with so.

Give Mary your number He is taking evening courses I'll ring Directory Enquiries Let's go to the White Horse Let's take three bottles They give him their keys We'll have breakfast early	**so**	he can get in and put the milk in the fridge. he can help his children with their homework. I get the right number. she can ring you back. we can have some fun. we have enough milk for the weekend. we have more time for sightseeing.

10I **Personalpronomen: Objektfall** (→ 5J, GI19)

He helps	**me** **you** **him** **her** **us** **them**	with	my your his her our their	work.	*mir* *dir/Ihnen* *ihm* *ihr* *uns* *ihnen*

Put in: me, you, him, her, us, them.
a. We have about 300 customers, and a lot of ..... don't pay on time. b. If you ring Passenger Inquiries, they will tell ..... the best way to get there. c. You can tell ..... that when she comes tomorrow. d. Can you give ..... your front-door key so I can get in? e. He can't help you if you don't tell ..... what you want. f. We're interested in ghosts. Can you show ..... a book about haunted houses in London?

10J **Have to = müssen** (→ GII40)

The milkman **has to** work on Bank Holidays. *Der Milchmann* **muß** *an Feiertagen arbeiten.*
Her English **has to** be very good. *Ihr Englisch* **muß** *sehr gut sein.* (→ 5C)

a. Die Firma muß für alles zahlen. b. Sie muß ihre Mutter in Leeds anrufen. c. Ich muß ihn jeden Morgen wecken. d. Du mußt heute abend zu deinem Nähkurs gehen. e. Wir müssen morgen um fünf Uhr aufstehen. f. Ich muß morgen nach Leicester fahren. g. Ihr müßt um elf Uhr in Wareham sein. h. Er muß seinen Kindern bei ihren Hausarbeiten helfen.

11

11A

CHILDREN SAVE WHALE

A whale lost its way in the North Sea and got stranded on an Essex beach yesterday. Children formed a chain to pour water over the thirty-foot, five-ton animal to keep it wet and cool. Then they dug a trench to help it to get back to the deep water. After nearly six hours the whale was able to slip into the River Blackwater, near Clacton, at high tide and swim away.

Mr Arthur Cox, a whale expert, said afterwards: "It's a good thing the children were there. They did a good job. I'm sure they saved the whale's life."

11B **Questions on 11A. One student asks another.**

a. Why did the whale get stranded?
b. Where did it get stranded?
c. Where did it lose its way?
d. Why did the children on the beach form a chain?
e. Why did they pour water on the whale?
f. Why did they dig a trench?
g. When did the whale swim away?
h. What's the Blackwater?

11C A letter from Clacton-on-Sea

Crown Hotel
Clacton-on-Sea
Essex

28 July 1975

Dear Doris,

As you can see, we are now at the seaside. Clacton-on-Sea is a pleasant resort about 70 miles from London. There are seven miles of sandy beaches, so you can always get away from the crowds if you walk far enough.

Yesterday there was a lot of excitement around here. Early in the morning a whale got stranded on the beach not far away from our hotel. It was low tide, and the poor thing lay there high and dry. It just couldn't help itself. Children tried to push the whale back into the deep water, but it was too heavy. So they poured water over it to keep it wet and cool. It was nearly six hours before high tide came and it was able to get away.

We took a lot of pictures, of course. We will show them to you when we see you next month.

We hope you are all well and not suffering too much from the heat.

Yours sincerely,

Mona and Fred

11D Questions on 11C. One student asks another.

a. Where are Mona and Fred writing from?
b. Where is Clacton?
c. How far is Clacton from London?
d. What's the weather like in Clacton?
e. What must you do if you want to get away from the crowds on the beach?
f. "The poor thing lay there high and dry." What does that mean?
g. Why couldn't the children push the whale back into the deep water?
h. When will Mona and Fred see Doris next?

11E **Vergangenheitsform der regelmäßigen Verben: Grundform + -(e)d** (→ GII23) ꝏ

Aussprache der -(e)d-Endung	**Grundform (Infinitiv)**	**Vergangenheitsform**
Normalerweise: -(e)d = [d]	form pour save	they **formed** [fɔːmd] a chain (*bildeten*) they **poured** [pɔːd] water over it (*gossen*) they **saved** [seivd] its life (*retteten*)
Nach [f], [k], [p], [s] und [ʃ]: -(e)d = [t]	help walk like	they **helped** [helpt] the whale (*halfen*) they **walked** [wɔːkt] away (*gingen*) they **liked** [laikt] the hotel (*mochten*)
Nach -t- und -d-: -ed = [id]	start translate	they **started** [ˈstɑːtid] early (*fingen an*) he **translated** [trænsˈleitid] it (*übersetzte*)

Schreibbesonderheiten

-*y* wird zu -*i*-, wenn nicht ein -*a*-, -*e*- oder -*o*- vorausgeht: try – **tried** (*versuchte*), aber stay – **stayed** (*wohnte*)

Gelegentliche Verdopplung des Endbuchstabens: slip – **slipped** (*glitt*), stop – **stopped** (*hörte auf*), dial – **dialled** (*wählte*), travel – **travelled** (*reiste*)

11F **Vergangenheitsform einiger unregelmäßiger Verben** ꝏ

come	high tide **came** [keim] (*kam*)
dig	they **dug** [dʌg] a trench (*gruben*)
do	they **did** [did] a good job (*taten / machten / leisteten*)
get	she **got** [gɔt] the recipe by phone (*bekam*)
lie	it **lay** [lei] there high and dry (*lag*)
lose	the whale **lost** [lɔst] its way (*verlor*)
say	he **said** [sed] that afterwards (*sagte*)
swim	the whale **swam** [swæm] away (*schwamm*)
take	we **took** [tuk] a lot of pictures (*nahmen / machten*)
be	{ it **was** [wɔz] low tide (*war*) { they **were** [wəːr] in Clacton last summer (*waren*)
don't	they **didn't** [ˈdidnt] suffer from the heat ("*taten nicht*")
can't	it **couldn't** [ˈkudnt] help itself (*konnte nicht*)

11 G **Talk about Mona and Fred's holiday in Clacton-on-Sea.**

a. Mona and Fred ..... in Clacton-on-Sea last year. b. They ..... at the Crown Hotel. c. It ..... very hot, but they ..... mind the heat. d. They ..... like the crowds, but if they ..... far enough on the beach, they ..... able to get away from them. e. One day there ..... a lot of excitement on the beach. f. When the holidaymakers ..... down to the beach, a whale ..... there high and dry. g. It ..... low tide, and the poor thing just ..... help itself. h. Children ..... to push the whale back into the deep water, but it ..... too heavy. i. So they ..... water over it to keep it wet and cool. j. It ..... nearly six hours before high tide ..... and the whale ..... able to swim away. k. Mona and Fred ..... a lot of pictures. l. A month later they ..... the photos to their friend Doris.

11 H **The students ask one another.** ǫǫ

Did the whale lose its way? – Yes, it did. Did the whale get stranded at high tide? – No, it didn't.

a. Did the children pour water over the whale? b. Did they dig a trench? c. Was the whale fifty feet long? d. Was the whale able to help itself? e. Were the children able to push the whale back into the deep water? f. Did the whale swim away at high tide? g. Did Mr Cox save the whale's life? h. Did Mona and Fred take many pictures? i. Is Clacton-on-Sea in Dorset? j. Is Clacton-on-Sea a pleasant resort?

11 I **One student asks a question, another student answers.**

a. What time did you get up yesterday? b. What time did you leave for work? (I left . . .) c. How did you travel to work? d. What time did you start work? e. What time did you have lunch? (I had lunch . . .) f. Where did you have lunch? g. What time did you stop work in the afternoon? h. What time did you get home? i. What time did you have your evening meal? j. What did you do in the evening? k. What time did you go to bed? (I went to bed . . .)

Weitere Vergangenheitsformen unregelmäßiger Verben

go: they **went** to Swanage in 1974 (*fuhren*)
have: they **had** a nice holiday in Clacton-on-Sea last year (*hatten*)
leave: they **left** for London yesterday (*fuhren ab*)

12

Inside the Cockney Pride pub in Jermyn Street, behind Piccadilly Circus

12A At the Prince of Wales pub

Alf What can I get you, Bob?
Bob A pint of bitter, please.
Alf And you, Chris?
Chris I think I'll have a half of lager, please.
(*Alf goes to the bar.*)
Barman Yes, sir?
Alf Two pints of bitter and a half of lager, please.
Barman Here you are, sir. One pound fifteen p, please.
Alf (*Returns with the glasses.*) Well, here we are . . . Cheers!
Bob and Chris Cheers!
Alf Nice place this, isn't it?
Bob Yes, rather pleasant, no jukebox, so you can still enjoy a quiet conversation.
Chris It's a bit dark though, don't you think?
Bob Well, it could be worse. I was in an old riverside pub the other night, it was that dark you couldn't see a thing. I was coming from the bar, had four pints in my hands, when I knocked into a suit of armour up against the wall and a great club thing fell on my toe. I staggered around holding my foot – the manager thought I was drunk and disorderly and threw me out.

12B Questions on 12A. One student asks another.

a. Alf went to the Prince of Wales pub yesterday evening. Who did he meet there?
b. Alf bought a round of drinks. What did he buy for Bob, what did he buy for Chris, and what did he buy for himself?
c. How much did he pay for the drinks? (He paid [peid] . . .)
d. If the price of bitter and lager is the same, how much did he pay for a half of bitter or lager?
e. What did Bob like about the pub?
f. What did Chris think about the pub?
g. Bob was in an old riverside pub the other night. What did he say about that pub?
h. Why did Bob knock into the suit of armour?
i. What fell on his toe?
j. Was it heavy?
k. Bob staggered around holding his foot. What do you think happened to the beer?
l. What did the manager think?
m. What did the manager do?

12C Vergangenheitsformen unregelmäßiger Verben

buy	Alf **bought** [bɔ:t] the first round of drinks (*kaufte*)
fall	a great club thing **fell** [fel] on Bob's toe (*fiel*)
meet	**I met** [met] him at the Cockney Pride pub yesterday (*traf*)
pay	**I paid** [peid] 46p for a pint of bitter (*bezahlte*)
think	the manager **thought** [θɔ:t] Bob was drunk (*dachte*)
throw	the manager **threw** [θru:] him out (*warf*)

Outside the Dog and Trumpet pub in Soho. What can you see in this picture?

12D **End of a pub crawl. One student is Jane, another is Bob.**

Jane What ..... you do last night, Bob?
Bob I ..... to one of those old pubs down by the Thames.
Jane ..... you like it?
Bob Yes, it ..... very nice – at first.
Jane At first?
Bob Yes. Don, Gerry, and Ted ..... there.
Jane So you ..... a good time together?
Bob Yes. First Don ..... a round of drinks.
Jane I see. And then?
Bob Then Gerry ..... to buy a round of drinks.
Jane Well, that's normal, isn't it?
Bob Then we ..... four pints from Ted.
Jane And then it was your turn to buy drinks.
Bob That's right. I ..... to the bar and ..... four pints of bitter.
Jane Four pints of bitter. Why not? Now come to the point!
Bob It ..... very dark. I ..... see a thing without my glasses.
Jane Well, old pubs are often dark, aren't they?
Bob Yes, probably. But there ..... a suit of armour up against the wall somewhere.
Jane A suit of armour? What's wrong with a suit of armour in a historical pub?
Bob Well, I ..... see it.
Jane You didn't see it?
Bob No, I ..... right into it.
Jane Good heavens! With the beer?
Bob Yes, with the beer. And a great club thing ..... on my toe.
Jane Oh no! ..... it very painful?
Bob Yes, very. I dropped the beer and ..... around holding my foot.
Jane Good Lord! What ..... all those people in the pub think of you?
Bob Well, the manager ..... I was drunk and disorderly and ..... me out.

12E

TOUR OF LONDON PUBS

For parties of 40–50 persons

Included are:

* Coach transportation within 30 miles of London
* Professional London guide
* A visit to 3 pubs
* 2 free drinks
* Darts match – Prize for the winner
* Lively songs from the pub pianist
* Sore head!

SCHEDULE

First stop

Arrive 7.30 p.m. City Pride Tavern, 84 Bishopsgate
Guide meets and welcomes party
Free drink of choice
Food available
Darts match – Winner gets prize

Second stop

Arrive 8.45 p.m. Henekey Inn, High Holborn
Free drink of choice
A little sightseeing if time permits

Third stop

Arrive 9.45 p.m. Cockney Pride Tavern, Piccadilly Circus
Resident pianist plays

11.00 Closing time. Home.

12F **Your club's outing this year will be a tour of London pubs. You are the club's secretary. Using 12E, draw up an information sheet for your fellow club members.**

This year we will visit three interesting London pubs.
We will travel by coach, and a professional London guide will point out the sights to us.
Our first stop will be the City Pride Tavern in Bishopsgate.
We will arrive there at 7.30 p.m.
(Now you go on.)

12G **In a letter, you are telling a friend about your club's outing:**

We visited three interesting London pubs.
We travelled by coach, and a guide pointed out the sights to us.
We first visited the City Pride Tavern in Bishopsgate . . .
(Now you go on.)

12H **Vergangenheitsformen unregelmäßiger Verben** QO

drink	I **drank** so much that I had a sore head afterwards (*trank*)
sing	the pianist **sang** some lively songs for us (*sang*)
win	I **won** [wʌn] the darts match (*gewann*)

Calling British airways

13

13 A

A British Airways. Good afternoon!
B Good afternoon! Is there a flight from London to Cologne tomorrow afternoon, please?
A Hold on, I'll have a look for you... I've got the BE 624 (six two four) at sixteen oh five.
B Can I book a seat on that flight for tomorrow?
A Just a moment, please. – All right, I've one seat confirmed on the BE 624, eighteenth July, London-Cologne, departing at sixteen oh five, arriving at seventeen ten . . .
B Yes . . .
A D'you want to book a return?
B No, it's just one-way.
A Can I have the passenger's name?
B My name is Schröder – S-C-H-R-O umlaut-D-E-R.
A And your initial?
B R for Robert.
A Can I have your phone number, please.
B It's 935 5599.
A Is that your home number?
B No, that's the number of the Mandeville Hotel, Mandeville Place, W.1.
A And your room number?
B 852. – Can I pick up the ticket at the West London Terminal?
A Yes, you can pick it up here. Can you be here one and three-quarter hours before departure.
B Yes, O.K. Thank you very much. Good-bye!
A Good-bye!

LONDON – COLOGNE/BONN

Frequency	Aircraft Dep	Arr	Via	Flight
Daily	1025	1145	non-stop	LH057
Daily	1605	1710	non-stop	BE624
Daily	1930	2050	non-stop	LH059

AF = Air France BE = British Airways LH = Deutsche Lufthansa
OS = Austrian Airlines PA = Pan American World Airways SR = Swissair

13B **Questions on 13A. One student asks another.**

a. How many flights are there daily from London to Cologne?
b. At what times do the flights leave?
c. At what times do the flights arrive?
d. Are they direct flights, or do they stop on the way?
e. Which flights are Lufthansa, and which British Airways?
f. At what time of the day does the passenger want to travel?
g. Which flight does the passenger book?
h. Which day does he book for?
i. Does he want a single or a return ticket?
j. What's the passenger's name?
k. Does he *live* in London?
l. What phone number does he give?
m. What's his address in London?
n. Where and when will Mr Schröder pick up his ticket?
o. How do you think Mr Schröder will travel from the West London Terminal to the airport?

13C **A British Airways booking office. One student is a passenger, another an airline clerk.**

A What's the fare to Berlin, please?
B Fifty-three pounds forty tourist class, and eighty pounds first class.
A Is that the return fare?
B No, single. The return fare is double the single fare.
A Isn't there a special weekend excursion fare if I travel on a Saturday and Sunday?
B Yes, there is. The tourist excursion return fare to Berlin is seventy-six pounds seventy.

Now you go on with the fares to Cologne, Düsseldorf, Frankfurt, Hamburg, Hanover, and Munich.

NORMAL SINGLE FARES (Return fares, valid 1 year, are double the single fares.)		Fares from London to	TOURIST EXCURSION RETURN FARES (Available only for travel on Saturdays and Sundays.)
First Class	Tourist Class		
£80.00	£53.40	Berlin	£76.70
£45.20	£30.10	Cologne	£43.20
£45.20	£30.10	Düsseldorf	£43.20
£57.10	£38.00	Frankfurt	£54.90
£61.40	£40.90	Hamburg	£59.10
£61.40	£40.90	Hanover	£59.10
£73.90	£49.20	Munich	£71.00

13D At the ticket counter

B Good afternoon. My name is Schröder. I'm booked on British Airways flight 624 to Cologne this afternoon. I'd like to pick up my ticket.

C Just a moment, Mr Schröder. I'll just check with the computer. – Yes, I see you've got a reservation for a single flight to Cologne. (*Writes out the ticket.*) – Here's your ticket, sir. Have a good flight!

B Thank you very much. Good-bye.

C Good-bye.

13E At the check-in desk

B Is this where I have to check in for the British Airways flight to Cologne?

D Yes, that's right. May I have your ticket, sir. And would you please put your baggage on the scales.

B I've only got a cabin bag.

D I see. Here's your boarding card, sir. Will you now please go to the international departures lounge. We'll call your flight in about twenty minutes.

13F On the way back from London. Please complete.

a. It was a quarter past two when Mr Schröder (arrive) at the British Airways ticket counter. b. The clerk (check) with the computer and then gave Mr Schröder his ticket. c. Mr Schröder (pay) £30.10 for the ticket. d. He (buy) a few newspapers and magazines at the bookstall and then (take) the bus to the airport. e. He (arrive) at the airport at a quarter past three and (go) straight to the check-in desk. f. He (get) his boarding card and then (go) through Passport Control to the international departures lounge.

13G **One student is Mr Schröder, another asks him questions.**

a. Where did you stay in London, Mr Schröder?
b. When did you fly back to Cologne? (I flew [flu:] . . .)
c. How did you travel to the airport?
d. Which airport did you leave from? (Heathrow)
e. Which airline did you fly?
f. What time did you leave, and what time did you arrive?
g. Was it a non-stop flight?
h. What was the fare from London to Cologne?
i. Where did you pick up your ticket?
j. Did you travel first class or tourist class?

13H **Zeitbestimmungen mit ago. Please answer.** (→ GII24)

When did he book his flight to Cologne? (two days ago)
He booked it two days ago.
(Er buchte ihn vor zwei Tagen / hat ihn vor zwei Tagen gebucht.)

a. When did they confirm the booking? (an hour ago) b. When did he pick up his ticket? (an hour ago) c. When did he pay? (a few days ago) d. When did he check in? (half an hour ago) e. When did they call our flight? (five minutes ago) f. When did the plane for Vienna leave? (twenty minutes ago)

13I **Vergangenheitsformen unregelmäßiger Verben**

fly	Mr Schröder **flew** [flu:] back on the eighteenth of July (*flog*)
give	the clerk at the check-in desk **gave** [geiv] him a boarding card (*gab*)

a [ei]	**j** [dʒei]	**s** [es]
b [bi:]	**k** [kei]	**t** [ti:]
c [si:]	**l** [el]	**u** [ju:]
d [di:]	**m** [em]	**v** [vi:]
e [i:]	**n** [en]	**w** ['dʌblju:]
f [ef]	**o** [əu]	**x** [eks]
g [dʒi:]	**p** [pi:]	**y** [wai]
h [eitʃ]	**q** [kju:]	**z** [zed]
i [ai]	**r** [ɑ:]	

13J **The students ask one another's names and spell them.**

A What's your name?
B My name is Brückmann.
A Would you spell your name, please?
B B - R - U umlaut - C - K - M - A - double N.
A And what's your first name, please, Mr Brückmann?
B My first name is Udo – U-D-O.

14A Letters after a visit

20 July 1976

Dear Morgan and Elaine,

I am writing to thank you again for entertaining me at your home during my recent visit to London. I very much enjoyed the evening we spent together, and it was a particular pleasure for me to come to your home.

The plane back to Cologne was very full, and the flight was rather bumpy. But otherwise it was a pleasant trip, and I was glad we arrived on time, because my wife was waiting for me at the airport. But there was an old gentleman on the plane who obviously didn't enjoy the flight at all. As we were getting off in Cologne, he walked up to the stewardess, shook her hand, and said: "Thank you for the two flights." The stewardess looked rather perplexed. "It was a pleasure to serve you, sir," she said, "but what do you mean by two flights? It was only one, wasn't it?" You'll never guess what the man answered: "No, for me it was two flights, young lady - my first and my last!"

With very best wishes to you both,
Yours,

Klaus

26 July 1976

Dear Klaus,

Thank you so much for your delightful letter of 20th July. We were sorry to hear that your flight home was not too pleasant, but we had a good laugh about the old gentleman on the plane who had two flights in one.

We were very glad that you were able to come to our home for the first of what we hope will be many visits. Next time you come, please let us know in advance so we can get some theatre tickets, or something like that, and have a proper evening out.

In the meantime, all our best wishes to you and your family.

Yours,

Morgan

14B An evening out with Morgan and Elaine

Next time Klaus is in London, Morgan and Elaine will have a proper evening out with him.
First they'll . . ., Then they'll . . ., etc. (Looking at the pictures, talk about what they'll do.)

Last time Klaus was in London, Morgan and Elaine had a proper evening out with him.
First they . . ., Then they . . ., etc. (Looking at the pictures, talk about what they did.)

14C Questions on 14A. One student asks another.

a. When did Klaus write the letter to Morgan and Elaine? (He wrote [rəut] . . .)
b. What did he say about the evening he spent with Morgan and Elaine?
c. Was his flight back to Cologne very pleasant?
d. What time did he arrive in Cologne? (See page 54.)
e. Who was waiting for him at the airport?
f. Did the old gentleman enjoy the flight?
g. Why do you think he didn't enjoy it?
h. Why was the stewardess perplexed?
i. Why could one say the old gentleman had two flights in one?
j. What does Morgan want to arrange when Klaus comes to London next time?

14D One student is Klaus, another asks him questions.

a. How did you like the evening you spent with Morgan and Elaine?
b. Did you enjoy your flight back to Cologne?
c. Was anybody waiting for you at Cologne Airport?
d. Did the plane arrive on time?
e. What was so funny about the old gentleman on the plane?

14E Vergangenheitsformen unregelmäßiger Verben

eat	last time we **ate** [et] a chicken curry at an Indian restaurant (*aßen*)
see	they **saw** [sɔ:] a show at a night club (*sahen*)
shake	he walked up to her and **shook** [ʃuk] her hand (*schüttelte*)
spend	when Klaus was in London, he **spent** [spent] a pleasant evening with Morgan and Elaine (*verbrachte*)
write	Klaus **wrote** [rəut] a letter to Morgan on 20th July (*schrieb*)

14F One student is Klaus, another asks him questions.

a. Which pub did you go to? (the Shakespeare's Head pub)
b. What did you drink? (two pints of best bitter)
c. Which theatre did you go to? (the Piccadilly Theatre)
d. What did you see? (saw [sɔ:] a play by Robert Bolt)
e. Which Indian restaurant did you go to? (the Islamabad restaurant in Soho)
f. What did you eat? (ate [et] a chicken curry)
g. Which night club did you go to? (the Red Mill Club in Soho)
h. What did you see? (a striptease revue)

14G **A visit to London. Please complete.**

a. During his visit to London last week, Klaus (have) a very pleasant evening out with Morgan and Elaine. b. First they (have) a few drinks at the Shakespeare's Head pub. c. There (be) a pianist at the pub who (sing) some nice old songs for them. d. Some of the men in the pub were (play) darts; others were just (drink). e. Next they (see) a play by Robert Bolt at the Piccadilly Theatre. f. After the theatre they (be) very hungry and (go) to an Indian restaurant in Berwick Street. g. Klaus (have) a chicken curry. h. He (like) it so much that he (ask) the waiter for the recipe. i. But he didn't (get) it. j. It (be) half past eleven when they (leave) the restaurant. k. Not far from the restaurant (be) a night club. l. A man (say): "This is the best night club in London. It's world-famous." m. They (go) in, (see) the show, and (drink) a lot. n. The next morning Klaus (have) a terrible headache.

14H **Ordnungszahlen und Datum**

Regel-mäßig:	the	**fourth** (4th) / **sixth** (6th) / **seventh** (7th) / **tenth** (10th) / **eleventh** (11th) / **twentieth** (20th) / **twenty-sixth** (26th) / **thirtieth** (30th)	of July
Un-regel-mäßig:	the	**first** (1st) / **second** (2nd) / **third** (3rd) / **fifth** (5th) / **eighth** (8th) / **ninth** (9th) / **twelfth** (12th)	of July

You write: He went back on 18th July / 18 July.
You say: He went back on the eighteenth of July.

Or you write: He went back on July 18th / July 18.
And you say: He went back on July the eighteenth.

Now read the following sentences aloud.

a. He wrote this letter on July 7. b. I booked the room on 24 August. c. Ron went to Swanage on 20th July. d. We had our club's outing on September 30 this year. e. On August 3rd we had dinner at the Star of India. f. She arrived here on a Sunday, I think it was July 22nd. g. They left Clacton-on-Sea on 31st July. h. Thank you so much for your delightful letter of 5 September. i. We've got theatre tickets for Saturday, 29th July. j. He'll be here again on August 12th. k. I think I took this picture on September 28.

15

15A

the samaritans – *can I help you?*

When the Reverend Chad Varah read, in the summer of 1953, that there were three suicides a day in Greater London, he did not write to The Times saying that the Government should do something about it. Instead, he made it known in the press that from 2 November 1953 people thinking of suicide could phone him at MANsion House 9000.
Chad Varah's one-man emergency service has since become a large organization called "The Samaritans". Thousands of lonely, miserable, and despairing people have phoned or called on The Samaritans in their hour of greatest need. They have found friendliness, understanding, and practical help.

At the 156 Samaritan branches in Britain there are now over 18,000 volunteers who give up a large part of their free time to help their fellow men. At any time of the day or night people who are in despair may ring one of the 156 emergency numbers to hear a friendly voice say: "The Samaritans – can I help you?"

15B **Questions on 15A.**

a. In what year did Chad Varah found The Samaritans?
b. Why did he start The Samaritans?
c. What was the first phone number of The Samaritans?
d. How many emergency numbers do The Samaritans have now?
e. Who are The Samaritans trying to help?
f. What do The Samaritans offer their "clients"?
g. How many Samaritan branches are there now in Britain?
h. How many volunteers are there in the Samaritans organization?
i. Do The Samaritans work for money?

15C And your neighbour as yourself

A Many people regard suicide as a sin, don't they?

B Well, most religions do. For Muslims it's worse than murder.

C And up to a few years ago it was a crime in Britain, too.

B It's still a "breach of the peace" in Scotland.

A Yes, that's true. But, of course, you don't help a desperate man if you tell him it's a sin or crime to commit suicide.

C That's how The Samaritans feel about it. They say: "If you're in despair, if you want to kill yourself, ring us up. We're always there, day and night, to listen to your problems, to talk to you, to help you, to make you feel less lonely."

B People who want to kill themselves are always lonely, aren't they?

A I'm sure most of them are. Old people, for example, or some young people in the big cities. They live alone, they don't mix with other people, there's no one who shows them love.

C But are The Samaritans successful in their fight against suicide? I mean, have they really reduced the suicide rate in this country?

B They say they have. The suicide rate has dropped by one third in nine years. Six thousand suicides or four thousand suicides a year, that's quite a difference.

C But the statistics can't tell us why the rate has dropped. So we'll never know if it was really The Samaritans who saved all those lives.

A I think it doesn't matter whether The Samaritans have saved twenty thousand, two thousand, two hundred or only two people. The important thing is that there are people like The Samaritans who think of others while most people think only of themselves.

15D Questions on 15C. One student asks another.

a. Why do many people regard suicide as a sin?

b. Until 1961, suicide was a crime in Britain. Do you think it was right to change that?

c. What do Muslims think of suicide?

d. Is suicide a crime in Scotland?

e. Do you think some people will not commit suicide if it's a sin or crime?

f. Talk about the suicide figures in 15G. Until which year did the rate go up? When did it start to drop? When did it start to go up again?

g. Do we know for sure that The Samaritans have reduced the suicide rate?

h. Do you think it's important to have The Samaritans even if they only reduce the suicide rate a little?

15E Grundzahlen ab 100 (→ 6G)

100 one hundred / a hundred
101 one / a hundred and one
181 one / a hundred and eighty-one
200 two hundred
346 three hundred and forty-six
1,000 one thousand / a thousand
1,101 one thousand one hundred and one
3,000 three thousand
100,000 one / a hundred thousand
1,000,000 one million / a million

15F Is there a need for The Samaritans?

Talk about the figures below.

Year	Number of new clients	Increase
1966	about 21,000	
		143 per cent (1966–1969)
1969	about 51,000	
		206 per cent (1969–1972)
1972	about 156,000	
		60 per cent (1972–1975)
1975	about 250,000	

15G NUMBER OF SUICIDES IN BRITAIN 1960–1974

1960	5,520	1965	5,576	1970	4,336
1961	5,608	1966	5,407	1971	4,322
1962	6,061	1967	5,102	1972	4,193
1963	6,159	1968	4,957	1973	4,259
1964	5,991	1969	4,732	1974	4,336

Talk about the figures on the left:
In nineteen sixty there were five thousand five hundred and twenty suicides in Britain.
In nineteen sixty-one there were five thousand six hundred and eight suicides in Britain. etc.

15H Other people's problems

Why do people take their own lives?
Because . . .
. . . they are depressed.
. . . they have lost someone close to them.
. . . their marriage has broken up.
. . . they have personal problems.
. . . they think they are a failure.
. . . they are in debt, unemployed, ill, or lonely.

How can we help people who have these problems?

15I Perfekt der regelmäßigen Verben: have/has + Grundform + -(e)d (→ GII25)

Many lonely people **have called** on The Samaritans. (*haben aufgesucht*)
Thousands of despairing people **have phoned** The Samaritans. (*haben angerufen*)
The suicide rate **has dropped** by one third. (*ist gefallen*)
Have The Samaritans **reduced** the suicide rate? (*haben verringert*)
How many lives **have** The Samaritans **saved**? (*haben gerettet*)

Die zur Bildung des Perfekts gebrauchte *-(e)d*-Form ist bei regelmäßigen Verben stets identisch mit der Vergangenheitsform (→ 11E).
Im Gegensatz zum Deutschen wird das Perfekt im Englischen immer mit *haben* gebildet:
they have walked = sie sind gegangen/gelaufen, he has travelled = er ist gereist.

15J Perfekt einiger unregelmäßiger Verben

become – became – become (*werden – wurde – geworden*):
Chad Varah's one-man service **has become** a large organization. (*ist geworden*)

break up – broke up – broken up (*zerbrechen – zerbrach – zerbrochen*):
Their marriage **has broken up**. (*ist zerbrochen/gescheitert*)

find – found [faund] – found (*finden – fand – gefunden*):
They **have found** friendliness and understanding. (*haben gefunden*)

lose – lost [lɔst] – lost (*verlieren – verlor – verloren*):
They **have lost** someone close to them. (*haben verloren*)

15K Practise definitions with who. (→ GII17)

A barman is a man		comes from Germany.	Give definitions
A clerk is a person		knows a lot about whales.	of the following:
A German is a person		serves customers in a shop.	An Austrian . . .
A guide is a person		serves drinks at a bar.	An Indian . . .
A passenger is a person		serves food or drinks in a restaurant.	A milkman . . .
A shop assistant is a person	**who**	serves passengers in a plane.	A poet . . .
A stewardess is a woman		shows the sights to tourists.	A policeman . . .
A tourist is a person		travels for pleasure.	A Samaritan . . .
A waitress is a woman		travels in a train, bus, plane, etc.	A Swiss . . .
A whale expert is a person		works in an office or at a counter.	A taxi driver . . .

16

16A Mail-order shopping

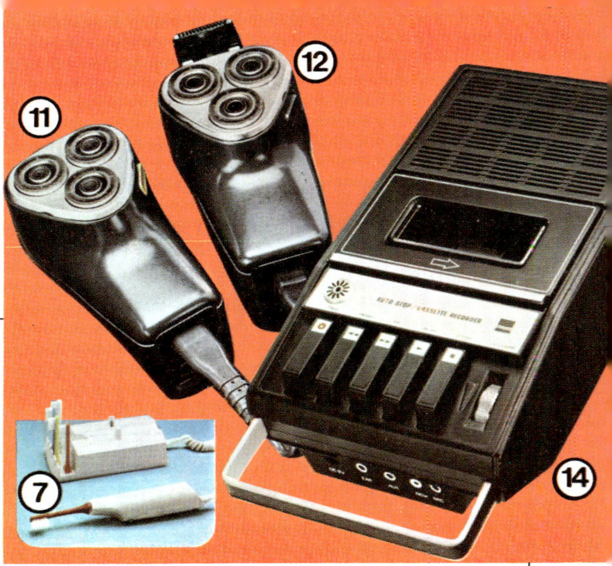

24 June 1976

Long & Company Limited
134-136 Hill Road
Leeds
LS2 9PR

Dear Sirs,

On May 20 I placed an order for £57.94 worth of goods from your catalogue "Spring & Summer 1976". I ordered a Sharp cassette recorder at £29.95, a Philishave 3 Special shaver at £18.49, and a Ronson battery toothbrush at £9.50.

After about two weeks the cassette recorder arrived, but since it was damaged, I returned it to you, asking for a new one. A few days later I received the Ronson toothbrush and a Philishave 3 Deluxe shaver at £19.75. Since the shaver was not the right model, I sent it back to you, asking you to send me a Philishave 3 Special instead. But it seems my note got lost somehow, because you returned the same shaver to me together with a bill for £3.50 for repairs!

I am returning the shaver to you under separate cover and would ask you to send me the correct model and an undamaged Sharp cassette recorder as soon as possible. Also, please cancel the enclosed bill for £3.50.

Yours faithfully,

Frank Burton

16B Questions on 16A. One student asks another.

a. When did Mr Burton order the goods?
b. What goods did he order?
c. What was the price of each item?
d. What was the price of the three items together?
e. When did the cassette recorder arrive?
f. Why did the customer send it back?
g. Did he receive the right toothbrush?
h. Why did he send the shaver back?
i. What was the difference between the "Special" and "Deluxe" models?
j. What did he get instead of the right shaver?
k. What did he ask the company to do with the repairs bill?
l. Do you often buy things by mail order?
m. What's your experience of mail-order buying?

16C A complaint

A Do you remember selling me this toaster yesterday?

B Yes, I think I do, sir. And a very good toaster it is too. Takes four slices of bread at once, has six heat settings, and at £13.99 it's almost a give-away.

A Yes, but it doesn't work.

B It doesn't work? These are very reliable toasters, sir, British-made, very good workmanship. We've never had any complaints.

A Well, you have a complaint now. I've tried this toaster three times. Each time I turned it on, the fuse went.

B That's bad. Shall we exchange it for a new one?

A No, I've lost my confidence in this kind of toaster. Can you recommend another brand?

B How about the "Good-as-Gold" Auto Super Deluxe toaster? It's got colour-selector control . . .

A Cut out the sales talk, young man. Instead, plug the darned thing in and see if it works.

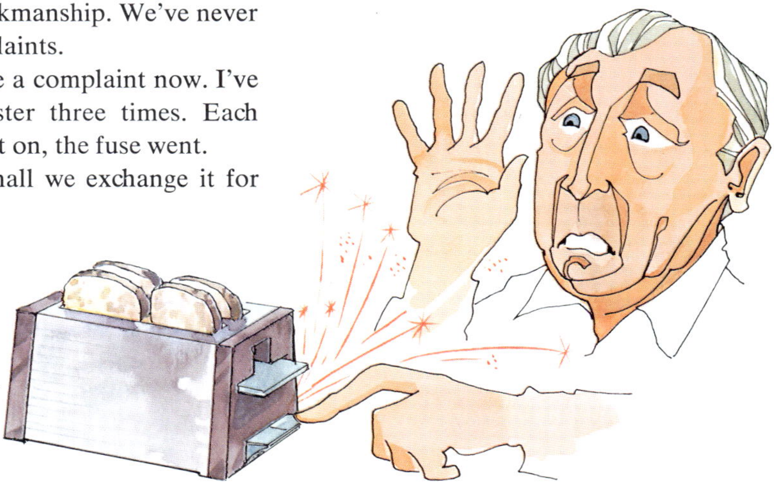

16D **Questions on 16C. One student asks another.**

a. What did the customer buy?
b. What kind of toaster was it?
c. How much did he pay for it?
d. Why was he bringing it back?
e. What happened each time he tried the toaster?
f. Did he want to exchange it for a new one of the same brand?
g. What kind of toaster did the assistant recommend this time?

16E **Perfekt oder Vergangenheitsform?** (→ GII26)

Perfekt	The catalogue **has arrived**. *Der Katalog ist angekommen.* The catalogue **has** just **arrived.** *Der Katalog ist gerade angekommen.* The catalogue **has** already **arrived.** *Der Katalog ist bereits angekommen.* **Has** the catalogue **arrived**? *Ist der Katalog angekommen?*
Vergangen-heitsform	The catalogue **arrived** yesterday. *Der Katalog ist gestern angekommen.* The catalogue **arrived** a few days ago. *Der K. ist vor ein paar Tagen angekommen.* The catalogue **arrived** last week. *Der Katalog ist vorige Woche angekommen.* When **did** the catalogue **arrive**? *Wann ist der Katalog angekommen?*

Das Perfekt ist im Englischen nur möglich, wenn weder ausgedrückt noch gefragt wird, *wann* in der Vergangenheit die Handlung stattfand. Mit *yesterday, . . . ago, last night/week/month/year* usw. muß stets die Vergangenheitsform gebraucht werden.

One student asks, another answers.

A	Have you ordered the new shavers? (yesterday)
B	Yes, I have.
A	When did you order them?
B	I ordered them yesterday.

a. Have you received the bill? (yesterday) b. Have you sent the damaged recorder back? (two days ago) c. Has the cassette recorder arrived? (this morning) d. Have you phoned Bill and Mary? (yesterday evening) e. Has Jack found the key? (five minutes ago) f. Have you written to Morgan? (last Sunday) g. Have you booked the tickets? (last week) h. Have the Turners sold their car? (last month)

16F **Please answer.**

> How often did you try? (about 15×) – I tried about fifteen times.
> How often has Janet been to Clacton? (4×) – She's been there four times.

a. How often did you meet her while you were there? (only 3×) b. How often did Jack phone you? (about 10×) c. How often did Jane visit you when you were in hospital? (6×) d. How often did they have to stop work? (7×) e. How often did he change his address during the last two years? (about 8×) f. How often have you written to Sandra? (5×) g. How often have you talked to the President? (never) h. How often does he go to the pub? (3× a week) i. How often does the President come here? (4× a year) j. How often does Mary go to her maths class? (3× a month)

16G **Weitere unregelmäßige Verbformen**

be – was/were – been (*sein – war(en) – gewesen*): Where **have** you **been**? (*bist gewesen*)
have – had – had (*haben – hatte – gehabt*): We **have** never **had** any complaints. (*haben gehabt*)
sell – sold – sold (*verkaufen – verkaufte – verkauft*):
Have they **sold** their car? (*haben verkauft*) Yes, they **sold** it last month. (*verkauften*)
send – sent – sent (*schicken – schickte – geschickt*):
Have you **sent** it back? (*hast zurückgeschickt*) Yes, I **sent** it back long ago. (*schickte zurück*)
write – wrote – written (*schreiben – schrieb – geschrieben*):
I **have** just **written** to her. (*habe geschrieben*)

16H **Make as many meaningful sentences as you can.**

He			(be)	by coach.
I		already	(break)	me.
Mr Burton		always	(help)	the house.
My husband		just	(like)	the shaver back.
My wife		never	(receive)	the suicide rate.
She	have	obviously	(reduce)	their new catalogue.
The Samaritans	has	often	(sell)	this hotel.
Their marriage		only	(send)	to England.
They		really	(talk)	to him.
We		sometimes	(travel)	up.
You			(visit)	us in our new home.

"My wife has just sold the house."

17

17A At the travel agent's

(C = Client, A = Agent)

C Well, have you arranged everything for us about the tour?

A Yes, I have, sir. Let me see . . . You'll leave from Heathrow at 12 o'clock sharp on October the first.

C By what airline?

A British Airways. – You'll arrive in Boston at a quarter past two in the afternoon.

C Are you sure we'll be travelling by plane and not by rocket?

A Yes, it does sound funny, doesn't it, two and a quarter hours flying time from London to Boston. But don't forget London time is five hours ahead of Boston.

C So our actual flying time will be – let me see – seven hours and fifteen minutes, is that right?

A Quite. Seven and a quarter hours if you're dead on time. – You'll spend two nights in Boston, so you'll have the whole of the second day for sightseeing.

C Any chance of hearing the Boston Symphony Orchestra?

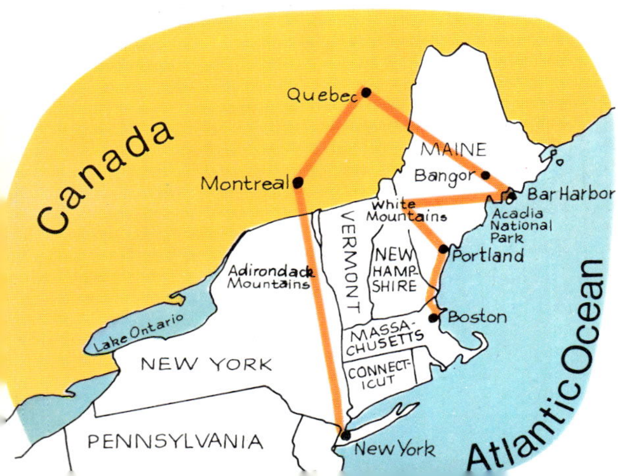

A Well, if you're interested, sir, we could find out for you. Shall I make a note of it?

C Yes, please do.

A Anyway, after Boston, on the third day, you'll travel along the Atlantic coast up to Portland, and on the fourth you'll make an excursion to the White Mountains.

C The White Mountains? Where are they?

A In northern New Hampshire. They're very beautiful. I've been there myself. Acadia National Park, where you'll be on the sixth day, is very pretty too. It's on Mount Desert Island, off the eastern coast of Maine.

C And from there we'll go on to Canada?

A Yes, that's right. You'll have one day for Quebec and two for Montreal.

C Oh, that's good.

A You'll spend the whole of the twelfth day travelling through the state of New York down to New York City.

C That's quite a long way, isn't it?

A Yes, almost four hundred miles. About the same distance as from London to Glasgow. – You then have three days for New York City, and you'll arrive back at Heathrow at nine forty a.m. on the sixteenth day. – You'll find all the details on this sheet here.

Congress Street – the heart of downtown Portland

Mount Desert Island, Maine: Northeast Harbour

Quebec: Château Frontenac and St Lawrence River

New York: street scene in downtown Manhattan

17B **Questions on 17A. One student asks another.**

a. What has the travel agent planned for the client?
b. Will the client be travelling alone?
c. When will the client leave for the United States?
d. Which airline will he fly by?
e. Where will he go first in the U.S.?
f. Why does the flying time seem to be so short?
g. What's the real flying time from London to Boston?
h. Where will the client spend the first night?
i. What will he do on the second day?
j. What would the client like to do in Boston if possible?
k. Where will the client go from Boston?
l. Where will he make an excursion to on the fourth day?
m. Where are the White Mountains, and where is Acadia National Park?
n. Which cities will the client visit in Canada?
o. Which route will he take to New York City?
p. How many days will he spend in New York City?
q. When will he get back to London?

17C Itinerary Mr and Mrs Cox

Explain the itinerary to Mr Cox (another student). Tell him about departure and arrival times, time differences between London and the eastern United States, the places he will visit in the U.S., the distances between them, etc.

1st day:	Depart Heathrow 12.00 (local time) Arrive Boston 14.15 (local time)
2nd day:	Boston - sightseeing
3rd day:	Afternoon - to Portland, Maine (109 miles)
4th day:	Portland - White Mountains excursion
5th day:	To Bangor, Maine
6th day:	To Bar Harbor, Mount Desert Island (42 miles) Visit Acadia National Park
7th day:	To Quebec (282 miles)
8th day:	Quebec - sightseeing
9th day:	To Montreal (155 miles)
10th day: 11th day:	Montreal - sightseeing
12th day:	To New York (388 miles)
13th day: 14th day:	New York - sightseeing
15th day:	Depart New York 22.00 (local time)
16th day:	Arrive Heathrow 09.40 (local time)

Kilometres		Miles
1.609	**1**	0.621
3.219	**2**	1.243
4.828	**3**	1.864
6.437	**4**	2.485
8.047	**5**	3.107
9.656	**6**	3.728
11.265	**7**	4.350
12.874	**8**	4.971
14.484	**9**	5.592
16.093	**10**	6.214

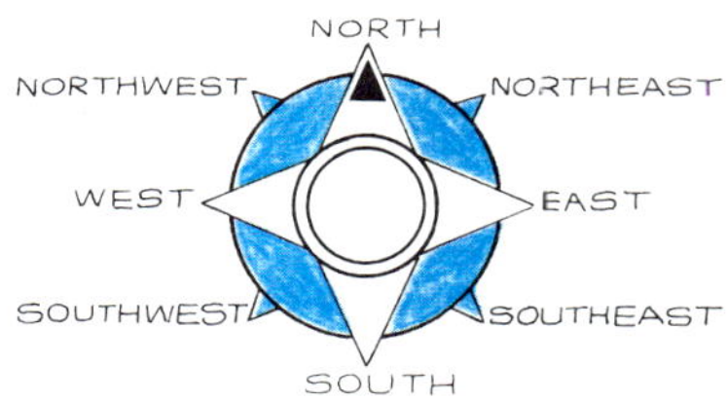

17D Locations

London Airport, at Heathrow, is 15 miles west of London.

Boston lies on the east coast of the United States, about 200 miles northeast of New York.

Portland is a city in southwest Maine, 150 miles northeast of Boston.

The **White Mountains** are a popular resort area in northern New Hampshire.

Mount Desert Island is off the eastern coast of Maine.

Canada is bounded on the north by the Arctic Ocean, on the west by the Pacific Ocean and Alaska, on the east by the Atlantic Ocean, and on the south by the U.S.A.

Quebec City, the capital of the province of Quebec, is situated on the north bank of the St Lawrence River.

Montreal is situated in southern Quebec, about 155 miles southwest of Quebec City.

New York State is about the size of England. It is situated in the northeastern part of the United States, with New York City at its southeastern end.

a. Talk about the location of Austria, Germany, and Switzerland. What countries, seas, oceans, mountains, rivers, lakes, etc. are these countries bounded by?
b. What "Land", state, province, Canton, etc. do you live in? Talk about its location.
c. Talk about the location of the town or village where you live. What part of the country is it situated in? How far away is it from other towns, villages, etc? What rivers, mountains, etc. are near your town or village?
d. How far away is the nearest railway station, airport, etc?

17E **Mr Cox gives a short account of his trip to America. Please complete.**

a. On Wednesday, 1st October, at 12 o'clock sharp, our British Airways Jumbo jet took off for Boston. b. After a smooth seven-and-a-half-hour flight we (arrive) in Boston, only fifteen minutes late, at half past two in the afternoon. c. We (not sleep) well the first night, though our hotel room (be) fairly quiet and comfortable. d. On the second day we (do) some sightseeing, and in the evening we heard a concert given by the Boston Symphony Orchestra. e. On the third day we (travel) over a hundred miles along the Atlantic coast up to Portland, and on the fourth we (make) an excursion to the White Mountains in northern New Hampshire. f. We (like) Acadia National Park on Mount Desert Island, which we (visit) on the sixth day. g. From Mount Desert Island we (go) to Quebec and Montreal in Canada. h. On our way back down to New York City we (come) through the Adirondack Mountains with their beautiful lakes, rivers, and forests. i. We (stop) to pay a short visit to the place where "John Brown's body lies a-mouldering in the grave", at John Brown's farm a few miles away from Lake Placid. j. We (spend) the last three days of our tour in New York City. k. After a long night flight we (arrive) back at Heathrow at 9.40 on the morning of October 16.

17F *Montreal: the Olympic Stadium ten months before the XXIst Games were due to open on 17 July 1976.*

Talk about the picture.
What can you see?
Say what you remember about the 1976 Games.
Did they go as planned?
Were they well organized?
Who were the outstanding athletes?

18

18A Living by the motorway

A The Hendersons have moved into their new house now.

B Have they? How nice! Whereabouts is it?

A In Harlington. Right next to the motorway. Where the big intersection is.

B But isn't it very noisy there? I mean, there are cars and lorries going past all the time…

A Yes, of course it's noisy. But they don't mind.

B They don't mind? You mean the noise doesn't get on their nerves?

A No, it doesn't at all.

B You can't be serious. Do you know what it's like at the side of a motorway? The noise drives you out of your mind.

A Yes, I know, but that's not the way the Hendersons feel. They actually like to be near the motorway, to watch the traffic . . . They say it's like a big promenade at the seaside – they always have something to look at.

B But how can anyone stand that awful noise? People get ill from too much noise, don't they?

A Yes, but it seems many of the people who live near the motorway are quite happy there. To Mrs Henderson it's a great advantage that no one can build on the motorway. She doesn't want to see other houses when she looks out of the window. She prefers the motorway. She also feels she has more privacy than other people. When she's sunbathing in the garden, nobody will notice her. The cars go much too fast.

18B Questions on 18A. One student asks another.

a. Where's the Hendersons' new house?
b. Why is it probably very noisy where the Hendersons live now?
c. Do the Hendersons mind the noise?
d. How do they feel about the motorway right next to their house?
e. What does Mrs Henderson mean when she says "no one can build on the motorway"?
f. Why does Mrs Henderson feel she has more privacy than other people?

Apartment houses in New York

Residential street in London

18 C **Talk about the way people live . . .**

. . . in a rented flat: pay high / low rent; don't own the flat / apartment; furnished – unfurnished; landlord – tenant; give (someone) notice; give one month's / six weeks' / six months' notice; advantages: less work than in a house of their own, repairs not their business, etc.; disadvantages: no garden, no pets(?), noise from other flats, etc.

. . . in a condominium / an owner-occupied flat: they don't rent but buy the flat; they own the flat / apartment but not the house or land; no landlord who can give them notice; advantages?; disadvantages?

. . . in a house of their own: detached – semidetached (which is better / cheaper?); good / bad neighbourhood; advantages: garden, pets, more space, etc.; disadvantages: more work (repairs!); can't just lock the door and go away; shops and stores not so near at hand, etc.

. . . in the slums of the big cities: old, ugly, dirty houses; in bad repair; overcrowded / too many people; not enough fresh air; children play in the street or backyard; vermin: cockroaches, mice, rats; often outside lavatories, no bathrooms, no hot water.

Detached one-family house in an American suburb

Flats in an East London slum

18D Talk about your home. One student asks, another answers.

a. Where do you live? (Near . . . Not far from . . .)
b. Have you got a furnished room, a flat, or a house?
c. What kind of house do you live in? (Old? New? Modern? Large? Small? How many storeys? A two-storey / three-storey / four-storey house.)
d. Which floor do you live on?
e. What rooms are there in your flat / house?
f. Have you got a garden? If so, what's it like?
g. Where do your children / other children play?
h. Have you got a balcony? If so, what do you use it for?
i. What kind of furniture do you like? (Old? Traditional? Modern? Practical? Heavy? Light?)
j. What kinds of pictures do you like to have on your walls?
k. Have you got a cellar? If so, what do you use it for?
l. How long have you lived in your present home? (Since 19 . . / For . . . years)
m. Do you like it? (Pretty? Cosy? Convenient? Quiet? Noisy?)
n. How do you like your neighbours?
o. Which is the best place to live? A big city, a suburb of a big city, a small town, a village, a faraway place in the country?

"Oh, while you're on your feet, dear . . . the milk."

18E -'s oder -s'? (→ GII2)

Singular	Plural
Mr **Henderson's** house	the **Hendersons'** house
one **month's** notice	six **months'** notice
Nicholson's London Guide	The **Samaritans'** Birmingham branch
Jack **Dixon's** job	

-'s or -s'? Put in the correct forms.

a. John (Brown) farm is near Lake Placid. b. The (Brown) farm is near Lake Placid. c. Mrs (Barton) flat is in Kensington. d. The (Barton) flat is in Kensington. e. Mr (Cox) trip to America was very expensive. f. The (Cox) trip to America was very expensive. g. Our (neighbour) children are a noisy lot, but they themselves are very quiet people. h. The (President) first name is Gerald, but his friends call him Jerry. i. He has to give his landlord two (week) notice if he wants to leave.

18F **Zusammengesetzte Adjektive (Grundzahl + Bindestrich + Singular-substantiv)** ᴏᴏ

after a **seven-hour** flight (*but:* after seven hours)
it's a **fifty-mile** journey (*but:* it's fifty miles away)
this is a **two-pint** bottle (*but:* these are two pints)
the **thirty-foot** whale lay there high and dry (*but:* the whale was 30 feet long)
he bought a **two-year-old** horse (*but:* this horse is two years old)

Translate accordingly.

a. ein zehntägiger Streik
b. ein achtstündiger Ausflug
c. ein zweiwöchiger Besuch
d. eine neunstündige Reise
e. eine zweistündige Unterhaltung
f. ein Zweifamilienhaus
g. eine Dreizimmerwohnung
h. ein vierstöckiges Haus
i. ein Drei-Sterne-Restaurant ("best cooking in the British Isles")

18G **Talk about your likes and dislikes.**

I like to I don't like to I've always liked to I've never liked to	be alone / mix with other people / go to cocktail parties sing songs / listen to good music / go to concerts watch television / go to the theatre / go to museums go to my English class / talk to interesting people have a drink at the pub / eat at Chinese restaurants sunbathe in the garden / do repairs in the house read books / magazines / newspapers study mail-order catalogues / go shopping in . . . play (table) tennis / football / chess travel to faraway countries / stay at expensive hotels visit beautiful places / swim in the sea

Beer and rolls at the local

Village pub in Cumbria

Village in Cumbria

19A

Beer flows free after 74 years

It was 74 years ago that 88-year-old Mr Charles Northam became a customer at the Black Dog in the village of Grigghall in Cumbria. Since then, he has drunk about 40,000 pints of his favourite mild there.

When the brewery discovered how long he had been a customer, they decided to give him free beer for the rest of his life.

In future, when Mr Northam walks the 700 yards from his cottage to the pub four times a week, the beer will be on the brewery.

He said yesterday: "This is very generous but it won't make any difference to my drinking habits. I never have more than $2\frac{1}{2}$ pints, and I won't change that. I'm not going to drink myself to death now."

His wife, Mrs Martha Northam, 83, a lifelong teetotaller, said: "I don't mind his drinking because he never has too much and is always home on time. But I do mind his getting free beer, because people might think I don't give him enough pocket money. It's not the beer that has kept him going all these years, it's my elderberry wine. He used to come in soaking wet after working in the fields all day and I used to give him the hot wine. He never caught a cold."

19B Questions on 19A. One student asks another.

a. How long has Mr Northam been a customer at the Black Dog?
b. At what age did he drink his first pint at the Black Dog?
c. How many pints of beer has Mr Northam drunk in 74 years?
d. What type of beer does he always drink?
e. Why did the brewery decide to give Mr Northam free beer for the rest of his life?
f. How many times a week does Mr Northam go to the pub?
g. How far is the pub away from his house?
h. In future the beer will be "on the brewery" – what does that mean?
i. How much beer does Mr Northam always drink when he's at the pub?
j. Is he going to drink more in future when he gets free beer?
k. If Mr Northam continues to drink his beer at the Black Dog up to the age of 95, how much will the brewery's generosity cost them? ($7 \times 52 \times 4 \times 2.5 = 3{,}640$ pints; 1 pint of mild = 35p)
l. Is Mrs Northam a beer drinker too?
m. Why doesn't she mind her husband's drinking?
n. What does she mind, and why?
o. Has the beer been bad for Mr Northam's health?
p. What does Mrs Northam say about her elderberry wine?

19C Use the short forms. (→ GI18)

It **will not** make any difference. It **won't** make any difference.
He has drunk 40,000 pints of mild in his life. **He's** drunk 40,000 pints of mild in his life.

a. Mr Northam *will not* have to pay for his beer in future. b. *They have* decided to give him free beer for the rest of his life. c. You *will not* believe how long *he has* been a customer at the Black Dog. d. There *will not* be many people in England *who have* drunk at the same pub for 74 years. e. *He has* never had more than 2½ pints, and he *will not* change that. f. He *will not* drink himself to death now. g. I hope people *will not* think I *do not* give you enough pocket money. h. You *will not* catch a cold if you drink the hot wine.

Farm in Cumbria

19D Talk about the differences between country life and city life.

a. Townspeople move about a great deal. Are you townspeople or country people? Are you still living where you were born? How often have you moved? Where have you lived?
b. Has Mr Northam moved about a lot? Or is he still living where he was born?
c. Does Mr Northam lead a very regular life? What about people in the cities?
d. What's Mr Northam's job? Do you think he's worked in many different jobs in his life? Ask your fellow students: Have they worked in the same job, at the same place, all their lives?
e. Use your imagination: How do country people like Mr Northam usually spend their day? What kind of work do they do? (work in the fields; feed the animals; milk the cows every twelve hours; work in the farm office; repair the farm machinery; drive to the market or to the shops)
f. What differences are there between your work and the work of people like Mr Northam? (work in an office / in a factory / in the open air; work from eight to five; work overtime)
g. What do people like Mr Northam do in their spare time? What do you do in your spare time?
h. Town life and country life – what are their advantages and disadvantages?
i. If you could start your life all over again, where would you rather live – in the country or in a big city?

19E **-self-Pronomen** (→ GII13)

I couldn't help **myself** (*ich konnte mir nicht helfen*)
you couldn't help **yourself** (*du . . . dir / Sie . . . sich*)
he couldn't help **himself** (*er . . . sich*)
she / Mary couldn't help **herself** (*sie . . . sich*)
it / the animal couldn't help **itself** (*es . . . sich*)
we couldn't help **ourselves** (*wir . . . uns*)
you couldn't help **yourselves** (*ihr . . . euch / Sie . . . sich*)
they / the children couldn't help **themselves** (*sie . . . sich*)

Put in: myself, yourself, himself, herself, ourselves, yourselves, themselves.
a. She made ..... a cup of tea. b. I'll serve ..... if you don't mind. c. Mr Northam isn't going to drink ..... to death now. d. We're only trying to protect ..... e. Many people have killed ..... because they were lonely. f. Must you always think of ..... first, Bob? g. Why don't you get ..... something to drink, children? h. Her husband talks about ..... most of the time. i. Did your wife enjoy ..... at the party last night?

19F Talk about what you used to do in the past. (→ GIII46)

When I was	a child, a little boy, a young girl, still at school, young,	I used to	drink go have hear live play spend travel watch work	a lot a lot of fun with my friends football in a furnished room in the fields in the garden in the street milk, not beer my holidays at the seaside pop music television to bed early	(all day). (every day). (most of the time).

19G One student asks, another student answers.

A He drinks, doesn't he? (his wife) *B* Yes, he does. *A* How does his wife feel about it? *B* She doesn't mind his drinking.	*A* You always come home late, don't you? (your wife) *B* Yes, I do. *A* How does your wife feel about it? *B* She doesn't mind my coming home late.

a. He watches television every evening, doesn't he? (his mother)
b. He plays football every week-end, doesn't he? (his family – they!)
c. She works in a night club, doesn't she? (Jack)
d. She always stays at expensive hotels, doesn't she? (her husband)
e. The children make a lot of noise, don't they? (the neighbours)
f. You call him Jerry, don't you? (he)
g. The dog wakes you up every night, doesn't he? (you)
h. We're in debt, aren't we? (you)

"My wife doesn't mind my having a quick one at the bar."

Anthony Booth as Mike, Una Stubbs as Rita, Warren Mitchell as Alf, and Dandy Nichols as Else, in Till Death Us Do Part (BBC Photograph)

A popular television series

Till Death Us Do Part is a comedy series that has appeared on BBC Television at intervals since 1966.

The series is about Alf Garnett, an East End working man in his mid-fifties. He lives in a small terraced house with his plump, stupid but good-hearted wife, their daughter Rita and her husband Mike, a lazy, long-haired layabout with half-baked Socialist opinions.

Alf Garnett is an unpleasant, ignorant, selfish, "bloody-minded" character who hates new ideas, coloured people, foreigners, and trade unions.

Viewers react to Alf Garnett in different ways. Some find him offensive, many regard him as a folk hero, others just think him funny. Almost everybody considers the series good entertainment.

Here are some typical Alf Garnett statements:

"There are too many long-haired layabouts in this country."

"Pakistanis and Indians are all lazy and dirty."

"Mixed marriages should not be allowed."

"Workers are trying to destroy the country with their bloody strikes and go-slows."

When 382 typical viewers were asked about the series, about half of them expressed the opinion that Alf was "right more often than he was wrong".

20B Questions on 20A. One student asks another.

a. What kind of programme is *Till Death Us Do Part*?
b. How long has it been on BBC Television?
c. Who is it about?
d. Describe the four main characters in the series.
e. What is Alf Garnett against? What does he hate?
f. What do TV viewers think of Alf Garnett?
g. What do they think of the series as a whole?
h. Look at the "typical Alf Garnett statements". Are there many people with similar views in this country?
i. Alf Garnett doesn't like Pakistanis, Indians, and blacks. Who are the "Pakistanis, Indians, and blacks" in this country?
j. What does Alf Garnett think of the workers and trade unions?
k. What is a "mixed marriage"?

20C Life in a multiracial society

Both Britain and the United States are multiracial societies. Both countries have a colour problem.

In Britain, the coloured population is about 1.5 million (= $2\frac{1}{2}$ per cent of the total population).

In the United States, the non-white population is over 25 million (= 12.6 per cent of the total population).

Coloured people in Britain are mainly immigrants (or the children of immigrants) from Commonwealth countries in the West Indies, Asia, and Africa.

Immigrants are often the victims of discrimination. It is difficult for them to find a decent place to live or a decent job. Like Alf Garnett, their white neighbours and workmates are often hostile to them.

In 1903 W. E. B. Du Bois said: "The problem of the twentieth century is the problem of the colour line." This is certainly true of the United States today. In her book *What America Means to Me*, Pearl S. Buck said: "It is not healthy when a nation lives within a nation, as coloured Americans are living inside America. A nation cannot live confident of its tomorrow if its refugees are among its own citizens."

a. Discuss the problem of discrimination. What people are the victims of discrimination?
b. What underprivileged groups are there in this country?
c. What disadvantages do you have if you are a member of an underprivileged group?
d. In what ways are foreigners at a disadvantage in this country? Do all foreigners have the same disadvantages?
e. Are there many mixed marriages nowadays? In what ways may the partners in a mixed marriage be different? (nationality, language, race, colour, religion, customs, etc.) What problems may these differences create?

20D "Stinker" Alfred – the German Alf Garnett

In 1974, Alfred Tetzlaff was as popular in Germany as Alf Garnett was in Britain. Wearing slippers, smoking a cigar, and calling his wife "silly cow", he had a young daughter who always wore jeans and a liberal son-in-law. He hated long hair, beards, and miniskirts, foreign workers, students, eggheads, and – above all – "the left".
Most people laughed at "the stinker", but some were worried about his popularity. Was Alfred becoming the hero of the nation? Was Germany going to be a nation of ugly little stinkers?
Wolfgang Menge, the author of the German *One Heart and One Soul* series, did not think so: "The whole thing works like a vaccine against smallpox," he said. "It acts like an infection, but instead of causing the illness, it prevents it."

A scene from the German TV series One Heart and One Soul*: Heinz Schubert as Alfred Tetzlaff, Elisabeth Wiedemann as Else, Hildegard Krekel as Rita, and Diether Krebs as Michael*

20E Questions on 20D. One student asks another.

a. Who was the German counterpart of Alf Garnett?

b. Was the German *One Heart and One Soul* series a success?

c. Describe Alfred Tetzlaff, his wife, his daughter, and his son-in-law.

d. Compare the two sons-in-law – Mike and his German counterpart Michael. Is there a difference between a "lazy, long-haired layabout with half-baked Socialist opinions" and a "liberal"?

e. What did Alfred hate?

f. Why were some people worried about Alfred Tetzlaff's popularity?

g. Did the author of the series think that Alfred Tetzlaff was "dangerous"? What did he mean when he compared Tetzlaff to a vaccine?

20F Talk about the topics of this lesson.

Till Death Us Do Part is a comedy series The series is about a working man Alf Garnett is an unpleasant character Wolfgang Menge is the man Heinz Schubert was the actor Some people think that a man "Stinker" Alfred is like a vaccine Do you know the American series Immigrants Britain is only one of many countries	that which who	calls come has appeared hates have is lives played protects wrote	a colour problem. coloured people and foreigners. from the West Indies, Asia, and Africa are often the victims of discrimination. his wife "silly cow" isn't very funny. in the East End of London. on BBC Television at intervals since 1966. people from smallpox. the counterpart of *Till Death Us Do Part*? the German counterpart of Alf Garnett. the German *One Heart and One Soul* series.

20G Television – who watches most?

Viewing time (hours : minutes) per head per week in the U.K.

Age group	5–14	15–19	20–29	30–49	50 & over
Viewing time	20:38	14:26	15:36	16:15	17:25

a. Discuss these figures.

b. How many hours do you and your family watch TV each week?

c. Here are the radio listening times for the five age groups, but in the wrong order: 1:53, 8:47, 10:12, 11:18, 12:01. What do you think, which figure belongs to which group?

d. Compare radio and television. Advantages? Disadvantages?

21

21 A **In business**

A You were a toolmaker before you went into business, weren't you, Mr Clark?

B Yes, I gave up my job at the factory three years ago. Then I sold my house to buy this shop here with the flat over it.

A And what do you sell?

B Oh, newspapers and magazines, biros, sweets, soft drinks and ices, cigarettes . . .

A You also have a kiosk, don't you?

B Yes, at Russell Hill station – three miles from here.

A That's a lot of work, isn't it? How do you manage it all?

B Well, my wife and my eldest son work with me. I work ninety hours a week, and so does my wife. The boy does less, of course, about thirty hours. You see, he's still at school, working for his exams just now . . .

A Are you better off now than you were in your old job?

B As a toolmaker I was earning between £50 and £60 a week. I did a lot of overtime, of course, but I worked much less than I do now. I had no worries and no debts. Today, my wife and I both work ninety hours, and we owe the bank £6,500.

A Wouldn't you like to go back to work in the factory?

B No, never! You know, it's nice to work in a shop, to meet people, to be your own master, even if you have a lot of problems. I've never been happier . . .

21 B **Questions on 21A. One student asks another.**

a. What did Mr Clark do before he went into business?
b. When did he give up his job at the factory?
c. Why did he give up his old job?
d. Why did he sell his house?
e. What does he sell in his shop?
f. Where's his kiosk?
g. What do you think he sells at his kiosk?
h. Who helps him with his work?
i. How many hours a week does he work? And his wife?
j. Why does his son work less?
k. Is Mr Clark better off now than in his old job?
l. If Mr Clark now works more and earns less than in his old job, why doesn't he go back to work as a toolmaker at the factory?

21 C **A small shopkeeper talks about his business**

Six days a week I start work at 5.30 a.m. and finish at 7 p.m.
On Sundays I work from 6.30 a.m. to 2 p.m.
My wife and I work in the shop and at the kiosk most of the time. My son Brian does the deliveries and also works at the kiosk and in the shop.
Together, the kiosk and the shop have a turnover of about £2,300 a month.
The neighbours say: "Two shops he's got now. He must be rolling in money." But they're forgetting that I have to find £113 a month for the mortgage alone. My interest payments last year on the loans and mortgage were £920. And the kiosk costs £56 a month in overheads.

a. How many hours does Mr Clark work each day?
b. What do his wife and his son Brian do?
c. What is Mr Clark's monthly profit if it is 10% / 15% of the turnover?
d. Compare Mr Clark's profit with what he earned as a toolmaker.
e. Is Mr Clark's business profitable?
f. What are Mr Clark's monthly expenses? (920 ÷ 12 = 76.66)
g. What does Mr Clark have to pay interest on?
h. Is it fair to say that the Clarks "must be rolling in money"?

21 D

A factory worker's day

At 7 a.m. Mike Briggs is finishing his breakfast in the front room of his terraced house in a London suburb.

Before he leaves for work, he takes a short stroll down the narrow path to the bottom of his back garden to have a look at his tomatoes, marrows, cabbages, beans, potatoes, and onions.

Working on the assembly line

At 7.30 Mike Briggs is on the shop floor to start work on the assembly line.

Eight hours of assembly-line work.

At 4 p.m. the whistle blows, and within minutes Mike Briggs is out of the factory and on his way home. He changes into his gardening clothes and goes outside.

After an hour or two of pottering about in the garden he has tea with his wife. While they eat, they watch their favourite series on television.

Afterwards he goes to the pub next door for a drink and a game of darts.

(Mike Briggs earns £60 a week.)

21 E **The Prime Minister talks about his working day**

I normally wake up about a quarter to eight and have breakfast at eight. At the same time I read the newspapers.

In the morning I usually work on boxes until the first meetings, which begin at 10 or 10.30.

Tuesdays and Thursdays I answer questions in the House. I never go out to lunch on these days. I just have a tray lunch and

discuss the questions with the No. 10 staff at 2.30. Then we go across to the House and I answer questions at 3.15.
Then there are usually meetings till dinner. I try to get away about 7 o'clock for a swim – but I don't always succeed – and after that there may be some official function, or I work in the flat (at No. 10), or I listen in the House.
As for television and radio – I very often hear the 8 o'clock news in the morning but don't often manage to watch television in the evenings.
I get to bed between midnight and half past twelve.
(The Prime Minister's salary is £20,000 a year.)

21 F **Compare the lives of Mike Briggs and John Clark.**

a. Which of the two men works longer hours?
b. Which has the more interesting job?
c. What is Mike Briggs' main interest in life?
d. What is John Clark's main interest in life?
e. What is it like to work on the assembly line? (monotonous, boring, tiring)
f. What is it like to work in a shop or kiosk like John Clark's?
g. Does Mike Briggs like his job? And what about John Clark?
h. Who earns more – Mike Briggs or John Clark?
i. Who would you rather be – Mike Briggs or John Clark? (Give reasons for your answer.)

21 G **Look at what the Prime Minister says about his working day.**

a. How many hours does he work every day?
b. Why is it important for the P.M. to read the papers every day?
c. John Clark spends most of the day behind the counter, and Mike Briggs is on the assembly line all day. Where does the P.M. spend most of his day?
d. Why doesn't the P.M. go out to lunch on Tuesdays and Thursdays?
e. What does the P.M. do in the evening?

21 H **Some comparisons. Please complete.** (→ GIII2–3)

a. John Clark now works twice . . . . much as he did when he worked in the factory, but he's much happier . . . . three years ago. b. Brian works less . . . . his father because he's still at school. c. As a shopkeeper John Clark earns . . . . than in his old job at the factory. d. He earns much . . . . money . . . . his neighbours think. e. His business isn't as profitable . . . . it could be. f. Mike Briggs starts work much . . . . than John Clark. g. But his job is more boring and tiring . . . . John Clark's. h. Mike Briggs likes his garden much . . . . than his job. i. The Prime Minister earns about six times . . . . much . . . . Mike Briggs, but his work is also much . . . . difficult. j. The Prime Minister starts work . . . . than John Clark and Mike Briggs but he works . . . . in the evening. k. The Prime Minister doesn't watch TV . . . . often as other people because he has . . . . time.

22A

22

Women in Britain

Women in Britain have the same political rights as men. And yet, although there are more women than men in Britain, only 27 out of the 635 members of Parliament are women.

Men and women are equal before the law, but it is usually more difficult for a woman to get credit than it is for a man.

Women form 37 per cent of the working population in Britain. Under the Equal Pay Act, every woman who does the same work as a man for the same employer at the same place of work has a right to the same rate of pay. But the average woman still earns much less than the average man mainly because she is less well-trained and works shorter hours.

Where both husband and wife have jobs outside the home, the woman's working week is about ten hours longer than the man's. It is the wife who does the cooking, the washing, the shopping, and the cleaning while the husband watches television or goes to the pub.

Average salaries of white-collar workers (U.K., 1974)

Men	£54 a week
Women	£29 a week

In at least one respect, though, men and women are apparently equal: According to a British Government survey, the most popular pastime for both sexes is watching television.

Average wages of blue-collar workers (U.K., 1974)			**Average hours worked per week**
Men	£1.08 an hour	£48.63 a week	45.1
Women	£0.72 an hour	£27.01 a week	37.4

22B Questions on 22A. One student asks another.

a. Give reasons why only 27 out of the 635 members of Parliament are women. What is the situation in this country?

b. What may be the reason why it is more difficult for a woman to get credit than for a man?

c. What does the Equal Pay Act say?

d. Why do women still earn much less than men?

e. Why is it that where both husband and wife have jobs, the woman works ten hours more than the man? Do you think it is fair?

22 C **Talk about "typical" women's and men's occupations.**

Give reasons why there are more women in some jobs than in others.

Percentage of women in selected occupations (United Kingdom)	
Typists	98.6%
Nurses	91.2%
Telephone operators	83.2%
Shop assistants	81.1%
Schoolteachers	64.1%
Butchers	6.7%
Postmen	6.5%
Soldiers	4.5%
Police	4.3%
Bus drivers	2.4%

No sex discrimination from the start – in the Salvation Army men and women have always had equal rights

22 D **Excuse me, would you mind answering a few questions . . .**

Is it better for a woman to look after the home or to work in a factory or office?
Can a woman have a family and a job at the same time?
Is it all right for a woman to go out to work and employ another woman to do the housework for her?
Should husbands help with the housework?
Is it really necessary for a housewife to iron things like handkerchiefs and shirts, blouses and dresses, underwear, nightdresses, and pyjamas?
Should a wife polish her husband's shoes?
Is it true that most housewives waste a lot of time because they don't organize their housework?

22 E Talk about women drivers / men drivers

Women Men	are	(much)	better / worse slower / faster safer / more dangerous more careful / more careless more / less polite more / less patient more / less aggressive more / less often drunk at the wheel	(drivers)	than	men. women.

22 F Vergleich mit as . . . as (→ GIII2)

Ann's working day is **as long as** Ted's.	*so lang wie*
Alfred Tetzlaff was **as popular as** Alf Garnett.	*so populär wie*
A plane is**n't as fast as** a rocket.	*nicht so schnell wie*
Women are**n't as aggressive as** men.	*nicht so aggressiv wie*

22 G Steigerung: Komparativ + than (→ GIII3)

A rocket is **faster than** a plane. He's much **happier than** he was three years ago.	*schneller als* *glücklicher als*
Men are **more aggressive than** women. His job is **more difficult / more interesting** now.	*aggressiver als* *schwieriger / interessanter*

Der Komparativ wird bei kürzeren Wörtern durch Anhängen von *-er*, bei längeren durch Voranstellen von *more* gebildet. Im einzelnen gelten folgende Regeln:

cheap – cheap**er** short – short**er**	Einsilbige Wörter hängen *-er* an.
dangerous – **more** dangerous interesting – **more** interesting	Wörter mit mehr als zwei Silben werden mit *more* gesteigert.
boring – **more** boring patient – **more** patient	Zweisilbige Wörter werden meistens mit *more* gesteigert.
early – earl**ier** pretty – prett**ier**	Zweisilbige Wörter auf *-y* hängen *-er* an, wobei das *-y* zu *-i-* wird.

Schreibregeln

late – la**ter**	*-e* am Wortende entfällt.
big – big**ger** hot – hot**ter**	Der Endbuchstabe wird nach kurzem, betontem *a, e, i* oder *o* verdoppelt.
dirty – dirt**ier** heavy – heav**ier**	Auslautendes *-y* wird bei mehrsilbigen Wörtern zu *-i-*.

Unregelmäßige Steigerung

bad – **worse** [wɜːs] good – **better** little – **less** many / much – **more**	*schlecht – schlechter* *gut – besser* *wenig – weniger* *viel / viele – mehr*

"I still say a holiday at the seaside is nicer than a holiday in the mountains."

22H Ausdruck eines geringeren Grades

Are women **less aggressive** than men?
Sind Frauen weniger aggressiv als Männer?

Are men **less careful** than women?
Sind Männer weniger vorsichtig als Frauen?

22I Say what you think.

Form sentences to express your opinion. There are usually four possibilities to choose from.

Opel cars / reliable / Ford cars.
Opel cars are *as reliable as* Ford cars.
Opel cars are*n't as reliable as* Ford cars.
Opel cars are *more reliable than* Ford cars.
Opel cars are *less reliable than* Ford cars.

a. A holiday at the seaside is / nice / a holiday in the mountains. b. Car parks are / important / children's playgrounds. c. Chess is / interesting / table tennis. d. Country life is / pleasant / town life. e. Work in the office is / tiring / work in the open air. f. A house is / convenient / a flat. g. Traditional furniture is / practical / modern furniture. h. Cigars are / dangerous / cigarettes. i. Beer is / good / wine. j. Miniskirts look / bad / jeans.

23 A Records

Superlatives are a favourite conversation topic. Men like to argue about which river is the longest, which car the fastest, which man the strongest, which bird the smallest. The *Guinness Book of Records* answers most questions of this kind.

Guinness tells us that the tallest man was 8 feet 11 inches, or 272 centimetres, that the oldest people were not older than 113 years, that the most intelligent animal is the chimpanzee, and that the most common illness is the common cold.

We also learn from Guinness that the language with the most words is English (790,000), that the world's most valuable painting is probably Leonardo's "Mona Lisa", that the biggest department store is Macy's in New York, and that the largest bookshop is Foyle's in London.

According to Guinness, the most successful songwriters so far have been John Lennon and Paul McCartney of the Beatles, who together wrote 30 songs which sold more than 1,000,000 records each.

The *Guinness Book of Records* has become so popular that it has set up a record itself: In November 1974, with sales of 23,950,000, it became the most successful of all commercially sold books. Congratulations, Guinness!

The world's shortest letters were exchanged between Victor Hugo (1802–85) and his publisher. The author was on holiday and wanted to know how his latest novel was selling.
He wrote: "?" – The reply was: "!"

Most successful songwriters John Lennon . . .

. . . and Paul McCartney of the Beatles

Macy's in New York – the world's biggest store

23 B Questions. One student asks another.

a. Why are superlatives a favourite conversation topic?
b. Guinness is a brewery. Can you think why a brewery would publish a book of records?
c. Talk about the problems that very tall people have.
d. What do you do when you have a cold?
e. How many words do you think people use in everyday conversation?
f. Where can you look at valuable paintings?
g. Where do you think you get better service – in a very large store or in a small shop? Give reasons.
h. What do you know about the Beatles? Do you like their music?

23 C Special exercise

Write down Victor Hugo's letter and his publisher's answer in full.

23 D Gothic made in U.S.A.

America, where everything is "bigger and better", has the biggest trees, the tallest buildings, the longest bridges, the fastest jets, and the most powerful corporations. But few people know that it also has the largest Gothic cathedral in the world: the cathedral of St John the Divine in New York City, though still unfinished, is larger than all the famous Gothic cathedrals in Europe.

a. What other American superlatives can you think of?
b. What's the world's tallest building at present?
c. The world's longest bridge is also in New York. Do you know its name?
d. Name some powerful American corporations. What do you know about them?
e. Why is it funny that the largest Gothic cathedral is in America?

Books by the mile – Foyle's in London

The largest white oak in the U.S. is in Maryland

Cathedral of St John the Divine in New York

23E

The laziest man in Britain

At the age of 47, Albert Thorogood became a folk hero, not because he had done something spectacular but because he had done a most nothing at all. Government officials discovered that in 25 years the able-bodied father of five had managed to work for only 33 weeks. For the rest of the time he had been on the dole, collecting about £12,000 in unemployment benefits.

a. What kind of people are "folk heroes" in this country?
b. Why did Albert Thorogood become a folk hero in Britain?
c. During his years on the dole "Idle Albert" got dozens of offers of jobs but he always found reasons not to accept them. What reasons do you think he gave for not accepting work?
d. How do you think "Idle Albert" usually passed the day?

23F Make sentences.

October 1975 / "Idle Albert" / collect / £12,000 in unemployment benefits. By October 1975 "Idle Albert" had collected £12,000 in unemployment benefits.
November 1974 / the *Guinness Book of Records* / sell / 23 million copies. By November 1974 the *Guinness Book of Records* had sold 23 million copies.

a. July 1974 / Mr Northam / drink / 40,000 pints of mild at the Black Dog.

b. 1975 / he / visit / over 150 countries. c. last year / the family / move / nine times. d. lunchtime / they / travel / 300 miles. e. five o'clock / the reporter / talk / to about 50 people. f. two o'clock / they / stop / work twenty times. g. the end of May / Long & Company / order / £40,000 worth of goods. h. the end of the week / he / write / to Sandra ten times. i. eleven o'clock / we / catch / 24 mice. j. the end of last year / she / be / to London fifteen times.

23G **Steigerung: Superlativ** (→ GIII4)

the **largest** / the **most valuable** painting in the world
das größte / das wertvollste Gemälde der Welt

Der Superlativ wird bei kürzeren Wörtern durch Anhängen von *-est*, bei längeren durch Voranstellen von *most* gebildet. Die Regeln für die Bildung des Superlativs entsprechen denen für die Bildung des Komparativs (→ 22G):

-est	**End-e entfällt**	**-y → -i-**	**most**
the fastest	the largest	the laziest	the most common
the greatest	the latest		the most intelligent
the longest		**Unregelmäßig**	the most popular
the nearest	**Verdopplung**	the best	the most powerful
the oldest	the biggest	the eldest	the most successful
the shortest		the most	the most valuable

23H **Make sentences.**

large store X is the largest store / one of the largest stores in . . . / in the world, etc.
good actor X is the best actor I know / one of the best actors I know.

a. fast car
b. old woman
c. pretty girl
d. tall building
e. long river
f. large mail-order company
g. interesting newspaper
h. powerful nation
i. expensive restaurant
j. intelligent man
k. beautiful woman
l. successful athlete
m. stupid TV show
n. important city

24

24A Man's best friend

A Did you know that Britain exports 20,000 dog skins to Belgium each year?

B Dog skins? You mean we kill dogs and sell their skins abroad?

A Yes, exactly that. They're made into gloves and other things.

B But where do they get the dogs from? I mean, people don't actually breed dogs for their skins, do they?

A Well, I'm afraid some people do just that, but most of the skins come from stray dogs which are destroyed in dogs' homes.

B Isn't it terrible to think that people might be wearing gloves or coats made from dogs?

A What's the difference though between a dog and a sheep? Nobody ever says people shouldn't wear sheepskin.

B Yes, but dogs are man's best friends. Just take our dog. He's a member of the family. We talk to him, and he understands us. When we're happy, he's happy, and when we're sad, he's sad. Dogs are much closer to us than sheep, aren't they?

A True, but not all people feel the way you do about dogs. Right now, at the beginning of the holidays, thousands of people are abandoning their dogs because they don't know what to do with them while they're away.

B And you mean these dogs will be destroyed and their skins eventually made into gloves?

A Well, they'll probably end up in a dogs' home, and if they don't find a new owner, they'll probably be destroyed, and if they're destroyed, their skins may well be sold to the leather trade . . .

24B Questions on 24A.

a. Did you know that dog skins are made into gloves and other articles of clothing?
b. Which country imports dog skins from England, and how many does it import?
c. What are the dog skins made into?
d. Where do most of the skins come from?
e. Why are stray dogs destroyed in dogs' homes?
f. Why are there so many stray dogs around in the summer?
g. What can one do with a dog or cat when one wants to go away on holiday?
h. What do you think of people who abandon or kill their pets when they go on holiday?

Skins for the leather trade?
Puppies for sale in Club Row Market

Mother saves girl from Alsatian

A two-year-old girl was taken to hospital yesterday after a dog had bitten her in the arm.

The child had gone into a neighbour's garden and put her arm through the iron grille of a shed where two Alsatians were kept. One of the dogs had gripped her arm.

The girl's screams were heard by her mother, who rushed out and freed her.

Among reactions to the incident were the following:

A neighbour said: "If an Alsatian attacks a child, it is dangerous and should be destroyed."

Another neighbour said: "People always blame the dog when such things happen, but in most cases it's the humans who're at fault. Children go into places where they shouldn't be, because parents don't control them properly."

The dog's owner said: "My dogs are normally quiet and well-behaved, but for some time now children have been getting into my garden and throwing stones at them. I see no reason why the dog should be destroyed, but I would be prepared to put a fine-wire mesh over the grille."

24D **Questions on 24C. One student asks another.**

a. Why was the little girl taken to hospital?
b. How did it happen that the child was bitten?
c. Why couldn't the girl run away?
d. Why was she lucky?
e. Do you think the dog should be destroyed?
f. What's a "dangerous" dog?
g. Are Alsatians sometimes dangerous?
h. Whose fault is it when children are nasty to dogs and get bitten?
i. Is it right to say that when a dog bites somebody, it's often the humans who are at fault? Give examples.
j. Does the owner think his dog is dangerous?
k. What reason does he give for the dog's aggressiveness?
l. What does he offer to do to prevent similar incidents in future?
m. Why would a fine-wire mesh be a good idea?

24E **Das Passiv** (→ GIII19)

Dog skins **are made** into gloves and coats. (*werden verarbeitet zu*)
Stray dogs **are destroyed** in dogs' homes. (*werden getötet*)

The girl **was taken** to hospital. (*wurde gebracht*)
The Alsatians **were kept** in a shed. (*wurden gehalten*)

Dangerous dogs should **be destroyed.** (*sollten getötet werden*)

Das Passiv wird im Deutschen mit *werden* gebildet, im Englischen jedoch mit *be* (= *sein*).

24F **Make meaningful sentences in the passive.**

Example: The little girl was saved by her mother.

Thousands of dogs			by her mother.
During the summer thousands of stray dogs		(abandon)	each summer.
The skins of stray dogs		(bite)	in a shed in the garden.
20,000 dog skins		(destroy)	in Club Row Market.
Dog skins	are	(export)	in dogs' homes.
Puppies	was	(hear)	in the arm.
The two Alsatians	were	(keep)	into gloves and other things.
The little girl		(make)	to Belgium each year.
The girl's screams		(sell)	to hospital.
The child		(take)	to the leather trade.

24G **Should / shouldn't + passive. Say what you think.** (→ GIII19, 44)

I think I don't think	a fine-wire mesh Alsatians children dangerous dogs dog skins dogs puppies stray dogs	should shouldn't	be	(abandon) (allow) (breed) (destroy) (keep) (make) (put) (sell)	by mail order. by their owners. for their skins. in a small flat. in dogs' homes. into articles of clothing. over the grille. to go into other people's gardens.

24H Verneintes Frageanhängsel ("nicht wahr?") (→ GII45)

	Bejaht		Verneint	
Dogs	are	closer to us than sheep,	**aren't they?**	*H. stehen uns näher als S., nicht wahr?*
It	was	only one,	**wasn't it?**	*Es war nur einer, nicht wahr?*
He	drinks	beer,	**doesn't he?**	*Er trinkt Bier, nicht wahr?*
People	get	ill from too much noise,	**don't they?**	*... werden krank ..., nicht wahr?*

Read the following sentences aloud, adding negative tags.

> They export dog skins to Belgium.
> They export dog skins to Belgium, don't they?

a. Most of the skins come from stray dogs. b. They're made into gloves and other things. c. There's a difference between dogs and sheep. d. Dogs are man's best friends. e. But many people abandon their dogs at the beginning of the holidays. f. You bought this puppy in Club Row Market. g. The girl was taken to hospital. h. The dog had bitten her in the arm. i. The girl had put her arm through the iron grille. j. The Alsatians were kept in a shed. k. People always blame the dog. l. But it's often the parents' fault.

24I Ask questions to which the following are answers. (→ GIII52)

> She bought the dog from *a trader in Club Row Market.*
> *Who* did she buy the dog from?

> Britain exports dog skins to *Belgium.*
> *Where* does Britain export dog skins to?

a. The little girl was saved by *her mother.* b. She talks to *the dog* when her husband is not at home. c. The children have been throwing stones at *the dogs.* d. They get the skins from *stray dogs which are destroyed in dogs' homes.* e. The injured child was taken to *St Mary's Hospital.* f. Ron is looking at *the puppies.* g. He's building a shed for *the animals.* h. These animals are killed for *their skins.* i. Dog skins are made into *gloves and coats.*

25

25A Chewing gum for the eyes

A How long has that boy been watching TV today?

B Oh, about four hours, I think.

A Isn't that a bit much? It says here in the paper that watching television can harm the development of young children.

B Really? But all children watch TV, don't they?

A Yes, I know. But all the same, this expert here says that TV rays can harm the brains of children up to the age of four or five.

B But Ben is already nine.

A Yes, but he's been a TV fan for years now. Maybe that's why he has to wear glasses. It says here that watching TV is also bad for young children's eyes.

B Are you trying to tell me it's my fault the boy has to wear glasses because I've always let him watch TV?

A No, it's just this article here – it worries me a bit. It also says TV takes away valuable time from other activities. The children don't play enough, they're passive most of the time, and they don't use their imagination.

B But if television is bad for young children, why doesn't the Government do something about it?

A What do you mean, the Government? This is a free country, isn't it? If we let our children spend most of their free time watching TV, that's our business after all, isn't it?

25B Questions on 25A.

a. Who do you think is A, who is B? Give reasons.
b. How long has the boy been watching television?
c. Is that more or less than the average daily viewing time? (Compare page 85.)
d. Why may TV be dangerous for young children?
e. Why might it be B's fault that the boy has to wear glasses?
f. What can children do instead of watching television?

"The commercials will be on in a minute – we can say grace then."

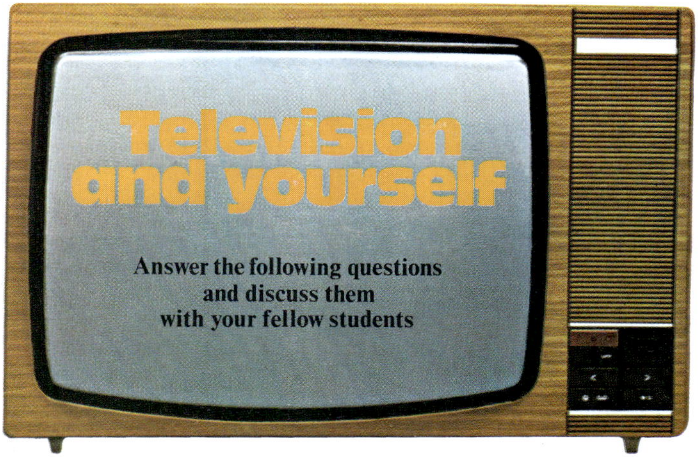

How much TV do you watch a day? (Too much? Effects?)

How much television a day is "normal"?

What are your favourite programmes? (Sports? News programmes? Documentaries? Educational programmes? Talk shows? Quiz shows? Variety shows? Comedies? Plays? Crime films? Horror films? Concerts? Operas?)

What is the funniest show on television?

What is the worst show?

What do you think of crime and violence on television? Is there too much of it on TV? Could it have dangerous effects?

What are educational programmes like? Do you like them?

What are the effects of television on children?

Should children be allowed to watch what they want?

What kind of programmes are unsuitable for children?

What kind of programmes are ideal for children?

What do you do when the commercials are on?

Do you buy the products that are advertised on television?

Do you remember any commercials that you have seen? If so, talk about them.

Do you always watch the news on television? Why or why not?

Who are your favourite announcers, entertainers, etc.? Talk about them.

Are political programmes necessary? Why or why not?

Television brings bloody war scenes into the living room. Is that a good thing?

There are a lot of American-made programmes shown by the West German, Austrian, and Swiss networks. Are they better or worse than homemade programmes?

Does TV in this country only cater for some people's tastes, or is it fair to everybody?

25D **Gebrauch des Perfekts** (→ GIII14)

a. How long **has** Mr Northam **been** a customer at the Black Dog?
Wie lange ist Herr Northam schon Kunde im Black Dog?

b. How long **has** that boy **been watching** TV today?
Wie lange sieht der Junge heute schon fern?

c. He **has been** a TV fan for years now.
Er ist nun schon seit Jahren ein Fernseh-Fan.

d. For some time now children **have been getting** into my garden and throwing stones at the dogs.
Schon seit einiger Zeit kommen immer wieder Kinder in meinen Garten und bewerfen die Hunde mit Steinen.

Zum Ausdruck von Handlungen, die aus der Vergangenheit in die Gegenwart dauern, steht im Englischen das Perfekt (a–c). Das Perfekt steht auch bei Handlungen, die sich innerhalb eines von der Vergangenheit in die Gegenwart reichenden Zeitraums mehrfach wiederholt haben (d). (Im Deutschen steht in allen diesen Fällen meist das Präsens.)

25E **Make sentences using the present perfect simple.**

They came here four weeks ago, and they're still here. (be) They've been here for four weeks now.
He bought the car in 1972, and he's still got it. (have) He's had the car since 1972.

a. He became unemployed six months ago, and he's still unemployed. (be)
b. We had sunshine when we arrived, and we've still got sunshine. (have)
c. He became a Socialist after the war, and he's still a Socialist. (be)
d. Ben became a TV fan when he was three years old, and he's still a TV fan. (be)
e. The dustmen went on strike two weeks ago, and they're still on strike. (be)
f. This series first appeared on BBC Television in 1966, and it's still on BBC Television. (be)
g. In November 1974, the *Guinness Book of Records* became the most successful of all commercially sold books, and it's still the most successful. (be)
h. The whale got stranded three hours ago, and it's still on the beach. (be)
i. We first had this problem about two years ago, and we've still got it. (have)

25F Make sentences using the present perfect progressive.

He started watching TV four hours ago, and he's still watching. He's been watching TV for four hours now.
He started wearing glasses when he was six, and he's still wearing glasses. He's been wearing glasses since he was six.

a. We started waiting two and a half hours ago, and we're still waiting.

b. He started suffering from headaches when he was a boy, and he's still suffering from headaches.

c. Albert Thorogood started doing nothing twenty-five years ago, and he's still doing nothing.

d. Our neighbour started breeding dogs in 1950, and he's still breeding dogs.

e. This country started exporting dog skins several years ago, and it's still exporting them.

f. The children started playing football at three o'clock, and they're still playing.

g. She started working for our company fifteen years ago, and she's still working for our company.

"We've been waiting for two and a half hours now."

h. I started learning English five years ago, and I'm still learning English.

i. My husband started pottering about in the garden after lunch, and he's still pottering about in the garden.

j. We started running intensive courses ten years ago, and we're still running them.

How long have you been in your present job / at your present school? *How long have you been living in your present home?* *How long have you been learning English?* *How long . . .?* (Go on asking each other questions of this kind.)

26

26A **Poetry** ∞

A I rather like reading poetry, don't you?

B There are some poets I like – A. E. Housman, for example, and Carl Sandburg.

A Oh, I remember learning a poem by Housman at school:
When I was one-and-twenty
I heard a wise man say,
"Give crowns and pounds and guineas
But not your heart away."

B Yes, that's a beautiful poem. Also the way it goes on:
"Give pearls away and rubies
But keep your fancy free."
But I was one-and-twenty,
No use to talk to me.

A It's tender and full of wisdom, isn't it? I wonder if young people nowadays like that kind of poetry.

B I'm sure some of them do. Old things are "in", aren't they? They call it nostalgia.

A Is it nostalgia that makes you like Carl Sandburg?

B No, it's that his poems are typically American somehow. You can almost smell the cities, the factories, the farms in them – and the people.

A He also collected American folk songs, didn't he?

B Yes, and he wrote a big biography of Abraham Lincoln.

A Which of his poems do you like best?

B That's hard to say. But there's one short one I like very much:
The fog comes
on little cat feet.
It sits looking
over harbour and city
on silent haunches
and then, moves on.

26B A song by the Beatles

She's leaving home

Wednesday morning at five o'clock as the day begins
silently closing her bedroom door
leaving the note that she hoped would say more
she goes downstairs to the kitchen
clutching her handkerchief
quietly turning the backdoor key
stepping outside she is free.
She (We gave her most of our lives)
is leaving (Sacrificed most of our lives)
home (We gave her everything money could buy)
she's leaving home after living alone
for so many years. Bye, bye.

Father snores as his wife gets into her dressing gown
picks up the letter that's lying there
standing alone at the top of the stairs
she breaks down and cries to her husband:
"daddy our baby's gone.
Why should she treat us so thoughtlessly
how could she do this to me."
She (We never thought of ourselves)
is leaving (Never a thought for ourselves)
home (We struggled hard all our lives to get by)
she's leaving home after living alone
for so many years. Bye, bye.

Friday morning at nine o'clock she is far away
waiting to keep the appointment she made
meeting a man from the motor trade.
She (What did we do that was wrong)
is having (We didn't know it was wrong)
fun (Fun is the one thing that money can't buy)
something inside that was always denied
for so many years. Bye, bye.
She's leaving home bye bye.

26C Questions on 26B.

a. What is this song about?
b. What kind of note is the girl leaving?
c. Who is speaking the sentences in brackets?
d. What do the parents say they did for the girl?
e. "She's leaving home after living alone for so many years." Who lived alone, and why?
f. What is the mother's first reaction when she finds out that her daughter has left home?
g. "We struggled hard all our lives to get by." What does that mean?
h. What day does the girl leave, and where is she two days later?
i. What might a "man from the motor trade" be?
j. What meaning do the sentences "We gave her everything money could buy" and "Fun is the one thing money can't buy" have in the context of the song?
k. ". . . something inside that was always denied for so many years" – What does that mean?

26D Please answer.

a. Are you at all interested in poetry? If so, which poets do you like?
b. Compare the three poems in this lesson. What are they about, what is their "message"?
c. Which of the three poems do you like best, and why?
d. Sandburg collected American folk songs. What similarities are there between songs and poems?
e. Are you interested in folk songs? What British or American folk songs do you know?
f. Is the Beatles song a folk song?
g. What is the difference between "good" and "bad" pop songs?
h. The Beatles were very popular in the sixties. Are they still well-known? What do you know about them?
i. What pop groups are popular at the moment? Do you like their music? Do you have any favourites?

26E A. E. Housman

was born on March 26, 1859, at Fockbury, Worcestershire.
After studying at Oxford he became first a clerk in the Patent Office and later a professor of Latin.
He published a little over 100 poems, which became very popular because their language was simple, their verse melodious, and their message clear.
Housman died on April 30, 1936.

26F Carl Sandburg

was born on January 6, 1878, in Galesburg, Illinois.
He began earning his living at the age of 11, left school at 13, worked at all sorts of odd jobs, fought in the Spanish-American War, studied at college, and finally became a journalist, writer, poet, and singer of folk songs.
Sandburg died on July 22, 1967.

26G **Relativsätze ohne Relativpronomen** (→ GIII55)

Durch Relativsätze werden Wörter bzw. Wortgruppen näher bestimmt. Relativsätze werden u. a. durch Relativpronomen wie *who* (→ 15K, 20F), *that* (→ 20F) oder *which* (→ 20F) eingeleitet. Mitunter kann das Relativpronomen im Englischen aber auch entfallen:

We gave her everything **(that) money could buy**.
Wir gaben ihr alles, was man mit Geld kaufen kann.

X is one of the best actors **(that) I know.**
X ist einer der besten Schauspieler, die ich kenne.

Make two sentences into one.

I very much enjoyed the evening. We spent it together.
I very much enjoyed the evening we spent together.

a. There's a short poem by Sandburg. I like it very much.
b. This is one of the songs. Paul McCartney wrote it.
c. She picked up the letter. Her daughter had written it.
d. This is the dog. We got it from the dogs' home.
e. These are the pictures. I took them in London.
f. I've read all the books. John gave me the books.
g. Have you ever met the girl? He's going to marry her.
h. She always buys the products. They advertise them on TV.

26H **Leaving home. Please complete.**

a. At five o'clock on Wednesday morning she silently closed her bedroom door and (go) downstairs to the kitchen. She had (write) a note for her parents so they would know that she had left them. She (go) to the back door, quietly (turn) the key and (step) outside. She (be) free!
b. Her father was still (snore) when her mother (get) into her dressing gown and (go) out of the bedroom. There was a letter (lie) there, and she (pick) it up and (read) it. When she understood what had (happen), she (break) down.
c. "Daddy, our baby's gone," she (cry). "Why should she (treat) us so thoughtlessly? How could she (do) this to me?"
d. When the father (talk) to friends later that day, he (say): "I don't (know) what we (do) that was wrong. We never (think) of ourselves, only of the girl. We (give) her everything money could buy ... (sacrifice) most of our lives ... We (struggle) hard all our lives to get by. And now this ..."
e. Two days later, on Friday morning, far away from home, the girl was (wait) to keep an appointment with a smart young car salesman. At last she would (be) able to do all the things that she had always (want) to do ...

27

27A The ideal secretary

(R = Reporter, G = Mr Green)

R Mr Green, your secretary, Janet Taylor, has just won the Ideal Secretary competition. What's your reaction?

G Oh, I was quite confident Janet would win. I'm sure she's the best secretary in the world – that's why I encouraged her to enter the competition.

R What do you feel makes an ideal secretary, Mr Green?

G Well, every secretary must have reasonable shorthand and typing speeds, of course. She must be familiar with office routine and all the rest. But above all, I think, a secretary must be loyal and reliable, and she must have a pleasant personality. She must be positive . . .

R It must be clear that she enjoys her work . . .?

G Yes, that's very important, perhaps most important of all. If you don't like a job, you'll never do it well . . . There are too many people around who don't give a damn about their work.

R What about looks? Does she have to be pretty?

G What's pretty? It's very much a matter of taste, isn't it? I'd say a pleasant, loyal, and reliable person is always pretty – to me at least!

R But she ought to be neat, oughtn't she?

G Yes, neatness is another matter. You can't have a secretary who's untidy.

R One last question, Mr Green. Miss Taylor has won a two-week holiday in New York, Bermuda, and Nassau. How will you manage while she's away?

G The organizers of the competition are giving me a free temporary secretary. It's part of the first prize. I only hope she's half as good as Janet . . .

27B The two bricklayers

Walking down the street, a man saw two bricklayers at work.
"What are you doing?" he asked the two men.
"I'm laying bricks," said the first.
"I'm building a great cathedral," replied the second.

a. Talk about the differences in the way the two bricklayers look at their jobs.
b. Does an ideal secretary look at her work like the first bricklayer or like the second? Give reasons.

27C Questions on 27A. One student asks another.

a. Why is the reporter interviewing Mr Green?
b. Did Mr Green know his secretary was going to enter the competition?
c. What are the main qualities of an ideal secretary?
d. What does Mr Green say about an ideal secretary's appearance?
e. Why is it important for a secretary to look neat?
f. Do you agree with Mr Green's statement that "there are too many people around who don't give a damn about their work"? Give examples.
g. What's the prize Miss Taylor has won?
h. Will Mr Green have to do without a secretary while Miss Taylor is away on her prize-winning trip?

We're looking for the ideal secretary

There's a wonderful prize for the lucky girl (or man) who wins the title.

The Ideal Secretary will win a flight to New York, Bermuda, and Nassau. PLUS an extra ticket for a friend or relation. PLUS £300 spending money. PLUS luxury accommodation for two at all places on the trip.

The Ideal Secretary will have above-average shorthand and typing speeds, a pleasant speaking voice, and a thorough knowledge of the working routine of an office.

The Ideal Secretary will get on well with all kinds of people. She will be intelligent, hard-working, efficient, tactful, and polite. She will have a good knowledge of English grammar and spelling.

There will be prizes for the boss of the winning secretary as well: a case (12 bottles) of finest Scotch whisky, PLUS 250 cigars, PLUS a temporary secretary while his own secretary is away on her or his prize-winning trip.

27D Exercises based on the newspaper cutting on the left

a. Talk once again about the qualities of the Ideal Secretary, using *should* throughout: "She should have above-average shorthand and typing speeds . . ." etc.
b. Janet Taylor has just won the Ideal Secretary competition. Talk about her qualities as a secretary, using as many superlatives as possible: "She had the best shorthand and typing speeds. She was the most intelligent of all the entrants." etc.

27E Two years ago.

Using 27A and the newspaper cutting on the left, talk about Janet Taylor winning the Ideal Secretary competition *two years ago*: "She won the Ideal Secretary competition in 19 . . The first prize included . . . She had the most pleasant personality of all the entrants . . ." etc.

27 F **Straight from the horse's mouth**

You are Janet Taylor. Write a letter to your parents in Scotland, telling them about your winning the first prize in the Ideal Secretary competition. Give as many details as possible about

a) the qualities you had to have to win the title,
b) the prizes for yourself and your boss, and
c) your boss's reaction to your becoming London's Ideal Secretary.

27 G **The ideal job**

Bosses are always looking for ideal secretaries and clerks but they don't always have "the ideal job" to offer.
Talk about the ideal office job:

Large organization? Medium-sized firm? Small office?
Distance from home?
Working hours (Per day? Lunch hour? 4-, 5-, 6-day week? Full-time? Part-time?)
Kind of room, desk, etc.?
Nature of work (Interesting? Important? Satisfying? Difficult? Responsible?)
Amount of work (Not too much – not too little?)
Boss's behaviour (Polite? Patient? Pleasant? Generous? Fussy? Hard to please?)
Colleagues (Friendly? Ready to help?)
Salary
Fringe benefits (Luncheon vouchers? Free lunches? Canteen? Paid holidays? Christmas bonus? Extra salary?)
Promotion prospects

27 H **Discuss the following:**

"Do your work with your whole heart and you will succeed – there is so little competition!"
(Elbert Hubbard, 1856–1915, American writer and publisher)

27I Talk about the ideal secretary / boss / colleague / job / office.

				loyal / reliable / pleasant / positive
				familiar with office routine
	must			interested in her / his work
The ideal secretary	should			pretty / good-looking / neat / untidy
The ideal boss	ought to			old / young / married / intelligent / stupid
The ideal colleague	has to	be	(too)	(im)patient / busy / hard-working / lazy
The ideal job	doesn't have to			aggressive / self-confident / selfish
The ideal office	shouldn't			polite / tactful / successful / fussy
	oughtn't to			difficult / boring / monotonous / tiring
				interesting / satisfying / exciting / hectic
				too far away from home / large / comfortable

27J Some – any (1) (→ GIII11)

Mit *any* wird oft eine Frage ausgedrückt, mit *some* eine bejahte Aussage:

Are there **any** fringe benefits? (attractive)
Yes, there are **some** attractive fringe benefits.

Answer the following sentences in the same way.
a. Are there any pictures in your office? (large colour photos on the walls) b. Are there any differences between the two recorders? (important) c. Are there any other prizes? (wonderful) d. Did he tell you any details? (interesting) e. Do you remember any TV commercials? (very stupid) f. Do you know any English songs? (very lively) g. Have you had any complaints? (very serious)

27K Some – any (2) (→ GIII11)

Any steht oft in verneinten Sätzen:

Are there **any** fringe benefits?
No, there aren't **any** fringe benefits.

Do Exercise 27J once again, giving negative answers as in the example.

"No, we've never had any complaints, sir."

Mugging 28

28A A mugging victim gives evidence

The moment I got into the fairly empty subway train, five young men surrounded me. Two of them stood in front of me, and the other three were behind me pushing me into them.

One went for my breast pocket and snatched my wallet while another took my brief-case.

All this happened within a few seconds while the doors were still open. The people in the carriage didn't take any notice.

I was not hurt. I was so surprised that I didn't resist or call for help. I saw them running out of the train and down the platform, but there was nothing I could do.

When I returned to the same station in the evening, I saw the five men again on another platform. They were obviously looking for another victim.

28B Questions on 28A. One student asks another.

a. Were there many people on the train?
b. How many muggers attacked the man?
c. How did they attack him?
d. What did they steal?
e. How long did the mugging take?
f. Why do you think the people in the carriage took no notice?
g. Why didn't the man call for help?
h. What conclusions do you draw from the fact that the muggers were still in the same station when the man came back in the evening?
i. How can the police prevent muggings on subway trains? Make suggestions.

28 C

A temporary occupation

Our correspondent reports from New York

Teddy S., who is now 21, became a mugger at the age of 15. He grew up in Harlem with 15 brothers and sisters.

"I just didn't have the things I needed – shoes, clothes, food," he explains. "So I either had to go to work or go out into the streets. Work was impossible – I was too young. Besides, mugging was like a game at first ..."

On an average night, Teddy and his friends attack eight victims, taking a total of about $400. They beat their victims only if they resist.

Teddy doesn't attack people with dogs because even a very small dog may bark so loudly that all hell breaks loose.

"You have to be young to make a living as a mugger," says Teddy. He is planning to give up mugging soon. He will finish college, take up a job, and get married. He would like to become a social worker.

28 D **Questions on 28C.**

a. Where did Teddy S. grow up?
b. In what kind of family did he grow up?
c. At what age did he become a mugger?
d. What reasons does he give for his becoming a criminal?
e. What's the average amount Teddy and his friends steal from each victim?
f. Do they beat their victims?
g. Why don't they attack people with dogs?
h. Why is Teddy planning to give up mugging?
i. What are his plans for the future?
j. Do you think it is in order if a robber becomes a social worker?

Harlem – New York's black ghetto

28 E Crime in the United States

Crime is one of the main problems facing the United States today. The crime rate has tripled in the last 15 years. In 1974 alone, serious crimes went up by 17 per cent to a record total of over ten million.

According to official estimates, fewer than half the crimes committed are reported to the police. An adult burglar has only one chance in 412 of going to jail for any single burglary; for young persons under 17, the figure is one in 659.

People are not in agreement about the causes of crime – and the cures. Liberals say that poverty, slums, poor education, and unemployment are natural causes of crime. Conservatives argue that everyone is the master of his fate and that a strong moral code, a respect for law and order, and harsh penalties are the best means to reduce crime. But people are becoming so fed up with crime that many a liberal has become a conservative. As one American mayor put it: "A conservative is a liberal who was mugged the night before."

Since both the police and the courts are understaffed, overworked, and in need of reform, more and more private citizens are taking personal action against crime:

- They patrol their own neighbourhoods and report suspicious activities to the police.
- They encourage victims to report all crimes and to testify against the criminals who committed them.
- They seek action against judges who are "soft on crime".

28 F Questions on 28E. One student asks another.

a. "The crime rate has tripled" – what does that mean?
b. How many crimes were reported in the United States in 1974?
c. If only about half the crimes committed are reported to the police, how many crimes were there really in 1974?
d. Do a high percentage of criminals go to jail for their crimes?
e. What's the difference in the way liberals and conservatives look at crime?
f. Why does many a liberal become a conservative?
g. Why are private citizens taking personal action against crime?
h. What are private citizens doing to reduce crime?

U.S. crime rate per 1,000 inhabitants

	Violent crime	Property crime
1960	1.6	17.1
1965	1.9	22.2
1970	3.6	35.8
1971	3.9	37.3
1972	3.9	35.2
1973	4.1	37.0

28G Talk about the crime figures on page 116.

By 1965 the rate for violent crimes had risen to one point nine. etc.
In 1972 the rate for violent crimes was the same as in 1971. etc.
In 19 . . the rate rose / went up / dropped / went down to . . . etc.
In 1965 there were nought point three more violent crimes than in 1960. etc.
In 1972 there were two point one fewer property crimes than in 1971. etc.

28H Talking about the future: going to

You are the leader of the Liberal-Socialist-Conservative Party, which has just won the election. In a speech on national television you are telling the country what the new government is going to do.

			abolish	crime / poverty / unemployment
			be (no more)	sex discrimination / race discrimination
			build	more hospitals / schools / colleges
			do something about	more universities / motorways
			do something for	taxes / wages / salaries
We			earn	unemployment benefits
This government	are		fight	strikes / go-slows
There		going to	get	muggings in our cities
Everybody	is		have (no more)	harsh penalties for all criminals
Women			help	the people in the slums and ghettos
			put an end to	a real democracy in this country
			raise	less / more
			reduce	the same pay as men
			take action against	as many women in Parliament as men
			work	

28I Not . . . any = no. Change these sentences.

The people in the carriage took **no** notice.
The people in the carriage did**n't** take **any** notice.

a. He made no suggestions. b. There were no suspicious activities last night. c. There have been no muggings in our town so far. d. There are no problems at the moment. e. As long as there is no money, there can be no reform. f. They've made no plans for the future. g. There's no difference between stealing from a poor man and stealing from a rich man. h. We have no evidence. i. Criminals have no respect for the law.

29A **A real globe-trotter**

29

According to the *Guinness Book of Records*, the world's most travelled man is J. Hart Rosdail, who was born in 1914. By 1975, Mr Rosdail, an elementary-school teacher from the American Midwest, had travelled 1,454,587 miles in 216 countries and territories. He recently discussed his travels with *Newsweek*.

Newsweek Why do you travel so much?

Rosdail There are a number of reasons. I'm interested in people: what they eat, what they wear, and what they do. Then, I'm a scenery nut. I love mountains, glaciers, and waterfalls.

N Do you have a favourite country?

R New Zealand is my favourite; it's a combination of Norway and Switzerland, both of which I like very much. I also like certain high areas in the Himalayas – and Angola and the Congo for their wonderful waterfalls . . .

N You don't seem very interested in cities.

R They're all pretty much alike. Each has its museums, art galleries, and high buildings. I grew up on a farm, and I like the wide open spaces.

N How do you usually travel?

R The best way to travel is to walk. If you're a little lazy, like myself, I recommend a bicycle – or, if you're still lazier, a car. But if you go on foot, you meet people along the road and they may invite you to spend the night. I've been invited 877 times either for a meal or an overnight stay.

N Then you don't stay in hotels or eat in restaurants?

R That's right. I'm one of those people who like to eat on time. I don't like to wait for meals even on airlines. So I carry my own food with me, and I eat when the time comes.

N What advice can you offer people who want to take unusual holidays?

R Travel light. Don't expect the same things you have at home. Be sure to read up on every place you want to see. If you know about something, then you may still decide that you don't have enough time to see it. But it's bad if you find out after the trip is over that there was something you shouldn't have missed.

29 B Questions on 29A. One student asks another.

a. There are only a handful of countries Mr Rosdail has not visited, among them North Korea, North Vietnam, and China. Why do you think he hasn't visited these countries?
b. Why does Mr Rosdail travel so much?
c. Why is New Zealand his favourite country?
d. Why isn't he interested in cities?
e. Why does he say the best way to travel is to walk?
f. Why would one think it's not always practical to travel by bicycle?
g. What advantages do you have if you go on foot?
h. Why does Mr Rosdail carry his own food with him?
i. Why is it good to travel light?

29 C Talk about the advantages and disadvantages of travelling . . .

. . . by ship

. . . by plane

. . . by train

. . . by car

29D **Holidays cheap and unusual**

You want to see the world, but you don't want to pay more than the absolute minimum for transport and accommodation? Then the trips offered by Rotel Tours, a West German travel firm, may be just the right thing for you. Each of the company's 42 Rotels, or rolling hotels, consists of a bus and a specially constructed trailer which combines the functions of a kitchen, dining area, dressing room, and dormitory.

During the trip the traveller has to do without many of the comforts of modern life: For washing and toilet facilities Rotels depend on camping grounds and hotels along the route. Only two meals a day are included: breakfast consisting of coffee or tea, bread, butter and jam, and supper with a choice of tinned ready-cooked dishes.

What makes Rotel travel attractive to many people is not only its low cost but also the fact that it makes it possible for them to get to remote places where there are no hotels or camping grounds. Or which tourist would have the means – and the courage! – to travel right across the Sahara, from Tunis to Accra, by private car? Rotel Tours offers the 30-day trip for 2,480 marks, including the flight from Germany to Tunisia.

29E **Questions on 29D. One student asks another.**

a. What exactly is a "Rotel"?
b. How many people can a Rotel accommodate?
c. What must the passengers do if they want to go to the toilet or take a shower?
d. What do you think the passengers can do if they want an additional meal or if they don't like tinned food?
e. Why is Rotel travel cheaper than other forms of travel?
f. Is Rotel travel only attractive because of its low cost?
g. What are the advantages and disadvantages of Rotel travel?
h. What do you personally think of this form of travel? Would it appeal to you?
i. What other cheap forms of travel are there?

29F Where West Germans spend their holidays

West Germany	41.1%	East Germany	2.6%
Austria	15.2%	Switzerland	2.5%
Spain	9.4%	Netherlands	2.3%
Italy	9.1%	Greece	1.1%
Yugoslavia	4.1%	United Kingdom	1.0%
France	3.9%		
Scandinavia	3.7%	Other countries	4.0%

a. Say (in complete sentences) what percentage of West Germans spend their holidays in which countries.
b. Can you think of reasons why Austria is the most popular country after West Germany? (Compare the figure for Austria with that for Switzerland.)
c. Very few West Germans go to Britain for their holidays. Why?
d. What languages do you need to get along in the various countries? Do you think the popularity of a country has something to do with the language spoken there?
e. What reasons may West Germans have for visiting East Germany?
f. Which of the 12 countries listed would be your favourite for spending a holiday? Give reasons for your choice.

29G The most popular holiday activities of West Germans

1.	Swimming	69%
2.	Walking, hiking	67%
3.	Doing nothing, sunbathing	65%
4.	Sightseeing	63%
5.	Sports and games (In this order: skiing, ball games, table tennis, tennis, sailing, boating, riding, skin diving, mountain climbing, cycling, fishing, waterskiing, golf.)	61%
6.	Shopping	59%
7.	Going to restaurants, eating well	59%
8.	Meeting people	58%
9.	Reading	56%
10.	Taking photos and filming	51%
11.	Being in company, dancing, flirting, playing cards	47%

a. Say (in complete sentences) what percentage of West Germans engage in which holiday activities.
b. Say which of these activities you engage in and why you like them.
c. Which of the listed activities are "good for the health", which are "less good for the health" or dangerous?
d. Which do you prefer: a long summer holiday only; a short winter holiday and a short summer holiday; a long winter holiday only?
e. A member of your family has been spending most of his / her holiday doing nothing, sunbathing, eating well, drinking beer, and playing cards. What do you say to him / her?

30

30A A sleepless night

I had been on the plane for seven hours, but at last I had arrived, hot and tired, at my destination.
Tomorrow there would be business meetings all day, too much sitting around, too much talking, too much smoking, too much drinking, too little exercise.
I was to spend the night at a hotel near the airport, a huge modern building, "the ultimate in luxury and convenience", as the prospectus said. "All The Service You Want . . ." it promised. "We've included everything one can possibly want in an up-to-the-minute hotel."
The room was the usual functional box: a double bed with one large double blanket tucked in on three sides, a bedside table, a desk, some chairs, and a TV.
On the desk there was a folded cardboard sign: "WHO CARES?" Opening it, I read: "WE DO." There followed one of those guest questionnaires: "Was your room kept spotlessly clean?" "Was the telephone service prompt?" And so on.
The room was clean enough. The trouble was that it had an unpleasant smell. The reason was obvious: there was no fresh air in the room, and there had been none for a long time.
It was a warm spring day, and the room was not only smelly, it was hot too. I tried to open the window, but it was sealed. I pressed a button, but the air conditioning didn't work.
I phoned the front desk. The telephone was answered promptly, and the lady who answered had a "voice with a smile".
"Can I have the window opened?"
"Sorry, sir, the windows have to be kept closed for correct temperature and maximum comfort of the guests."
"Can I have some sort of air conditioning in the room?"
"I'm sorry, sir, but it's not warm enough for the air conditioning to be turned on."
"But I'm dying of heat and there's no air in this room and it stinks!"

"I'm sorry, sir, but the air conditioning can't be turned on till June the tenth." The smile was gone from the voice now.
"Then, can I at least have a fan to stir the air up a bit?"
"I'm sorry, sir, but there are no fans in the building. There's no requirement for fans."
The telephone clicked, and I was alone, alone in a vast, efficient, computer-run hotel in the American Midwest. There was something missing from this perfectly organized hotel, something that the old hotels of the past had even if they were not always spotlessly clean. I had a whole sleepless night to think what it was.

30 B **Questions on 30A. One student asks another.**

a. For how long had the writer been travelling?
b. Where had he probably come from?
c. How was he feeling?
d. What had he come to the Midwest for?
e. Was he looking forward to the meetings?
f. What does he mean by "too little exercise"?
g. Where was he going to spend the night?
h. What does "huge" mean?
i. What's meant by an "up-to-the-minute" hotel?
j. What was there in the room? Was it a cosy room?
k. Is a double bed "with one large double blanket tucked in on three sides" comfortable for two people?
l. What was the idea of the "WHO CARES?" sign?
m. What was the trouble with the room, and what was the cause of the trouble?
n. Why couldn't the window be opened?
o. Who did the writer phone, and why?
p. What does the writer mean by "she had a voice with a smile"?
q. What did the lady at the desk say about the window and the air conditioning?
r. Who had probably decided that there should be no air conditioning before June the tenth?
s. What did the writer mean when he said there was something missing from the hotel?

30 C **Two hotels – two worlds**

Describe these two hotels. What are the differences between them? What purposes are they good for? (Holiday? Honeymoon? Business meetings?) Which do you like better?

30 D **Kann das Relativpronomen wegfallen?** (→ GIII55)

In 26G sahen wir, daß das den Relativsatz einleitende Relativpronomen im Englischen mitunter weggelassen wird. Eine Regel wurde nicht gegeben und soll auch hier noch nicht gegeben werden. Entscheiden Sie bei den folgenden Sätzen nach Gefühl, ob das Relativpronomen wegfallen kann oder nicht.

a. I've never seen a place *that* was so beautiful. b. Have you read up on all the places *that* you want to see? c. This hotel offers you all the service *that* you want. d. It's the service *that* makes this hotel so attractive. e. He just didn't have anybody *who* needed him. f. He just didn't have the things *that* he needed. g. What's the prize *that* Miss Taylor has won? h. Which is the girl *who* won the prize? i. The United States is a country *that* has a very high crime rate. j. There are only a handful of countries *that* Mr Rosdail hasn't visited. k. The trailer *which* he has constructed combines the functions of a kitchen, dining area, and dormitory. l. He has constructed a trailer *which* combines the functions of a kitchen, dining area, and dormitory. m. She always buys the things *that* they advertise on TV.

30 E **Give definitions.**

a. A hotel is a place where . . .
b. A restaurant is a place where . . .
c. A dining room is a . . .
d. A dormitory is a . . .
e. A kitchen is a . . .
f. An art gallery is a . . .
g. A museum is a . . .
h. A teetotaller is a person who . . .
i. A journalist is a person who . . .
j. A secretary is a . . .
k. A travel agent is a . . .
l. A talk show is a TV programme in which . . .
m. A quiz show is . . .

"Isn't she smart, darling? She always picks the things they advertise on television."

30 F Das Partizip Perfekt als Mittel der Satzverkürzung (→ GIII38)

We always buy the products **that are advertised** on television.
We always buy the products **advertised** on television.
Wir kaufen immer die Erzeugnisse, für die im Fernsehen Reklame gemacht wird.

Shorten the following sentences as in the example.
a. Do you think the popularity of a country has something to do with the language *which is spoken* there? b. Fewer than half the crimes *that are committed* are reported to the police. c. Chad Varah's one-man emergency service has become a large organization *which is called* "The Samaritans". d. We heard a concert *which was given* by the Boston Symphony Orchestra. e. We did some exercises *which were based* on an article from a newspaper. f. Isn't it terrible to think that people might be wearing gloves or coats *which were made* from dogs? g. He slept in a double bed with one large double blanket *that was tucked* in on three sides. h. Which of the 12 countries *that are listed* below would be your favourite for spending a holiday? i. Many of the films *which are shown* by our networks come from America.

30 G Talk about yourself.

I was born on . . . in . . .
I grew up in . . .
I went to school in . . .
I studied / served my apprenticeship . . .
From . . . to . . . I worked as a(n) . . .
I now work in / at . . .
I've worked in my present job since / for . . .
I've been learning English since / for . . .
I'm learning English because . . .
I'm (not) married. (I've got . . . children, aged . . .)
I live in . . .
I've lived at my present address since / for . . .
From . . . to . . . I lived in . . .
My hobbies are . . .
I like (to) . . .
I'm interested in . . .
I usually spend my holidays in / at . . .
I'm going to spend my next holiday in . . .
I hope to . . . one day.
For me, the most important thing in life is . . .

My name is Mildgyth Gwendolen Buccleuch . . .

LEKTIONSWORTSCHATZ

Lektion 1

1A	at the hotel	[ət ðə həu'tel]	im Hotel ("in dem Hotel")
	good morning	[gud 'mɔ:niŋ]	guten Morgen; guten Tag
	my name is Turner	[mai 'neim iz 'tə:nə]	mein Name ist / ich heiße Turner
	is there a letter for me?	[iz ðər ə 'letə fɔ 'mi]	ist ein Brief für mich da?
	Mrs Mary Turner from Leeds	['misiz 'mɛəri 'tə:nə frəm 'li:dz]	Frau Mary Turner aus Leeds
	that's (= that is) right	['ðæts 'rait]	das ist richtig; das stimmt
	yes, here's (= here is) a letter for you	['jes 'hiəz ə 'letə fɔ ju]	ja, hier ist ein Brief für Sie
	madam	['mædəm]	gnädige Frau; gnädiges Fräulein
	thank you	['θæŋk ju]	danke
1B	what's (= what is) your name?	['wɔts jɔ: 'neim]	wie ist Ihr Name? ("was ist Ihr Name?"); wie heißen Sie?
	please	[pli:z]	bitte
	sir	[sə:]	mein Herr
	and your first name?	[ən jɔ 'fə:st neim]	und Ihr Vorname ("erster Name")?
	Mr Egli	['mistər 'eigli]	Herr Egli
	are you German?	[ɑ ju 'dʒə:mən]	sind Sie / bist du Deutscher?
	no, I'm (= I am) Swiss	['nəu aim 'swis]	nein, ich bin Schweizer
	I'm from Bern in Switzerland	[aim frəm 'bə:n in 'switsələnd]	ich bin aus Bern in der Schweiz
	ticket	['tikit]	(Fahr-/Flug-/Eintritts-)Karte
1C	where are you from?	['wɛər ə ju 'frɔm]	wo sind Sie / stammen Sie her?
	Miss Bauer	['mis 'bauə]	Fräulein Bauer
	where's (= where is) that?	['wɛəz 'ðæt]	wo ist das?
	Germany	['dʒə:məni]	Deutschland
	it's (= it is) in Austria	[its in 'ɔstriə]	es ist in Österreich
	a town near Vienna	[ə 'taun niə vi'enə]	eine Stadt in der Nähe von Wien
	Austrian	['ɔstriən]	Österreicher(in)
	yes, I am	['jes ai 'æm]	ja(, das bin ich)
	Baden is my home town	['bɑ:dn iz mai 'həum 'taun]	Baden ist meine Heimatstadt
1D	how d'you (= do you) do	['hau djə 'du:]	guten Tag! *(Vorstellungsformel)*
	this is my friend Rolf Schmidt	['ðis iz mai 'frend]	dies ist mein Freund Rolf Schmidt
	that's a town in Bavaria	['ðæts ə 'taun in bə'vɛəriə]	das ist eine Stadt in Bayern
	is this your first visit to London?	[iz 'ðis jɔ 'fə:st vizit tə 'lʌndən]	ist dies Ihr erster Besuch in London?
	on holiday	[ɔn 'hɔlədi]	auf Urlaub; in Ferien
	how nice	['hau 'nais]	wie nett; wie schön
	have a good time!	['hæv ə 'gud 'taim]	viel Spaß! ("eine gute Zeit!")
1E	hello!	['he'ləu]	hallo!; (guten) Tag!
	good-bye!	['gud-'bai]	auf Wiedersehen!
	Janet / Sandra	['dʒænit / 'sɑ:ndrə]	*(weibliche Vornamen)*
	what a surprise!	['wɔt ə sə'praiz]	was für eine Überraschung!
	nice to see you	['nais tə 'si: ju]	schön, dich zu sehen
	how are you?	['hau 'ɑ: ju]	wie geht es dir?
	oh, fine, thanks!	['əu 'fain 'θæŋks]	o gut / prima, danke!
	I'm very well	[aim 'veri 'wel]	es geht mir sehr gut
	but how's your father?	[bət 'hauz jɔ 'fɑ:ðə]	aber wie geht es deinem Vater?
	is he still in hospital?	[iz i 'stil in 'hɔspitl]	ist er noch im Krankenhaus?
	no, he isn't (= is not)	['nəu hi 'iznt]	nein(, er ist nicht)
	he's quite well again	[hiz 'kwait 'wel əgen]	er ist wieder ganz gesund
	his leg is much better	[hiz 'leg iz 'mʌtʃ 'betə]	sein Bein ist viel besser

you = du / Sie / ihr / dich / euch / dir / Ihnen

your = dein(e) / Ihr(e) / euer / eure

	he's alone at the moment	[hiz ə'ləun ət ðə 'məumənt]	er ist allein im Augenblick
	my mother is in Ireland	[mai 'mʌðər iz in 'aiələnd]	meine Mutter ist in Irland
	with her sister	[wið hə 'sistə]	mit / bei ihrer Schwester
	oh, is she?	['əu 'iz ʃi]	o, ist sie das?
	well, I'm glad your father is all right	['wel aim 'glæd jɔ 'fɑːðər iz 'ɔːl 'rait]	nun, ich bin froh, daß dein Vater (wieder) in Ordnung ist
	give him my regards	['giv im mai ri'gɑːdz]	grüß ihn von mir ("gib ihm meine Grüße")
	there's my bus at last	['ðεəz mai 'bʌs ət 'lɑːst]	da ist endlich mein Bus
	now	[nau]	jetzt; nun
	bye, Janet!	['bai 'dʒænit]	tschüs, Janet!
	all the best!	['ɔːl ðə 'best]	alles Gute!
1F	put in	['put 'in]	setze ein; setzen Sie ein
1G	use the short forms	['juːz ðə 'ʃɔːt 'fɔːmz]	gebrauche(n Sie) die Kurzformen
1H	please answer	['pliːz 'ɑːnsə]	antworte(n Sie) bitte
	Sandra's father	['sɑːndrəz 'fɑːðə]	Sandras Vater
1L	questions on 1A–1E (= one A to one E)	['kwestʃənz ɔn 'wʌn 'ei tə 'wʌn 'iː]	Fragen zu 1A–1E
1M	in the classroom	[in ðə 'klɑːsrum]	im Klassenzimmer; in der Klasse
	is this your first English lesson?	[iz ðis jɔ 'fəːst 'iŋgliʃ 'lesn]	ist dies Ihre erste Englischstunde?

Lektion 2

2A	a letter from New York	[ə 'letə frəm nju 'jɔːk]	ein Brief aus New York
	July 7, 1975 (= July seven, nineteen seventy-five)	[dʒuː'lai 'sevn 'naintiːn 'sevnti-'faiv]	7. Juli 1975
	Dear Rita and Mark	['diə 'riːtə ən mɑːk]	Liebe Rita und Mark
	we are now in New York	[wiə 'nau in nju 'jɔːk]	wir sind jetzt in New York
	it is very hot	[its 'veri 'hɔt]	es ist sehr heiß
	in the streets	[in ðə 'striːts]	in / auf den Straßen
	between the skyscrapers	[bi'twiːn ðə 'skaiskreipəz]	zwischen den Wolkenkratzern
	our hotel room is nice and cool	[auə həu'tel 'rum iz 'nais ən 'kuːl]	unser Hotelzimmer ist schön kühl
	it is air-conditioned	[its 'εə-kəndiʃnd]	es ist klimatisiert
	there are fine museums in New York	[ðər ə 'fain mju'ziəmz in nju 'jɔːk]	es gibt / sind schöne Museen in New York
	bridge – bridges	[bridʒ – 'bridʒiz]	Brücke – Brücken
	park – parks	[pɑːk – pɑːks]	Park – Parks
	Central Park with its lakes	['sentrəl 'pɑːk wið its 'leiks]	der Central Park mit seinen Seen
	meadow – meadows	['medəu – 'medəuz]	Wiese – Wiesen
	tree – trees	[triː – triːz]	Baum – Bäume
	a wonderful place to relax	[ə 'wʌndəful pleis tə ri'læks]	ein herrlicher Ort zum Entspannen
	there are always surprises in New York	[ðər ər 'ɔːlwiz sə'praiziz in nju 'jɔːk]	in New York gibt es immer Überraschungen
	like the "Little Church Around the Corner"	[laik ðə 'litl 'tʃəːtʃ əraund ðə 'kɔːnə]	wie die "Kleine Kirche um die Ecke"
	right in the middle of	['rait in ðə 'midl əv]	direkt in der Mitte von
	a lot of tall buildings	[ə 'lɔt əv 'tɔːl 'bildiŋz]	eine Menge hoher Gebäude
	many people are out of work	['meni 'piːpl ər aut əv 'wəːk]	viele Leute / Menschen sind arbeitslos
	there is too much crime	[ðəz 'tuː 'mʌtʃ 'kraim]	es gibt zuviel Kriminalität
	not only unsafe	[nɔt əunli 'ʌn'seif]	nicht nur unsicher / gefährlich
	they are dirty, too	[ðεə 'dəːti 'tuː]	sie sind auch schmutzig
	because	[bi'kɔz]	weil
	dustman – dustmen	['dʌstmən – 'dʌstmən]	Müllabfuhrmann – Müllabfuhrmänner

	they are on strike	[ðɛər ɔn 'straik]	sie sind im Streik / streiken
	a city full of problems	[ə 'siti 'ful əv 'prɔbləmz]	eine Stadt voller Probleme
	with best wishes	[wið 'best 'wiʃiz]	mit besten Wünschen
	Yours, Gabi and Carsten	['jɔːz 'gɑːbi ən 'kɑːstn]	Eure Gabi und Carsten

Bildtexte auf den Seiten 10–11

	the Guggenheim Museum	[ðə 'gugənhaim mju'ziəm]	das Guggenheim-Museum
	on the edge of Central Park	[ɔn ði 'edʒ əv 'sentrəl 'pɑːk]	am Rande des Central Park
	Brooklyn Bridge	['bruklin 'bridʒ]	*(Brücke in New York)*
2B	they are in their room	[ðɛər in ðɛə 'rum]	sie sind in ihrem Zimmer
2C	write down the complete letter	['rait 'daun ðə kəm'pliːt 'letə]	schreiben Sie / schreibe / schreibt den vollständigen Brief nieder
	we are often in Central Park	[wiər 'ɔfn in 'sentrəl 'pɑːk]	wir sind oft im Central Park
	we are glad you are all well	[wiə 'glæd juər 'ɔːl 'wel]	wir sind froh / freuen uns, daß ihr alle gesund seid
2E	talk about New York	['tɔːk əbaut nju 'jɔːk]	reden Sie über New York
2F	please complete	['pliːz kəm'pliːt]	bitte vervollständigen Sie
2H	why is the room nice and cool?	['wai iz ðə 'rum 'nais ən 'kuːl]	warum ist das Zimmer schön kühl?
2I	the streets are so hot	[ðə 'striːts ə səu 'hɔt]	die Straßen sind so heiß

Lektion 3

3A	calling from the seaside	['kɔːliŋ frəm ðə 'siːsaid]	*(etwa:)* Anruf von der (See-) Küste
	Gerry / Ron	['dʒeri / rɔn]	*(männliche Vornamen)*
	are you back at last?	[ə ju 'bæk ət 'lɑːst]	bist du endlich wieder zurück?
	at home	[ət 'həum]	zu Hause
	we're (= we are) still in Swanage	[wiə 'stil in 'swɔnidʒ]	wir sind immer noch in Swanage *(Seebad i. Südengl., 8100 Einw.)*
	it's just wonderful down here	[its 'dʒʌst 'wʌndəful 'daun 'hiə]	es ist einfach herrlich hier unten
	we've (= we have) got sunshine all day	[wiːv gɔt 'sʌnʃain 'ɔːl 'dei]	wir haben den ganzen Tag Sonnenschein
	the sea is nice and warm	[ðə 'siː iz 'nais ən 'wɔːm]	das Meer ist schön warm
	pleasant	['pleznt]	angenehm; freundlich; nett
	not too expensive	['nɔt 'tuː iks'pensiv]	nicht zu teuer
	it has everything	[it hæz 'evriθiŋ]	es hat alles
	a heated swimming pool	[ə 'hiːtid 'swimiŋ puːl]	ein beheiztes Schwimmbad
	flower gardens	['flauə gɑːdnz]	Blumengärten
	playgrounds for the children	['pleigraundz fə ðə 'tʃildrən]	Spielplätze für die Kinder
	the food is good too	[ðə 'fuːd iz 'gud 'tuː]	das Essen ist auch gut
	I'm glad you're (= you are) all happy	[aim 'glæd juər 'ɔːl 'hæpi]	ich bin froh, daß ihr alle glücklich seid
	what about tennis?	['wɔt əbaut 'tenis]	wie ist / steht es mit Tennis?
	two tennis courts	['tuː 'tenis kɔːts]	zwei Tennisplätze
	there are also lots of other things	[ðər ər 'ɔːlsəu 'lɔts əv 'ʌðə θiŋz]	es gibt auch eine Menge ("Mengen") von anderen Dingen
	table tennis / mini golf	['teibl tenis / 'mini gɔlf]	Tischtennis / Minigolf
	they even have a motorboat	[ðei 'iːvn hæv ə 'məutəbəut]	sie haben sogar ein Motorboot
	for their guests	[fə ðɛə 'gests]	für ihre Gäste
	have you got a pleasant room?	['hæv ju gɔt ə 'pleznt 'rum]	habt ihr ein nettes Zimmer?
	it's (= it is) large and quiet	[its 'lɑːdʒ ən 'kwaiət]	es ist groß und ruhig
	it's (= it has) got a balcony	[its gɔt ə 'bælkəni]	es hat einen Balkon
	it hasn't (= has not) got a TV	[it 'hæznt gɔt ə 'tiː'viː]	es hat keinen Fernseher

	thank goodness!	['θæŋk 'gudnis]	Gott sei Dank!
	they're (= they are) so busy they have no time for television anyway	[ðεə 'səu 'bizi ðei hæv 'nəu 'taim fə 'teliviʒn 'eniwei]	sie sind so beschäftigt, daß sie zum Fernsehen sowieso keine Zeit haben
	I've (= I have) got a lot to do	[aiv gɔt ə 'lɔt tə 'du:]	ich habe eine Menge zu tun
	at the office	[ət ði 'ɔfis]	im Büro
	everybody else is on holiday	['evribɔdi 'els iz ɔn 'hɔlədi]	alle anderen sind ("jeder sonst ist") auf Urlaub
	you know . . .	[jə 'nəu]	weißt du / wissen Sie . . .
3B	Ron and his family	['rɔn ən hiz 'fæmili]	Ron und seine Familie
	what's the weather like?	['wɔts ðə 'weðə laik]	wie ist das Wetter?
3D	the streets aren't dirty	[ðə 'stri:ts 'ɑ:nt 'də:ti]	die Straßen sind nicht schmutzig
	are the hotels very expensive there?	[ɑ: ðə həu'telz veri iks'pensiv ðεə]	sind die Hotels dort sehr teuer?
3J	a golf course	[ə 'gɔlf kɔ:s]	ein Golfplatz
	a private beach	[ə 'praivət 'bi:tʃ]	ein Privatstrand / eigener Strand
	have they got boats?	[hæv ðei gɔt 'bəuts]	haben sie Boote?
	have the rooms got air conditioning?	[hæv ðə 'rumz gɔt 'εə kəndiʃniŋ]	haben die Zimmer eine Klimaanlage?
	balcony – balconies	['bælkəni – 'bælkəniz]	Balkon – Balkons
3K	or	[ɔ:]	oder

Lektion 4

4A	booking a room	['bukiŋ ə 'rum]	Zimmerreservierung, -buchung
	a double room for three nights	[ə 'dʌbl 'rum fə 'θri: 'naits]	ein Doppelzimmer für drei Nächte
	twin-bedded room	['twin-bedid rum]	Zimmer mit zwei Einzelbetten
	we have one room left	[wi həv 'wʌn 'rum 'left]	wir haben ein Zimmer übrig/frei
	on the ground floor	[ɔn ðə 'graund 'flɔ:]	im Erdgeschoß
	has it got a bath?	[hæz it gɔt ə 'bɑ:θ]	hat es ein Bad?
	it's nice and quiet	[its 'nais ən 'kwaiət]	es ist schön ruhig
	it's at the back	[its ət ðə 'bæk]	es ist hinten ("an der Rückseite")
	how much is it?	['hau 'mʌtʃ iz it]	wieviel kostet es?
	it's eight pounds fifty	[its 'eit 'paundz 'fifti]	es kostet acht Pfund fünfzig
	what about breakfast?	['wɔt əbaut 'brekfəst]	wie ist es mit dem Frühstück?
	is that included?	[iz 'ðæt in'klu:did]	ist das mit eingeschlossen?
	yes, of course	['jes əv 'kɔ:s]	ja, natürlich
	a full English breakfast	[ə 'ful 'iŋgliʃ 'brekfəst]	ein komplettes engl. Frühstück
	included in the price	[in'klu:did in ðə 'prais]	im Preis inbegriffen
4B	a reservation letter	[ə rezə'veiʃn letə]	eine briefliche Zimmerreservierung ("Reservierungsbrief")
	August 4, 1975 (= August four, nineteen seventy-five)	['ɔ:gəst 'fɔ: 'nainti:n 'sevnti-'faiv]	4. August 1975
	Dear Sirs	['diə 'sə:z]	Sehr geehrte Herren
	please reserve a single room	['pli:z ri'zə:v ə 'siŋgl 'rum]	bitte reservieren Sie ein Einzelzimmer
	for the night of September 10 (= September ten)	[fə ðə 'nait əv sep'tembə 'ten]	für die Nacht des 10. September/ vom 10. zum 11. September
	Yours faithfully	['jɔ:z 'feiθfəli]	hochachtungsvoll
	Mandeville Hotel	['mændəvil həu'tel]	*(Hotel in London W. 1)*
4C	plans for the evening	['plænz fə ði 'i:vniŋ]	Pläne für den Abend
	my wife	['mai 'waif]	meine (Ehe-)Frau
	my husband	['mai 'hʌzbənd]	mein (Ehe-)Mann
	what shall we do tonight?	['wɔt ʃəl wi 'du: tə'nait]	was sollen / wollen wir heute abend tun / machen?
	we can watch television	[wi kən 'wɔtʃ 'teliviʒn]	wir können fernsehen

	we can't watch television every evening	[wi 'kɑ:nt 'wɔtʃ 'teliviʒn 'evri 'i:vniŋ]	wir können nicht jeden Abend fernsehen
	what about a drink at the White Horse, then?	['wɔt əbaut ə 'driŋk ət ðə 'wait 'hɔ:s ðen]	wie wäre es dann mit einem Drink im "Weißen Pferd"?
	have a lot of fun	[hæv ə 'lɔt əv 'fʌn]	eine Menge / viel Spaß haben
	what about me?	['wɔt əbaut 'mi:]	was ist mit mir?
	pub	[pʌb]	(Gast-)Wirtschaft; Lokal; Kneipe
	you can go there	[ju kən 'gəu 'ðɛə]	du kannst da hingehen
	when I'm at my dressmaking class	[wen 'aim ət mai 'dresmeikiŋ klɑ:s]	wenn ich bei / in meinem Nähkurs bin
	go to a restaurant	[gəu tu ə 'restrɑ̃:]	in ein Restaurant gehen
	Chinese / Indian	['tʃai'ni:z / 'indiən]	chinesisch / indisch
	have a good meal	[hæv ə 'gud 'mi:l]	gut essen
	that's a good idea	['ðæts ə 'gud ai'diə]	das ist eine gute Idee
	have dinner	[hæv 'dinə]	zu Abend essen *(dinner = Hauptmahlzeit!)*
	at the Star of India	[ət ðə 'stɑ:r əv 'indiə]	im "Stern von Indien"
	watch the Midnight Movie	['wɔtʃ ðə 'midnait 'mu:vi]	sich den Mitternachtsfilm anschauen
	on television	[ɔn 'teliviʒn]	im Fernsehen
	afterwards	['ɑ:ftəwədz]	danach
4D	going to the theatre	['gəuiŋ tə ðə 'θiətə]	auf dem Weg ("Gehen") ins Theater
	haven't you got them?	['hævnt 'ju: gɔt ðəm]	hast du sie (denn) nicht?
	wait a moment!	['weit ə 'məumənt]	(warte) einen Augenblick!
	perhaps they're in my other suit	[pə'hæps ðɛər in mai 'ʌðə 'su:t]	vielleicht sind sie in meinem anderen Anzug
	let's get a move on	['lets 'get ə 'mu:v ɔn]	wir müssen uns beeilen
	Mike is waiting for us	['maik iz 'weitiŋ fər əs]	Mike wartet auf uns
4G	information about a room	[infə'meiʃn əbaut ə 'rum]	Auskunft über ein Zimmer
	student	['stju:dnt]	Lernende(r); Schüler(in)
	another is the clerk	[ə'nʌðər iz ðə 'klɑ:k]	ein anderer ist der (Hotel-)Angestellte
	A / B	[ei / bi:]	*(Buchstaben des Alphabets)*
4H	have a swim	[hæv ə 'swim]	schwimmen gehen
	a game of chess	[ə 'geim əv 'tʃes]	eine Partie Schach
	breakfast in bed	['brekfəst in 'bed]	Frühstück im Bett
4I	make plans for the evening	['meik 'plænz fə ði 'i:vniŋ]	machen Sie Pläne für den Abend
4J	breakfast menu	['brekfəst menju:]	Frühstückskarte
	fruit juice	['fru:t dʒu:s]	Fruchtsaft
	fresh grapefruit	['freʃ 'greipfru:t]	frische Grapefruit
	corn flakes and porridge	['kɔ:n fleiks ən 'pɔridʒ]	Maisflocken und Haferbrei
	grilled bacon	['grild 'beikən]	gegrillter Speck
	sausage and tomato	['sɔsidʒ ən tə'mɑ:təu]	Wurst und Tomate
	fried egg	['fraid 'eg]	Spiegelei
	toast / marmalade	[təust / 'mɑ:məleid]	Toast / Orangenmarmelade
	jam / tea / coffee	[dʒæm / ti: / 'kɔfi]	Marmelade / Tee / Kaffee
	order from the menu	['ɔ:də frəm ðə 'menju:]	bestellen Sie von der Karte
	what will you have?	['wɔt wil ju 'hæv]	was möchten Sie haben?
	I'll (= I will) have . . .	[ail hæv]	ich hätte gern ("möchte haben")
4K	sometimes	['sʌmtaimz]	manchmal
4L	please translate	['pli:z træns'leit]	bitte übersetzen Sie

Lektion 5

5A	Susan	['su:zn]	*(weiblicher Vorname)*
	this is Helga	['ðis iz 'helgə]	*(am Telefon:)* hier ist Helga

	where are you ringing from?	['wɛər ə ju 'riŋiŋ frɔm]	von wo rufst du an?
	a phone box in Piccadilly	[ə 'fəun bɔks in pikə'dili]	eine Telefonzelle am Piccadilly
	I'm staying at a hotel near Oxford Street	[aim 'steiiŋ ət ə həu'tel 'niər 'ɔksfəd stri:t]	ich wohne in einem Hotel in der Nähe der Oxford Street
	are you working?	[ə ju 'wə:kiŋ]	arbeitest du?
	are you just having a holiday?	[ə ju 'dʒʌst hæviŋ ə 'hɔlədi]	machst du nur mal Ferien?
	I'm taking an English course	[aim 'teikiŋ ən 'iŋgliʃ 'kɔ:s]	ich besuche einen Englischkurs
	at a language school	[ət ə 'læŋgwidʒ sku:l]	an einer Sprachschule
	run an intensive course	['rʌn ən in'tensiv 'kɔ:s]	einen Intensivkurs veranstalten
	one of those intensive courses	['wʌn əv ðəuz in'tensiv 'kɔ:siz]	einer von diesen Intensivkursen
	business English	['biznis iŋgliʃ]	Geschäfts-/Wirtschaftsenglisch
	very advanced stuff	['veri əd'vɑ:nst 'stʌf]	sehr fortgeschrittenes Zeug
	I see	['ai 'si:]	aha!; ah so!
	then you must be pretty busy	[ðen ju məst bi 'priti 'bizi]	dann mußt du ziemlich beschäftigt sein
	but all the same	[bət 'ɔ:l ðə 'seim]	aber wie dem auch sei
	you must come and see us soon	[ju məs 'kʌm ən 'si: əs 'su:n]	du mußt uns bald besuchen (kommen)
	come round to dinner	['kʌm 'raund tə 'dinə]	zum Essen (vorbei)kommen
	tomorrow evening	[tə'mɔrəu 'i:vniŋ]	morgen abend
	a lovely idea	[ə 'lʌvli aidiə]	eine reizende Idee
	at what time?	[ət 'wɔt 'taim]	um welche Zeit?
	any time after six	['eni 'taim 'ɑ:ftə 'siks]	jederzeit nach sechs (Uhr)
	see you tomorrow	['si: jə tə'mɔrəu]	bis morgen! ("sehe dich morgen")
5B	one student asks another	['wʌn 'stju:dnt 'ɑ:sks ə'nʌðə]	ein Kursteilnehmer fragt den anderen
	who is she ringing?	['hu: iz ʃi 'riŋiŋ]	wen ruft sie an?
5C	by the way	['bai ðə 'wei]	übrigens
	Brian	['braiən]	*(männlicher Vorname)*
	the Ashley School of English	[ði 'æʃli 'sku:l əv 'iŋgliʃ]	"die Ashley-Schule für Englisch"
	how many hours?	[hau meni 'auəz]	wie viele (Zeit-)Stunden?
	between 15 and 30 (= fifteen and thirty) a week	[bi'twi:n 'fif'ti:n ən 'θə:ti ə 'wi:k]	zwischen 15 und 30 die Woche
	good heavens!	['gud 'hevnz]	du lieber Himmel!
	that's hard work	[ðæts 'hɑ:d 'wə:k]	das ist schwere Arbeit
	is English that important to her?	[iz 'iŋgliʃ 'ðæt im'pɔ:tənt tə hə:]	ist Englisch so / dermaßen wichtig für sie?
	after all, she's got a top job	['ɑ:ftər 'ɔ:l ʃiz gɔt ə 'tɔp 'dʒɔb]	schließlich hat sie eine führende Stellung
	with an American company	[wið ən ə'merikən 'kʌmpəni]	bei einer amerikanischen Firma
	it has to be very good	[it 'hæs tə bi 'veri 'gud]	es muß sehr gut sein
	not far from the school	[nɔt fɑ: frəm ðə 'sku:l]	nicht weit von der Schule
	it isn't cheap	[it 'iznt 'tʃi:p]	es ist nicht billig
	pay for everything	['pei fər 'evriθiŋ]	(für) alles bezahlen
5D	who is paying for the hotel?	['hu:z peiiŋ fə ðə həu'tel]	wer bezahlt (für) das Hotel?
5H	an unpleasant surprise	[ən ʌn'pleznt sə'praiz]	eine unangenehme Überraschung
5I	the unhappy children	[ði ʌn'hæpi 'tʃildrən]	die unglücklichen Kinder
	read these sentences aloud	['ri:d ði:z 'sentənsiz ə'laud]	lesen Sie diese Sätze laut
5J	this is for him / her	[ðis iz fə 'him / 'hə:]	dies ist für ihn / sie
	this is for them (= Kay and Ron)	['ðis iz fə 'ðem]	dies ist für sie (= Kay und Ron)
	I've got a job with an American company, so it's very important to me	[aiv gɔt ə 'dʒɔb wið ən ə'merikən 'kʌmpəni səu its 'veri im'pɔ:tnt tə mi]	ich habe eine Stellung bei einer amerikanischen Firma, deshalb ist es sehr wichtig für mich

6A	eating out	['i:tiŋ 'aut]	auswärts essen / speisen
	waiter / customer	['weitə / 'kʌstəmə]	Kellner / Kunde, Kundin
	can I take your order?	[kən ai teik jɔ:r 'ɔ:də]	kann ich Ihre Bestellung aufnehmen?
	I think I'll have ...	[ai 'θiŋk ail hæv]	ich glaube, ich nehme ("werde haben") ...
	a tomato soup to start with	[ə tə'mɑ:təu su:p tə 'stɑ:t wið]	als erstes eine Tomatensuppe
	I'd (= I would) like a fillet steak	[aid laik ə 'filit 'steik]	ich hätte gern ("würde mögen") ein Filetsteak
	large or medium?	['lɑ:dʒ ɔ: 'mi:diəm]	groß oder mittel(groß)?
	well done	['wel 'dʌn]	(gut) durchgebraten
	very well, sir	['veri 'wel sə:]	sehr wohl, mein Herr
	what do you serve with the steak?	['wɔt du ju 'sə:v wið ðə 'steik]	was servieren Sie / gibt es zum Steak?
	we serve all grills with lettuce	[wi 'sə:v 'ɔ:l 'grilz wið 'letis]	wir servieren alle Grillgerichte mit (Kopf-)Salat
	grilled tomatoes	['grild tə'mɑ:təuz]	gegrillte Tomaten
	can I have some chips as well?	[kən ai hæv səm 'tʃips əz 'wel]	kann ich auch (ein paar) Pommes frites haben?
	certainly, sir	['sə:tnli sə:]	selbstverständlich, mein Herr
	would you like anything to drink?	[wud ju 'laik 'eniθiŋ tə 'driŋk]	hätten Sie gern ("würden Sie mögen") etwas zu trinken?
	what kind of beer do you have?	['wɔt kaind əv 'biə du ju hæv]	was für (eine Art von) Bier haben Sie?
	lager / bitter	['lɑ:gə / 'bitə]	*(englische Biersorten)*
	a half of bitter	[ə 'hɑ:f əv 'bitə]	ein halbes Pint (Bitter-)Bier *(1 pint* [paint] *= 0,57 l)*
6B	a misunderstanding	[ə 'misʌndə'stændiŋ]	ein Mißverständnis
	do you serve fish?	[du ju sə:v 'fiʃ]	servieren / haben Sie Fisch?; bedienen Sie Fische?
	waitress	['weitrəs]	Kellnerin
	we serve everyone	[wi 'sə:v 'evriwʌn]	wir bedienen jeden
6C	sorry, no cream	['sɔri 'nəu 'kri:m]	bedaure / leider keine Sahne
	bring me a cup of coffee	['briŋ mi ə kʌp əv 'kɔfi]	bringen Sie mir eine Tasse Kaffee
	a cheese sandwich	[ə 'tʃi:z 'sænwidʒ]	ein Käse-Sandwich
	without cream	[wi'ðaut 'kri:m]	ohne Sahne
	I'm sorry	[aim 'sɔri]	es tut mir leid
	we haven't got any cream	[wi 'hævnt 'gɔt əni 'kri:m]	wir haben keine Sahne
	coffee without milk	['kɔfi wi'ðaut 'milk]	Kaffee ohne Milch
6D	lunch	[lʌntʃ]	Mittagessen
	cream of tomato	['kri:m əv tə'mɑ:təu]	Tomatenkrem(suppe)
	chicken soup	['tʃikin 'su:p]	Hühnersuppe
	grilled Dover sole	['grild 'dəuvə 'səul]	gegrillte Seezunge
	mixed grill	['mikst 'gril]	gemischter Braten vom Grill
	(mixed) salad	[('mikst) 'sæləd]	(gemischter) Salat
	onion	['ʌnjən]	Zwiebel
	vegetable(s)	['vedʒtəbl(z)]	Gemüse
	French fried potatoes	['frentʃ 'fraid pə'teitəuz]	Pommes frites
	boiled potatoes	['bɔild pə'teitəuz]	Salzkartoffeln ("gekochte K.")
	spinach	['spinidʒ]	Spinat
	sweets	[swi:ts]	Süßigkeiten; Süßspeisen
	apple pie	['æpl 'pai]	(warmer) gedeckter Apfelkuchen
	per portion	[pə 'pɔ:ʃn]	pro Portion
	value-added tax included	['vælju-'ædid tæks in'klu:did]	einschließlich Mehrwertsteuer
	I think I'll take ...	[ai 'θiŋk ail 'teik]	ich glaube, ich nehme ...

6E	p / pence	[piː / pens]	*(100 pence = £1* ['wʌn 'paund])
	ask the prices of the dishes on the menu	['ɑːsk ðə 'praisiz əv ðə 'diʃiz ɔn ðə 'menjuː]	fragen Sie nach den Preisen der Gerichte auf der Speisekarte
6G	how many rooms do you need?	[hau meni 'rumz də ju niːd]	wie viele Zimmer brauchen Sie?
	how many eggs do you want?	[hau meni 'egz də ju wɔnt]	wie viele Eier möchten Sie?
	at what time can I come?	[ət 'wɔt 'taim kən ai 'kʌm]	um welche Zeit kann ich kommen?
	what's the house number?	['wɔts ðə 'haus nʌmbə]	was / wie ist die Hausnummer?

thirteen ['θəː'tiːn] – thirty ['θəːti]	seventeen ['sevn'tiːn] – seventy ['sevnti]
fourteen ['fɔː'tiːn] – forty ['fɔːti]	eighteen ['ei'tiːn] – eighty ['eiti]
fifteen ['fif'tiːn] – fifty ['fifti]	nineteen ['nain'tiːn] – ninety ['nainti]
sixteen ['siks'tiːn] – sixty ['siksti]	

6H	tourist	['tuərist]	Tourist(in)
	what time do you serve meals?	['wɔt 'taim də ju 'səːv 'miːlz]	um welche Zeit servieren Sie die Mahlzeiten?
	from seven to ten thirty	[frəm 'sevn tə 'ten 'θəːti]	von sieben bis zehn Uhr dreißig
	not much time for sightseeing	[nɔt mʌtʃ 'taim fə 'saitsiːiŋ]	nicht viel Zeit für Besichtigungen
	ask questions	['ɑːsk 'kwestʃənz]	Fragen stellen
	give answers	['giv 'ɑːnsəz]	Antworten geben
	like the following	['laik ðə 'fɔləuiŋ]	wie die folgenden
	on Sundays	[ɔn 'sʌndeiz]	an Sonntagen; sonntags
6K	practise questions with "do"	['præktis 'kwestʃənz wið 'duː]	üben Sie Fragen mit "do"
	enough time	[i'nʌf 'taim]	genug Zeit

Lektion 7

7A	shopping	['ʃɔpiŋ]	Einkauf(en)
	assistant	[ə'sistənt]	Verkäufer(in)
	can I help you?	[kən ai 'help ju]	kann ich Ihnen helfen?
	I'm looking for a book about London	[aim 'lukiŋ fər ə 'buk əbaut 'lʌndən]	ich suche ein ("bin schauend nach einem") Buch über London
	a guide of some sort	[ə 'gaid əv 'sʌm 'sɔːt]	irgendeine Art von Führer
	this little red book here	[ðis litl 'red buk hiə]	dieses kleine rote Buch hier
	everybody uses it	['evribɔdi juːziz it]	jeder benutzt es
	policeman – policemen	[pə'liːsmən – pə'liːsmən]	Polizist – Polizisten
	taxi driver	['tæksi draivə]	Taxifahrer
	I know it's very good	[ai 'nəu its veri gud]	ich weiß, daß es sehr gut ist
	I've already got it	[aiv 'ɔːlredi 'gɔt it]	ich habe es bereits
	I don't actually want a guide	[ai 'dəunt 'æktʃuəli 'wɔnt ə 'gaid]	ich möchte eigentlich keinen Führer
	a book with photos	[ə 'buk wið 'fəutəuz]	ein Buch mit Fotos
	when I get back to Germany	['wen ai 'get 'bæk tə 'dʒəːməni]	wenn ich nach Deutschland zurückkomme
	have a look at this book	['hæv ə 'luk ət 'ðis buk]	schauen Sie sich dieses Buch an
	it shows all the London sights in colour	[it 'ʃəuz 'ɔːl ðə 'lʌndən 'saits in 'kʌlə]	es zeigt alle Londoner Sehenswürdigkeiten in Farbe
	the texts are not only in English but in French as well	[ðə 'teksts ə 'nɔt 'əunli in 'iŋgliʃ bət in 'frentʃ əz 'wel]	die Texte sind nicht nur in englisch, sondern auch in französisch
	the pictures are really splendid	[ðə 'piktʃəz ə 'riəli 'splendid]	die Bilder sind wirklich großartig
	but there's something else	[bət ðəz sʌmθiŋ 'els]	aber da ist noch etwas anderes
	I'm interested in	[aim 'intrəstid in]	ich interessiere mich für
	ghosts and such things	['gəusts ən 'sʌtʃ 'θiŋz]	Gespenster und solche Dinge

	do you have any books about	[du ju hæv əni 'buks əbaut]	haben Sie (irgendwelche) Bücher über
	this house is haunted	['ðis 'haus iz 'hɔːntid]	in diesem Haus spukt es
	house – houses	[haus – 'hauziz]	Haus – Häuser
	hundreds of them	['hʌndrədz əv ðəm]	Hunderte von ihnen
	a book on the subject	[ə 'buk ɔn ðə sʌbdʒikt]	ein Buch über das Thema
	oh yes, we do!	['əu 'jes wi 'duː]	o doch(, wir haben eins)!
	paperback	['peipəbæk]	Taschenbuch
	it tells you a lot	[it 'telz ju ə 'lɔt]	es sagt / erzählt Ihnen viel
	haunted places	['hɔːntid 'pleisiz]	Stellen / Orte, wo es spukt
	author	['ɔːθə]	Autor; Verfasser
	the president of the club	[ðə 'prezidənt əv ðə 'klʌb]	der Vorsitzende des Vereins
	so he knows his stuff	[səu hi 'nəuz iz 'stʌf]	deshalb weiß er (genau) Bescheid
	how much does it cost?	[hau mʌtʃ dəz it 'kɔst]	wieviel kostet es?
7B	a man or a woman	[ə 'mæn ɔr ə 'wumən]	ein Mann oder eine Frau
	does she want a guide?	[dʌz ʃi wɔnt ə 'gaid]	will / möchte sie einen Führer?
	which is one of the best guides to London?	['witʃ iz wʌn əv ðə 'best 'gaidz tə 'lʌndən]	welches ist einer der besten Londonführer?
	how does she know . . .	['hau dəz ʃi 'nəu]	woher weiß sie . . .
	Nicholson	['niklsən]	*(Familienname)*
	who does she want it for?	['huː dəz ʃi 'wɔnt it fɔː]	für wen möchte sie es?
	what is good about that book?	[wɔts 'gud əbaut ðæt buk]	was ist gut an diesem Buch?
	what else is she interested in?	['wɔt 'els iz ʃi 'intrəstid in]	für was interessiert sie sich sonst noch?
	the title of the paperback	[ðə 'taitl əv ðə 'peipəbæk]	der Titel des Taschenbuchs
	why does he say that?	['wai dəz i 'sei 'ðæt]	warum sagt er das?
7E	add a sentence	['æd ə 'sentəns]	fügen Sie einen Satz hinzu
	I drink whisky	['ai 'driŋk 'wiski]	ich trinke Whisky
7G	an interesting church	[ən 'intrəstiŋ 'tʃəːtʃ]	eine interessante Kirche
	the United States	[ðə juː'naitid 'steits]	die Vereinigten Staaten
7K	where do you live?	['wɛə də ju 'liv]	wo leben / wohnen Sie?
	travel to work	['trævl tə 'wəːk]	zur Arbeit fahren
	I go to work by bus	[ai gəu tə 'wəːk bai 'bʌs]	ich fahre mit dem Bus zur Arbeit
	go by tram	['gəu bai 'træm]	mit der Straßenbahn fahren
	go by car / by train	['gəu bai 'kɑː / bai 'trein]	mit dem Auto / mit dem Zug fahren
	go by underground	['gəu bai 'ʌndəgraund]	mit der Untergrundbahn fahren
	go on foot	['gəu ɔn 'fut]	zu Fuß gehen
	start work in the morning	['stɑːt 'wəːk in ðə 'mɔːniŋ]	morgens mit d. Arbeit anfangen
	do you have lunch at work?	[du ju hæv 'lʌntʃ ət 'wəːk]	essen Sie “auf der Arbeit” zu Mittag?
	stop work in the afternoon	['stɔp 'wəːk in ði ɑːftə'nuːn]	nachmittags mit der Arbeit aufhören
	get home	['get 'həum]	nach Hause kommen
	in the evening / afternoon	[in ði 'iːvniŋ / ɑːftə'nuːn]	am Abend / am Nachmittag
	read a newspaper	['riːd ə 'njuːspeipə]	eine Zeitung lesen
	listen to music	['lisn tə 'mjuːzik]	Musik hören
	go for a walk	['gəu fər ə 'wɔːk]	einen Spaziergang machen
	sport / gardening / politics	[spɔːt / 'gɑːdniŋ / 'pɔlətiks]	Sport / Gartenarbeit / Politik
	foreign countries	['fɔrən 'kʌntriz]	fremde Länder

Lektion 8

8A	calling passenger inquiries	['kɔːliŋ 'pæsinʒə in'kwaiəriz]	Anruf bei der Zugauskunft
	may I help you?	['mei ai 'help ju]	darf / kann ich Ihnen helfen?
	Dorset	['dɔːsit]	*(südengl. Grafschaft, 561 663 Ew.)*
	go to Swanage direct	['gəu tə 'swɔnidʒ dai'rekt]	direkt nach Swanage fahren

	if you hold on a moment	[if ju 'həuld 'ɔn ə 'məumənt]	wenn Sie einen Augenblick am Apparat bleiben
	the best way to get there	[ðə 'best 'wei tə 'get ðɛə]	die beste Art, dort hinzukommen
	Wareham	['wɛərəm]	*(Stadt in Dorset, 4580 Einw.)*
	mile	[mail]	*(= 1,609 km)*
	station	['steiʃn]	Bahnhof
	a journey of thirty-six minutes	[ə 'dʒə:ni əv 'θə:ti-'siks 'minits]	eine Reise / Fahrt von sechsunddreißig Minuten
	about every one to two hours	[əbaut evri 'wʌn tə 'tu: 'auəz]	etwa alle ein bis zwei Stunden
	shall I give you the times?	[ʃəl ai giv ju ðə 'taimz]	soll ich Ihnen die Zeiten geben?
	yes, please do	['jes 'pli:z 'du:]	ja, bitte tun Sie das
	around lunchtime	[ə'raund 'lʌntʃtaim]	um die Mittagszeit herum
	if you leave at eleven thirty	[if ju 'li:v ət i'levn 'θə:ti]	wenn Sie um elf Uhr dreißig abfahren
	Waterloo	[wɔ:tə'lu:]	*(Bahnhof in London S.E.1)*
	you'll (= you will) arrive in Wareham	[jul ə'raiv in 'wɛərəm]	Sie werden in Wareham ankommen
	anything a little later?	['eniθiŋ ə litl 'leitə]	irgendwas ein bißchen später?
	you'll get to Wareham at . . .	[jul get tə 'wɛərəm ət]	Sie werden in Wareham um . . . ankommen
	that'll (= that will) do very nicely	['ðætl du 'veri 'naisli]	*(etwa:)* das genügt mir vollkommen
	thank you very much for your help	[θæŋk ju 'veri 'mʌtʃ fə jɔ 'help]	vielen Dank für Ihre Hilfe
	not at all	['nɔt ə'tɔ:l]	keine Ursache! („überhaupt nicht")
8B	passenger	['pæsinʒə]	Fahrgast
	excuse me	[iks'kju:z mi]	entschuldigen Sie bitte
	when's (= when is) the next train to Oxford?	['wenz ðə 'nekst 'trein tu 'ɔksfəd]	wann ist / geht der nächste Zug nach Oxford?
	railway official	['reilwei ə'fiʃl]	Eisenbahnbeamter
	fourteen oh five	['fɔ:ti:n əu 'faiv]	vierzehn Uhr fünf
	isn't there one before that?	['iznt ðə wʌn bə'fɔ: ðæt]	ist denn da keiner vorher?
	we never run one before the next one	[wi 'nevə 'rʌn wʌn bəfɔ: ðə 'nekst wʌn]	wir lassen nie einen vor dem nächsten fahren
8C	how long do we stop at York?	['hau 'lɔŋ də wi stɔp ət 'jɔ:k]	wie lange halten wir in York?
8D	where does he want to go?	['wɛə dəz i wɔnt tə 'gəu]	wo will / möchte er hinfahren?
	how long does it take?	['hau 'lɔŋ dəz it 'teik]	wie lange dauert es?
	when will you arrive?	['wen wil ju ə'raiv]	wann werden Sie ankommen?
8E	get lunch	['get 'lʌntʃ]	(ein) Mittagessen bekommen
	on the train	[ɔn ðə 'trein]	im Zug
	a lot of money	[ə 'lɔt əv 'mʌni]	eine Menge / viel Geld
8F	departure	[di'pɑ:tʃə]	Abfahrt; Abflug; Abreise
	platform	['plætfɔ:m]	Bahnsteig

Bexleyheath ['beksli'hi:θ]	Folkestone ['fəukstən]	Orpington ['ɔ:piŋtən]
Chatham ['tʃætəm]	Gravesend ['greivz'end]	Ramsgate ['ræmzgeit]
Dartford ['dɑ:tfəd]	Greenwich ['grenidʒ]	Sevenoaks ['sevnəuks]

via Greenwich	['vaiə 'grenidʒ]	über Greenwich
(not) calling at London Bridge	[('nɔt) 'kɔ:liŋ ət 'lʌndən 'bridʒ]	hält (nicht) am Bahnhof London Bridge
all trains call at Waterloo	['ɔ:l 'treinz 'kɔ:l ət wɔ:tə'lu:]	alle Züge halten am Waterloo-Bahnhof
Charing Cross Station	['tʃæriŋ 'krɔs 'steiʃn]	Bahnhof Charing Cross

	the train for Dartford	[ðə 'trein fə 'dɑ:tfəd]	der Zug nach Dartford
	at eight minutes past three	[ət 'eit minits pɑ:st 'θri:]	um acht Minuten nach drei
	now you go on	[nau 'ju: 'gəu 'ɔn]	nun machen Sie weiter
8G	at various times during the English lesson	[ət 'vɛəriəs 'taimz djuəriŋ ði 'iŋgliʃ 'lesn]	zu verschiedenen Zeiten während der Englischstunde
	they ask one another	[ðei 'ɑ:sk wʌn ənʌðə]	sie fragen einander
	it's six o'clock	[its 'siks ə'klɔk]	es ist sechs Uhr
	it's (a) quarter past six	[its (ə) 'kwɔ:tə pɑ:st 'siks]	es ist Viertel nach sechs
	it's half past six	[its 'hɑ:f pɑ:st 'siks]	es ist halb sieben
8H	St Pancras / Euston	[snt 'pæŋkrəs / 'ju:stən]	*(Londoner Bahnhöfe)*
	Nottingham / Leicester / Derby	['nɔtiŋəm / 'lestə / 'dɑ:bi]	*(englische Städte)*
	heavy type denotes ...	['hevi taip di'nəuts]	Fettdruck bedeutet ...
	through train	['θru: trein]	durchgehender Zug
	restaurant car	['restərɔŋ kɑ:]	Speisewagen
	buffet car	['bufei kɑ:]	Büfettwagen
	whole / part	[həul / pɑ:t]	ganz / Teil-
	Mondays / Fridays / Saturdays	['mʌndiz / 'fraidiz / 'sætədiz]	montags / freitags / samstags
	excepted	[ik'septid]	ausgenommen; außer
	change at Leicester	['tʃeindʒ ət 'lestə]	in Leicester umsteigen
	a British Rail timetable	[ə 'britiʃ 'reil 'taimteibl]	ein Fahrplan der brit. Eisenbahn
	a.m. (= ante meridiem)	['ei 'em]	vor 12 Uhr mittags
	p.m. (= post meridiem)	['pi: 'em]	nach 12 Uhr mittags
8I	make sentences of this type	['meik 'sentənsiz əv 'ðis 'taip]	bilden Sie Sätze dieses Typs

Lektion 9

9A	telephone box	['telifəun bɔks]	Telefonzelle
	Chinatown	['tʃainətaun]	Chinesenviertel
	you can get a lot out of your phone	[ju kən get ə 'lɔt aut əv jɔ: 'fəun]	Sie können aus Ihrem Telefon eine Menge herausholen
	for example	[fər ig'zɑ:mpl]	zum Beispiel
	you can hear tourist information	[ju kən hiə 'tuərist infə'meiʃn]	Sie können Touristeninformationen hören
	dial a number	['daiəl ə 'nʌmbə]	eine Nummer wählen
	or you may dial	[ɔ: ju mei 'daiəl]	oder Sie können wählen
	poets reading their own poems	['pəuits ri:diŋ ðər 'əun 'pəuimz]	Dichter, die ihre eigenen Gedichte lesen
	if you don't know what to cook for dinner	[if ju 'dəunt 'nəu wɔt tə 'kuk fə 'dinə]	wenn Sie nicht wissen, was Sie zum Dinner kochen sollen
	the recipe of the day	[ðə 'resipi əv ðə 'dei]	das Rezept des Tages
	a bedtime story	[ə 'bedtaim 'stɔ:ri]	eine Gutenachtgeschichte
	information on almost anything under the sun	[infə'meiʃn ɔn ɔ:lməust 'eniθiŋ ʌndə ðə 'sʌn]	Auskünfte über nahezu alles unter der Sonne
	The Daily Telegraph	[ðə 'deili 'teligrɑ:f]	*(große engl. Tageszeitung)*
	information service	[infə'meiʃn sə:vis]	Auskunfts- / Informationsdienst
	problems so big that	['prɔbləmz 'səu 'big ðət]	Probleme, die so groß sind, daß
	find understanding	['faind ʌndə'stændiŋ]	Verständnis finden
	advice	[əd'vais]	Rat
	call "The Samaritans"	[kɔ:l ðə sə'mæritnz]	"Die Samariter" anrufen (→ 15A–F)
	meet other people	['mi:t ʌðə 'pi:pl]	andere Menschen kennenlernen
	make a friend	['meik ə 'frend]	einen Freund gewinnen
	men and women	['men ən 'wimin]	Männer und Frauen
	talk on tape	['tɔ:k ɔn 'teip]	auf (Ton-)Band sprechen
	look for a partner	['luk fər ə 'pɑ:tnə]	einen Partner suchen

9D	directory	[di'rektəri]	Telefonbuch; Fernsprechbuch
	directory enquiries	[di'rektəri in'kwaiəriz]	Fernsprechauskunft
	emergencies	[i'mə:dʒənsiz]	Notfälle
	fire / police / ambulance	['faiə / pə'li:s / 'æmbjuləns]	Feuer / Polizei / Krankenwagen
	pop music	['pɔp mju:zik]	Popmusik; Schlagermusik
	telegrams (inland)	['teligræmz ('inlənd)]	Telegramme (Inland)
	Speaking Clock	['spi:kiŋ 'klɔk]	Zeitansage ("sprechende Uhr")
	weather forecast	['weðə fɔ:kɑ:st]	Wettervorhersage
	London area	['lʌndən 'ɛəriə]	Raum London; Londoner Raum
	find out	['faind 'aut]	herausfinden
	report an accident	[ri'pɔ:t ən 'æksidənt]	einen Unfall melden
	send a telegram	['send ə 'teligræm]	ein Telegramm schicken
	phone somebody	['fəun sʌmbədi]	jemanden anrufen
9E	if so	['if 'səu]	wenn ja
9F	what time do you get up?	['wɔt 'taim də ju 'get 'up]	um welche Zeit stehen Sie auf?

Lektion 10

10A	the milkman	[ðə 'milkmən]	der Milchmann
	Jack Dixon	['dʒæk 'diksn]	*(Name)*
	that doesn't mean	[ðæt 'dʌznt mi:n]	das bedeutet nicht
	he just puts milk bottles on people's doorsteps	[hi 'dʒʌst puts 'milk bɔtlz ɔn 'pi:plz 'dɔ:steps]	er stellt einfach Milchflaschen auf die Türstufen der Leute
	apart from milk	[ə'pɑ:t frəm 'milk]	abgesehen von / neben Milch
	the modern milkman	[ðə 'mɔdn 'milkmən]	der moderne Milchmann
	he sells all sorts of other things as well	[hi 'selz ɔ:l sɔ:ts əv 'ʌðə θiŋz əz 'wel]	er verkauft auch alle möglichen anderen Dinge
	bread	[bred]	Brot
	even tights	['i:vn 'taits]	sogar Strumpfhosen
	he wakes people up	[hi 'weiks pi:pl 'ʌp]	er weckt die Leute (auf)
	so they can get to work on time	[səu ðei kən get tə 'wə:k ɔn 'taim]	damit sie pünktlich zur Arbeit kommen
	some of his customers	['sʌm əv iz kʌstəməz]	einige seiner Kunden
	front-door key	[frʌnt-'dɔ: ki:]	Haus(tür)schlüssel
	so he can get in	[səu i kən 'get 'in]	damit er hereinkann
	put the milk in the fridge	['put ðə 'milk in ðə 'fridʒ]	die Milch in den Kühlschrank stellen
	while they are out	[wail ðɛər 'aut]	während sie außer Haus sind
	he is up at five	[hi:z 'ʌp ət 'faiv]	er ist um fünf Uhr auf
	he doesn't get home until six	[hi 'dʌznt 'get 'həum əntil 'siks]	er kommt erst um sechs ("nicht bis sechs") nach Hause
	he doesn't mind that	[hi 'dʌznt 'maind 'ðæt]	das macht ihm nichts aus
	what he doesn't like is having to work on Bank Holidays	[wɔt i 'dʌznt laik iz hæviŋ tə 'wə:k ɔn 'bæŋk 'hɔlədiz]	was ihm nicht gefällt, ist, daß er an (Bank-)Feiertagen arbeiten muß

Holidays in England and Wales	
Bank Holidays	Other holidays
New Year's Day (January 1) Easter Monday Spring Bank Holiday (last Monday in May or first in June) Late Summer Bank Holiday (last Monday in August or first in September) First weekday after Christmas	Good Friday Christmas Day (December 25)

enjoy something	[in'dʒɔi sʌmθiŋ]	sich an etwas erfreuen
enjoy a day off	[in'dʒɔi ə 'dei 'ɔf]	einen freien Tag haben

	about 450 (= four hundred and fifty) customers	[əbaut 'fɔː hʌndrəd ən 'fifti 'kʌstəməz]	ungefähr / etwa 450 Kunden
	unpaid bills run to £300 (= three hundred pounds)	['ʌnpeid 'bilz rʌn tə 'θriː hʌndrəd 'paundz]	unbezahlte Rechnungen belaufen sich auf £300
	as much as	[əz 'mʌtʃ əz]	so viel wie; nicht weniger als
	milkmen are born, not made	['milkmən ə 'bɔːn 'nɔt 'meid]	Milchmänner werden geboren, nicht gemacht
	I say / he says	[ai 'sei / hi 'sez]	ich sage / er sagt
	it is clear he likes his job	[its 'kliə hi 'laiks iz 'dʒɔb]	es ist klar / deutlich, daß er seinen Beruf liebt / gern hat
	he has better things in mind	[hi hæz 'betə θiŋz in maind]	er hat bessere Dinge im Sinn
	evening courses in maths	['iːvniŋ kɔːsiz in 'mæθs]	Abendkurse in Mathematik
	he can help them with their homework	[hi kən 'help ðəm wið ðɛə 'həumwəːk]	er kann ihnen bei ihren Hausarbeiten helfen
	he hopes they will make it to the university one day	[hi 'həups ðeil meik it tə ðə juːni'vəːsiti 'wʌn 'dei]	er hofft, daß sie eines Tages auf die Universität gehen werden
10B	does he mind the long working hours?	[dʌz i 'maind ðə 'lɔŋ 'wəːkiŋ auəz]	macht ihm die lange Arbeitszeit was aus?
	how does he feel about Bank Holidays?	['hau dəz i 'fiːl əbaut 'bæŋk 'hɔlədiz]	wie denkt er über Bankfeiertage?
	all of his customers	['ɔːl əv iz 'kʌstəməz]	alle seine Kunden
	how much do they owe him?	['hau 'mʌtʃ du ðei 'əu him]	wieviel schulden sie ihm?
10D	average	['ævridʒ]	Durchschnitt; Durchschnitts-
	the average Briton	[ði 'ævridʒ 'britn]	der Durchschnittsbrite
	he eats about four and a half eggs	[hi 'iːts əbaut 'fɔːr ən ə 'hɑːf 'egz]	er ißt etwa viereinhalb Eier
	a pint of milk	[ə 'paint əv 'milk]	ein Pint Milch *(= 0,57Liter)*
	he smokes about 60 cigarettes a week	[hi 'sməuks əbaut 'siksti sigə'rets ə 'wiːk]	er raucht etwa 60 Zigaretten in der / pro Woche
	for about 17 hours	[fər əbaut 'sevntiːn 'auəz]	etwa 17 Stunden lang
	each week	['iːtʃ 'wiːk]	jede Woche
10E	policemen keep order	[pə'liːsmən 'kiːp 'ɔːdə]	Polizisten halten Ordnung
	they protect property	[ðei prə'tekt 'prɔpəti]	sie schützen (das) Eigentum
	they give information to strangers	[ðei giv infə'meiʃn tə 'streindʒəz]	sie geben / erteilen Fremden Auskunft
	they arrest criminals	[ðei ə'rest 'kriminlz]	sie verhaften Verbrecher
	they carry guns	[ðei 'kæri 'gʌnz]	sie tragen Schußwaffen
	the men in the pictures	[ðə 'men in ðə 'piktʃəz]	die Männer auf den Bildern
10F	shop assistant	['ʃɔp əsistənt]	(Laden-)Verkäufer(in)
	Bill drives a taxi	['bil 'draivz ə 'tæksi]	Bill fährt ein Taxi
	Lucy Butler	['luːsi 'bʌtlə]	*(Name)*
	she works in a shop	[ʃi 'wəːks in ə 'ʃɔp]	sie arbeitet in einem Laden
	Mike is at the university	['maik iz ət ðə juːni'vəːsiti]	Mike ist auf der Universität
10G	he knows her address	[hi 'nəuz ər ə'dres]	er kennt ihre Adresse
10H	we'll have breakfast early	[wiːl hæv 'brekfəst 'əːli]	wir werden früh frühstücken
	she can ring you back	[ʃi kən 'riŋ ju 'bæk]	sie kann dich zurückrufen
	have some fun	[hæv səm 'fʌn]	etwas Spaß haben; sich amüsieren
	the weekend	[ðə 'wiːk'end]	das Wochenende
	more time for sightseeing	['mɔː 'taim fə 'saitsiːiŋ]	mehr Zeit für Besichtigungen

Lektion 11

11A	children save whale	['tʃildrən 'seiv 'weil]	Kinder retten Wal
	lose – lost	[luːz – lɔst]	verlieren – verlor
	it lost its way	[it 'lɔst its 'wei]	er verirrte sich ("verlor seinen Weg")
	in the North Sea	[in ðə 'nɔːθ 'siː]	in der Nordsee

	get stranded – got stranded	['get / 'gɔt 'strændid]	stranden – strandete
	on an Essex beach	[ɔn ən 'esiks 'bi:tʃ]	an einem Strand in Essex
	yesterday	['jestədi]	gestern
	they formed a chain	[ðei 'fɔ:md ə 'tʃein]	sie bildeten eine Kette
	to pour water over the whale	[tə 'pɔ: 'wɔ:tər əuvə ðə 'weil]	um Wasser über den Wal zu gießen
	the thirty-foot animal	[ðə 'θə:ti-'fut 'æniməl]	das dreißig Fuß lange Tier *(1 foot = 30,48 cm)*
	the five-ton animal	[ðə 'faiv-'tʌn 'æniməl]	das fünf Tonnen schwere Tier
	to keep it wet	[tə 'ki:p it 'wet]	um es naß / feucht zu halten
	dig – dug	[dig – dʌg]	graben – grub
	dig a trench	['dig ə 'trentʃ]	einen Graben graben / ausheben
	get back to the deep water	['get 'bæk tə ðə 'di:p 'wɔ:tə]	ins tiefe Wasser zurückkommen
	nearly six hours	['niəli 'siks 'auəz]	nahezu / fast sechs Stunden
	was able to slip	[wəz 'eibl tə 'slip]	konnte ("war imstande zu") gleiten / rutschen
	into the River Blackwater	[intə ðə 'rivə 'blækwɔ:tə]	in den Blackwater-Fluß
	Clacton(-on-Sea)	['klæktən(-ɔn-'si:)]	*(engl. Seebad, 38 500 Einw.)*
	at high tide	[ət 'hai 'taid]	bei Flut
	swim away – swam away	['swim ə'wei – 'swæm ə'wei]	wegschwimmen – schwamm weg
	Arthur Cox	['ɑ:θə 'kɔks]	*(Name)*
	expert	['ekspə:t]	Experte; Expertin
	say – said	[sei – sed]	sagen – sagte
	it's a good thing the children were there	[its ə 'gud θiŋ ðə 'tʃildrən wə ðɛə]	es ist gut, daß die Kinder da waren
	do – did	[du: – did]	tun – tat
	they did a good job	[ðei 'did ə 'gud 'dʒɔb]	sie taten / leisteten gute Arbeit
	I'm sure they saved the whale's life	[aim 'ʃɔ: ðei seivd ðə 'weilz 'laif]	ich bin sicher, daß sie dem Wal das Leben retteten
11C	crown	[kraun]	Krone
	as you can see	[æz ju kən 'si:]	wie du sehen kannst
	at the seaside	[ət ðə 'si:said]	an der See
	resort	[ri'zɔ:t]	(Erholungs-)Ort
	sandy beaches	['sændi 'bi:tʃiz]	Sandstrände
	get away from the crowds	['get ə'wei frəm ðə 'kraudz]	den (Menschen-)Massen entgehen
	if you walk far enough	[if ju 'wɔ:k 'fɑ:r inʌf]	wenn man weit genug geht / läuft
	there was a lot of excitement	[ðə wəz ə 'lɔt əv ik'saitmənt]	es herrschte große Aufregung
	around here	[ə'raund 'hiə]	hier herum
	not far away	['nɔt 'fɑ:r ə'wei]	nicht weit weg
	it was low tide	[it wəz 'ləu 'taid]	es war Ebbe
	the poor thing	[ðə 'puə 'θiŋ]	das arme Ding
	lie – lay	[lai – lei]	liegen – lag
	high and dry	['hai ən 'drai]	auf dem trock(e)nen
	it just couldn't help itself	[it 'dʒʌst 'kudnt 'help itself]	es konnte sich einfach nicht helfen
	try – tried	[trai – traid]	versuchen – versuchte
	they tried to push the whale	[ðei 'traid tə 'puʃ ðə weil]	sie versuchten, den Wal zu schieben
	it was too heavy	[it wəz 'tu: 'hevi]	er war zu schwer
	before high tide came	[bəfɔ: 'hai 'taid keim]	bevor die Flut kam
	come – came	[kʌm – keim]	kommen – kam
	it was able to get away	[it wəz 'eibl tə 'get ə'wei]	er konnte wegkommen
	take – took	[teik – tuk]	nehmen – nahm
	take a lot of pictures	['teik ə 'lɔt əv 'piktʃəz]	viele Bilder machen
	we will show them to you	[wi:l 'ʃəu ðəm tə ju]	wir werden sie euch zeigen
	next month	['nekst 'mʌnθ]	nächsten Monat

	we hope you are not suffering too much from the heat	[wi 'həup juə 'nɔt 'sʌfəriŋ 'tu: 'mʌtʃ frəm ðə 'hi:t]	wir hoffen, daß ihr nicht zu sehr unter der Hitze leidet
	Yours sincerely	['jɔ:z sin'siəli]	*(Briefschluß, etwa:)* Eure
11D	where are they writing from?	['wɛər ə ðei 'raitiŋ frɔm]	von wo schreiben sie?
	when will they see them next?	['wen wil ðei 'si: ðəm 'nekst]	wann werden sie sie das nächste Mal sehen?
11G	holidaymaker	['hɔlədimeikə]	Urlauber(in); Feriengast
	come down to the beach	['kʌm 'daun tə ðə 'bi:tʃ]	zum Strand herunterkommen

11H

the whale was fifty **feet** [fi:t] long	*der Wal war fünfzig Fuß lang*
aber: it was a fifty-**foot** [fut] whale	*es war ein fünfzig Fuß langer Wal*

Lektion 12

12A	inside the Cockney Pride pub	['in'said ðə 'kɔkni 'praid pʌb]	im Cockney-Pride-Pub (cockney = waschechter Ostlondoner; pride = Stolz)
	Jermyn Street	['dʒə:min stri:t]	*(Straße in London S.W.1)*
	behind Piccadilly Circus	[bihaind 'pikədili 'sə:kəs]	hinter dem Piccadilly Circus
	the Prince of Wales	[ðə 'prins əv 'weilz]	der Prinz von Wales
	Alf / Bob / Chris	[ælf / bɔb / kris]	*(männliche Vornamen)*
	what can I get you?	['wɔt kən ai 'get ju]	was kann ich dir holen?
	go – goes	[gəu – gəuz]	gehen – geht
	barman	['ba:mən]	Büfettier
	here you are, sir	[hiə ju 'a: sə]	bitte sehr, mein Herr
	return	[ri'tə:n]	zurückkehren; zurückkommen
	glass – glasses	[gla:s – 'gla:siz]	Glas – Gläser
	well, here we are	['wel 'hiə wi 'a:]	so, bitte schön!
	cheers!	[tʃiəz]	Prost!; zum Wohl!
	rather pleasant	['ra:ðə 'pleznt]	recht nett / angenehm
	jukebox	['dʒu:kbɔks]	Musikautomat
	conversation	[kɔnvə'seiʃn]	Unterhaltung; Gespräch
	a bit dark though	[ə bit 'da:k ðəu]	allerdings ein bißchen dunkel
	don't you think?	['dəunt jə 'θiŋk]	meint ihr nicht?
	well, it could be worse	['wel it 'kud bi 'wə:s]	nun, es könnte schlimmer sein
	an old riverside pub	[ən 'əuld 'rivəsaid 'pʌb]	ein altes Lokal am Fluß(ufer)
	the other night	[ði 'ʌðə 'nait]	neulich abends
	it was that dark you couldn't see a thing	[it wəz 'ðæt 'da:k ju 'kudnt si: ə 'θiŋ]	es war so dunkel, daß man nichts sehen konnte
	I had four pints in my hands	[ai hæd 'fɔ: 'paints in mai 'hændz]	ich hatte vier Pint(gläser) in den Händen
	when I knocked into a suit of armour up against the wall	[wen ai 'nɔkt intu ə 'su:t əv 'a:mər 'ʌp əgenst ðə 'wɔ:l]	als ich gegen eine Ritterrüstung stieß, die an der Wand stand
	a great club thing fell on my toe	[ə 'greit 'klʌb θiŋ fel ɔn mai 'təu]	ein großes keulenartiges Ding fiel mir auf den Zeh
	fall – fell	[fɔ:l – fel]	fallen – fiel
	I staggered around holding my foot	[ai 'stægəd ə'raund 'həuldiŋ mai 'fut]	ich wankte herum und hielt mir den Fuß
	manager	['mænidʒə]	Geschäftsführer
	think – thought	[θiŋk – θɔ:t]	denken – dachte
	drunk and disorderly	['drʌŋk ən dis'ɔ:dəli]	betrunken und "Ärgernis erregend"
	throw out – threw out	['θrəu 'aut – 'θru: 'aut]	hinauswerfen; rauswerfen
12B	who did he meet there?	['hu: did i 'mi:t ðɛə]	wen traf er dort?
	he met . . .	[hi 'met]	er traf . . .
	buy – bought	[bai – bɔ:t]	kaufen – kaufte
	a round of drinks	[ə 'raund əv 'driŋks]	eine Runde / "Lage" (Drinks)

	what did he buy for himself?	['wɔt did i bai fər im'self]	was kaufte er für sich (selbst)?
	the price is the same	[ðə 'prais iz ðə 'seim]	der Preis ist derselbe
	what did he think about the pub?	['wɔt did i 'θiŋk əbaut ðə 'pʌb]	was hielt er von dem Lokal?
	what happened to the beer?	['wɔt 'hæpnd tə ðə 'biə]	was passierte mit dem Bier?
12C	outside the pub	['aut'said ðə 'pʌb]	vor dem Lokal
	dog and trumpet	['dɔg ən 'trʌmpit]	Hund und Trompete
	Soho	['səuhəu]	*(Londoner Stadtviertel)*
12D	end of a pub crawl	['end əv ə 'pʌb krɔːl]	Ende eines Kneipenbummels
	Jane	[dʒein]	*(weibl. Vorname)*
	last night	['lɑːst 'nait]	gestern abend
	down by the Thames	['daun bai ðə 'temz]	unten an der Themse
	(at) first	[(ət) 'fəːst]	zuerst
	together	[tə'geðə]	zusammen
	that's normal, isn't it?	[ðəts 'nɔːməl iznt it]	das ist normal, nicht wahr?
	it was your turn	[it wəz 'jɔː təːn]	du warst an der Reihe
	come to the point!	['kʌm tə ðə 'pɔint]	komm zur Sache!
	without my glasses	[wi'ðaut mai 'glɑːsiz]	ohne meine Brille
	probably	['prɔbəbli]	wahrscheinlich
	somewhere	['sʌmwɛə]	irgendwo
	wrong	[rɔŋ]	falsch; unrichtig; verkehrt
	a historical pub	[ə his'tɔrikl 'pʌb]	eine historische (alte) Kneipe
	was it very painful?	[wɔz it 'veri 'peinful]	war es sehr schmerzhaft?
	drop – dropped	[drɔp – drɔpt]	fallen lassen – ließ fallen
	good Lord!	['gud 'lɔːd]	(ach,) du großer / lieber Gott!
12E	tour of London pubs	['tuər əv 'lʌndən 'pʌbz]	Pub-Tour in London
	parties of 40–50 persons	['pɑːtiz əv 'fɔːti tə 'fifti 'pəːsnz]	Gruppen von 40–50 Personen
	coach transportation	['kəutʃ trænspɔː'teiʃn]	Busbeförderung
	within 30 miles	[wi'ðin 'θəːti 'mailz]	im Umkreis von 30 Meilen
	professional	[prə'feʃnəl]	beruflich; Berufs-
	2 free drinks	['tuː 'friː 'driŋks]	2 kostenlose Drinks
	darts	[dɑːts]	Pfeilwerfen (dart = Wurfpfeil)
	match	[mætʃ]	(Wett-)Spiel, Kampf; Partie
	prize for the winner	['praiz fə ðə 'winə]	Preis für den Sieger
	lively songs	['laivli 'sɔŋz]	flotte Lieder
	pianist	['piənist]	Pianist(in); Klavierspieler(in)
	sore head	['sɔː 'hed]	Brummschädel ("weher Kopf")
	schedule	['ʃedjuːl]	Zeitplan
	first stop	['fəːst stɔp]	erster Aufenthalt
	tavern	['tævən]	Wirtshaus; Schenke
	Bishopsgate	['biʃəpsgeit]	*(Straße in London E.C.2)*
	welcome somebody	['welkəm sʌmbədi]	jemanden begrüßen
	free drink of choice	['friː 'driŋk əv 'tʃɔis]	kostenloser Drink nach Wahl
	available	[ə'veiləbl]	verfügbar; z. Verfügung stehend
	second stop	['sekənd stɔp]	zweiter Aufenthalt
	inn	[in]	Gasthaus; Gasthof; Wirtshaus
	High Holborn	['hai 'həubən]	*(Straße in London W.C.1)*
	if time permits	[if 'taim pə'mits]	wenn es die Zeit zuläßt
	third stop	['θəːd stɔp]	dritter Aufenthalt
	resident pianist plays	['rezidənt 'piənist pleiz]	"ansässiger" Pianist spielt
	closing time	['kləuziŋ taim]	Polizeistunde; Feierabend
12F	your club's outing this year	[jɔː 'klʌbz 'autiŋ ðis 'jiə]	Ihr diesjähriger Vereinsausflug
	secretary of a club	['sekrətri əv ə 'klʌb]	Schriftführer(in) eines Vereins
	draw up an information sheet	['drɔː 'ʌp ən infə'meiʃn ʃiːt]	ein Informationsblatt aufsetzen
	club members	['klʌb membəz]	Vereinsmitglieder
	fellow club members	['feləu 'klʌb membəz]	Vereinskameraden, -kameradinnen

	we will visit	['wi:l 'vizit]	wir werden besuchen
	point out the sights to somebody	['pɔint 'aut ðə 'saits tə sʌmbədi]	jemandem die Sehenswürdigkeiten zeigen
12H	I drink / drank a lot	[ai 'driŋk / 'dræŋk ə 'lɔt]	ich trinke / trank eine Menge
	we sing / sang a lot	[wi 'siŋ / 'sæŋ ə 'lɔt]	wir singen / sangen viel
	win – won	[win – wʌn]	gewinnen – gewann

Lektion 13

13A	British Airways	['britiʃ 'ɛəweiz]	*(brit. Luftverkehrsgesellschaft)*
	good afternoon!	[gud ɑ:ftə'nu:n]	guten Tag!
	a flight to Cologne	[ə 'flait tə kə'ləun]	ein Flug nach Köln
	book a seat	['buk ə 'si:t]	einen Platz buchen / reservieren
	one seat confirmed	['wʌn 'si:t kən'fə:md]	einen Platz bestätigt (d. h. fest gebucht, "O. K.")
	eighteenth (of) July	['eiti:nθ (əv) dʒu'lai]	achtzehnter Juli
	departing / arriving	[di'pɑ:tiŋ / ə'raiviŋ]	abfliegend / ankommend
	d'you (= do you) want to book a return?	[dju 'wɔnt tə buk ə ri'tə:n]	möchten Sie einen Rückflug buchen?
	initial	[i'niʃl]	Anfangsbuchstabe; Initiale
	home number	['həum nʌmbə]	Privatnummer
	pick up the ticket	['pik ʌp ðə 'tikit]	die Karte / d. Flugschein abholen
	West London (Air) Terminal	['west 'lʌndən ('ɛə) 'tə:minl]	*(Fluggastabfertigungsgebäude in der Londoner Innenstadt)*
	before departure	[bə'fɔ: di'pɑ:tʃə]	vor dem Abflug
	O.K.	['əu'kei]	gut!; in Ordnung!
	frequency	['fri:kwənsi]	Häufigkeit
	aircraft	['ɛəkrɑ:ft]	Flugzeug; Maschine
	daily / non-stop	['deili / 'nɔn-'stɔp]	täglich / ohne Zwischenlandung
13B	a direct flight	[ə dai'rekt 'flait]	ein Direktflug
	which day does he book for?	['witʃ 'dei dəz i 'buk fɔ:]	für welchen Tag bucht er?
	single ticket	['siŋgl tikit]	einfache Karte; Einfachflugschein
	return ticket	[ri'tə:n tikit]	Rückfahrkarte; Rückflugschein
	travel to the airport	['trævl tə ði 'ɛəpɔ:t]	zum Flughafen fahren
13C	booking office	['bukiŋ ɔfis]	(Büro für) Platzbuchung
	airline clerk	['ɛəlain klɑ:k]	Angestellter der Fluggesellschaft
	what's the fare to Berlin?	['wɔts ðə 'fɛə tə bə:'lin]	was ist der Flugpreis nach Berlin?
	tourist class	['tuərist klɑ:s]	Touristenklasse
	double the single fare	['dʌbl ðə 'siŋgl fɛə]	das Doppelte des Einfachflugpreises
	a special weekend excursion fare	[ə 'speʃl wi:kend iks'kə:ʃn fɛə]	ein besonderer Wochenendausflugstarif
	Munich	['mju:nik]	München
	valid 1 year	['vælid 'wʌn 'jiə]	ein Jahr gültig
	travel on Saturdays and Sundays	[trævl ɔn 'sætədiz ən 'sʌndiz]	Reisen an Samstagen und Sonntagen
13D	at the ticket counter	[ət ðə 'tikit kauntə]	am Flugscheinschalter
	I'm booked on flight . . .	[aim 'bukt ɔn flait]	ich bin auf Flug . . . gebucht
	I'd like to pick up my ticket	[aid 'laik tə pik ʌp mai 'tikit]	ich möchte gern meinen Flugschein abholen
	check with the computer	['tʃek wið ðə kəm'pju:tə]	am Computer überprüfen
	write out the ticket	['rait 'aut ðə 'tikit]	den Flugschein ausschreiben
13E	check-in desk	[tʃek-'in desk]	(Fluggast-)Abfertigungsschalter
	is this where I have to check in?	[iz 'ðis wɛər ai hæf tə 'tʃek 'in]	muß ich mich hier abfertigen lassen?

	would you please put your baggage on the scales	[wud ju pli:z put jɔ: 'bægidʒ ɔn ðə 'skeilz]	würden Sie bitte Ihr Gepäck auf die Waage stellen
	cabin bag	['kæbin bæg]	Bordtasche
	boarding card	['bɔ:diŋ kɑ:d]	Einsteigkarte
	international departures lounge	[intə'næʃnəl di'pɑ:tʃəz launʒ]	Abflughalle Ausland
	we'll call your flight	[wi:l 'kɔ:l jɔ: 'flait]	wir werden Ihren Flug aufrufen
13F	on the way back	[ɔn ðə 'wei 'bæk]	auf dem Rückweg / Rückflug
	he gave him his ticket	[hi 'geiv im iz 'tikit]	er gab ihm seinen Flugschein
	a few newspapers	[ə fju: 'nju:speipəz]	ein paar / einige Zeitungen
	magazine	[mægə'zi:n]	Magazin; "Illustrierte"
	bookstall	['bukstɔ:l]	Bücherstand; Zeitungsstand
	go straight to the desk	['gəu 'streit tə ðə 'desk]	direkt zum Schalter gehen
	go through Passport Control	['gəu θru: 'pɑ:spɔ:t kən'trəul]	durch die Paßkontrolle gehen
13G	Heathrow	['hi:θ'rəu]	*(Londoner Hauptflughafen)*
	which airline did you fly?	['witʃ 'ɛəlain did ju 'flai]	mit welcher Fluggesellschaft flogen Sie?
13H	he booked it two days ago	[hi 'bukt it tu: 'deiz əgəu]	er buchte ihn vor zwei Tagen
	when did they confirm the booking?	[wen did ðei kən'fə:m ðə 'bukiŋ]	wann bestätigten sie d. Buchung / haben sie die Buchung bestätigt?
	half an hour ago	['hɑ:f ən 'auər əgəu]	vor einer halben Stunde
	the plane for Vienna	[plein]	das Flugzeug nach Wien
13J	spell a name	['spel ə 'neim]	einen Namen buchstabieren

Lektion 14

14A	Morgan and Elaine	['mɔ:gən ən i'lein]	*(männl. u. weibl. Vorname)*
	I am writing to thank you	[aim 'raitiŋ tə 'θæŋk ju]	ich schreibe, um Ihnen zu danken
	entertain somebody	[entə'tein sʌmbədi]	jemanden gastlich aufnehmen
	recent	['ri:snt]	kürzlich
	spend – spent	[spend – spent]	verbringen – verbrachte
	the evening we spent together	[ði 'i:vniŋ wi 'spent tə'geðə]	der Abend, den wir zusammen verbrachten
	it was a particular pleasure for me	[it wəz ə pə'tikjulə 'pleʒə fə mi:]	es war mir ein besonderes Vergnügen / eine besondere Freude
	a rather bumpy flight	[ə 'rɑ:ðə 'bʌmpi 'flait]	ein ziemlich unruhiger Flug
	but otherwise it was a pleasant trip	[bət 'ʌðəwaiz it wəz ə 'pleznt 'trip]	aber (an)sonst(en) war es eine angenehme Reise
	an old gentleman	[ən 'əuld 'dʒentlmən]	ein alter Herr
	who obviously didn't enjoy the flight at all	[hu 'ɔbviəsli 'didnt in'dʒɔi ðə 'flait ət 'ɔ:l]	dem der Flug offensichtlich gar nicht gefiel
	as we were getting off	[æz wi wə 'getiŋ 'ɔf]	als wir ausstiegen
	he walked up to the stewardess	[hi 'wɔ:kt 'ʌp tə ðə stjuə'des]	er ging zu der Stewardeß
	shake – shook	[ʃeik – ʃuk]	schütteln – schüttelte
	he shook her hand	[hi 'ʃuk hə 'hænd]	er schüttelte ihr die Hand
	she looked perplexed	[ʃi 'lukt pə'plekst]	sie sah verblüfft / verdutzt aus
	what do you mean by two flights?	['wɔt du ju 'mi:n bai 'tu: flaits]	was meinen Sie mit zwei Flügen?
	it was only one, wasn't it?	[it wəz əunli 'wʌn 'wɔznt it]	es war doch nur einer, nicht wahr?
	you'll never guess	[jul 'nevə 'ges]	Sie werden nie erraten
	young lady	['jʌŋ 'leidi]	junge Dame
	both	[bəuθ]	beide
	delightful	[di'laitful]	reizend; entzückend; köstlich
	20th July (= the twentieth of July)	[ðə 'twentiəθ əv dʒu'lai]	20. Juli
	we had a good laugh	[wi həd ə 'gud 'lɑ:f]	wir haben herzlich gelacht

	next time you come	['nekst taim ju 'kʌm]	wenn Sie das nächste Mal kommen
	in advance	[in əd'vɑːns]	im voraus; vorher
	have a proper evening out	[həv ə 'prɔpər 'iːvniŋ 'aut]	einmal richtig ausgehen
	in the meantime	[in ðə 'miːntaim]	in der Zwischenzeit; inzwischen
14B	etc. (= et cetera)	[ət'setrə]	usw.; etc.
14C	he wrote a letter	[hi 'rəut ə 'letə]	er schrieb einen Brief
	see page 54 (= fifty-four)	['siː 'peidʒ 'fifti-'fɔː]	siehe Seite 54
	why could one say ...	['wai kud wʌn 'sei]	warum könnte man sagen ...
	what does he want to arrange?	['wɔt dəz i wɔnt tu ə'reindʒ]	was will er arrangieren?
14D	how did you like ...	['hau did ju 'laik]	wie gefiel Ihnen ...
	was anybody waiting for you?	[wəz 'enibɔdi 'weitiŋ fɔ ju]	wartete (irgend) jemand auf Sie?
	funny	['fʌni]	komisch; lustig; drollig
14F	a play by Robert Bolt	[ə 'plei bai 'rɔbət 'bəult]	ein Stück von Robert Bolt
	Islamabad	[iz'lɑːməbæd]	*(Hptst. v. Pakistan, 80 000 Ew.)*
	chicken curry	['tʃikin 'kʌri]	Hühner-Curry(gericht)
	night club	['nait klʌb]	Nachtklub
	mill	[mil]	Mühle
	a striptease revue	[ə 'striptiːz ri'vjuː]	eine Striptease-Revue
14G	they are hungry	[ðɛə 'hʌŋgri]	sie sind hungrig / haben Hunger
	Berwick Street	['berik striːt]	*(Straße in Soho, London W.1)*
	ask for the recipe	['ɑːsk fə ðə 'resipi]	nach dem Rezept fragen
	they leave / left the place	[ðei 'liːv / 'left ðə pleis]	sie verlassen / verließen den Ort
	it's world-famous	[its 'wəːld-'feiməs]	er ist weltberühmt
	go in	[gəu 'in]	hineingehen; reingehen
	see a show	['siː ə 'ʃəu]	eine Show / Vorführung sehen
	have a terrible headache	[hæv ə 'teribl 'hedeik]	schreckliche Kopfschmerzen haben
14H	the thirtieth / ninth / twelfth of July	[ðə 'θəːtiəθ / 'nainθ / 'twelfθ əv dʒu'lai]	der dreißigste / neunte / zwölfte Juli

Lektion 15

15A	the Reverend	[ðə 'revrənd]	"der ehrwürdige" *(Titel engl. Geistlicher)*
	Chad Varah	['tʃæd 'vɑːrə]	*(engl. Geistlicher, geb. 1911)*
	he reads – he read	[hi 'riːdz – hi 'red]	er liest – er las
	in the summer of 1953 (= nineteen fifty-three)	[in ðə 'sʌmər əv 'naintiːn 'fifti-'θriː]	im Sommer (des Jahres) 1953
	three suicides a day	['θriː 'suisaidz ə 'dei]	drei Selbstmorde am / pro Tag
	Greater London	['greitə 'lʌndən]	Groß-London
	The Times	[ðə 'taimz]	*(große engl. Tageszeitung)*
	the Government should do something about it	[ðə 'gʌvnmənt ʃud 'duː sʌmθiŋ ə'baut it]	die Regierung sollte etwas dagegen tun / sollte da etwas unternehmen
	instead	[in'sted]	statt dessen
	made it known in the press	['meid it 'nəun in ðə 'pres]	machte in der Presse bekannt
	November	[nəu'vembə]	November
	people thinking of suicide	['piːpl θiŋkiŋ əv 'suisaid]	Menschen, die an Selbstmord denken
	MAN(sion House)	['mænʃən haus]	*(ehem. Londoner Telefonbezirk)*
	become – became – become	[bi'kʌm – bi'keim – bi'kʌm]	werden – wurde – geworden
	it has since become	[it əz 'sins bi'kʌm]	er ist seitdem geworden
	a large organization	[ə 'lɑːdʒ ɔːgənai'zeiʃn]	eine große Organisation
	called The Samaritans	['kɔːld ðə sə'mæritnz]	genannt/namens The Samaritans

	thousands of lonely people	['θauzəndz əv 'ləunli 'pi:pl]	Tausende v. einsamen Menschen
	miserable	['mizərəbl]	traurig; unglücklich; elend
	despairing people	[dis'pεəriŋ 'pi:pl]	verzweifelte Menschen
	call on somebody	['kɔ:l ɔn sʌmbədi]	jemanden aufsuchen
	hour of greatest need	['auər əv 'greitist 'ni:d]	Stunde der größten Not
	find – found – found	[faind – faund – faund]	finden – fand – gefunden
	friendliness and practical help	['frendlinəs ən 'præktikl 'help]	Freundlichkeit und praktische Hilfe
	branch	[brɑ:ntʃ]	Zweigstelle; Filiale
	Britain	['britn]	Großbritannien
	over eighteen thousand volunteers	['əuvər 'eiti:n 'θauzənd vɔlən'tiəz]	über achtzehntausend Freiwillige
	who give up a large part of their free time	[hu 'giv ʌp ə 'lɑ:dʒ 'pɑ:t əv ðεə 'fri: 'taim]	die einen großen Teil ihrer Freizeit opfern
	fellow men	['feləu 'men]	Mitmenschen
	despair	[dis'pεə]	Verzweiflung
	a friendly voice	[ə 'frendli 'vɔis]	eine freundliche Stimme
15B	found an organization	['faund ən ɔ:gənai'zeiʃn]	eine Organisation gründen
	offer somebody something	['ɔfə sʌmbədi sʌmθiŋ]	jemandem etwas anbieten
	client	['klaiənt]	Klient(in); Kunde; Kundin
15C	and your neighbour as yourself	[ən jɔ 'neibər əz jɔ:'self]	und deinen Nächsten wie dich selbst *(aus Lukas 10, 27)*
	regard something as a sin	[ri'gɑ:d sʌmθiŋ əz ə 'sin]	etwas für eine Sünde halten
	most religions do	['məust ri'lidʒənz du:]	die meisten Religionen tun es
	Muslim	['muzlim]	Moslem; Mohammedaner
	worse than murder	['wə:s ðən 'mə:də]	schlimmer als Mord
	up to a few years ago	[ʌp tu ə 'fju: 'jiəz əgəu]	bis vor ein paar Jahren
	suicide was a crime	['suisaid wəz ə 'kraim]	Selbstmord war ein Verbrechen
	breach of the peace	['bri:tʃ əv ðə 'pi:s]	("Bruch des Friedens") Friedensbruch; grober Unfug
	Scotland	['skɔtlənd]	Schottland *(5,2 Mill. Einw.)*
	that's true	['ðæts 'tru:]	das ist wahr; das stimmt
	you don't help a desperate man	[ju 'dəunt 'help ə 'despərət 'mæn]	man hilft einem verzweifelten Menschen nicht
	commit suicide	[kə'mit 'suisaid]	Selbstmord begehen
	if you want to kill yourself	[if ju wɔnt tə 'kil jɔ:self]	wenn du dich umbringen willst
	ring us up	['riŋ əs 'ʌp]	ruf uns an
	talk to somebody	['tɔ:k tə sʌmbədi]	mit jemand(em) reden / sprechen
	feel less lonely	['fi:l 'les 'ləunli]	sich weniger einsam fühlen
	people who want to kill themselves	['pi:pl hu wɔnt tə 'kil ðəmselvz]	Menschen, die sich umbringen wollen
	most of them are lonely	['məust əv ðəm ə 'ləunli]	die meisten v. ihnen sind einsam
	mix with other people	['miks wíð 'ʌðə 'pi:pl]	Umgang mit anderen Menschen haben
	no one	['nəu wʌn]	niemand
	show somebody love	['ʃəu sʌmbədi 'lʌv]	jemandem Liebe erweisen
	successful in their fight against suicide	[sək'sesful in ðεə 'fait əgenst 'suisaid]	erfolgreich in ihrem Kampf gegen den Selbstmord
	have they reduced	[həv ðei ri'dju:st]	haben sie reduziert / verringert
	the suicide rate	[ðə 'suisaid reit]	die Selbstmordquote / -ziffer
	the rate has dropped by one third	[ðə 'reit əz 'drɔpt bai 'wʌn 'θə:d]	die Quote / Ziffer ist um ein Drittel gefallen
	that's quite a difference	[ðæts 'kwait ə 'difrəns]	das ist ein ziemlicher Unterschied
	the statistics	[ðə stə'tistiks]	die Statistiken
	save lives	['seiv 'laivz]	Menschenleben retten
	it doesn't matter whether ...	[it 'dʌznt 'mætə weðə]	es ist gleichgültig / egal, ob ...
15D	until 1961 (= nineteen sixty-one)	[əntil 'nainti:n 'siksti-'wʌn]	bis 1961

	change something	['tʃeindʒ sʌmθiŋ]	etwas ändern
	figures	['figəz]	(vor allem statistische) Zahlen
	go up	['gəu 'ʌp]	in die Höhe gehen
	do we know for sure . . .	[du wi nəu fə 'ʃuə]	wissen wir sicher . . .
	even if	['i:vn 'if]	auch wenn
15E	million	['miljən]	Million
15F	is there a need for . . .	[iz ðər ə 'ni:d fə]	besteht ein Bedarf an . . .
	the figures below	[ðə 'figəz bi'ləu]	die nachstehenden Zahlen
	an increase	[ən 'inkri:s]	ein Zuwachs; eine Steigerung
	per cent	[pə 'sent]	Prozent
15G	the figures on the left	[ðə 'figəz ɔn ðə 'left]	die linksstehenden Zahlen
15H	he took his own life	[hi tuk iz 'əun laif]	er nahm sich das Leben
	they took their own lives	[ðei tuk ðər 'əun 'laivz]	sie nahmen sich das Leben
	depressed	[di'prest]	deprimiert; bedrückt
	lose – lost – lost	[lu:z – lɔst – lɔst]	verlieren – verlor – verloren
	someone close to them	[sʌmwʌn 'kləus tə ðəm]	jemand, der ihnen nahestand
	their marriage has broken up	[ðεə 'mæridʒ əz 'brəukn 'ʌp]	ihre Ehe ist gescheitert
	break – broke – broken	[breik – brəuk – 'brəukn]	brechen – brach – gebrochen
	personal problems	['pə:snl 'prɔbləmz]	persönliche Probleme
	I'm a failure	[aim ə 'feiljə]	ich bin ein Versager
	they are in debt	[ðεər in 'det]	sie sind verschuldet
	unemployed	['ʌnim'plɔid]	arbeitslos; erwerbslos
	he's ill	[hiz 'il]	er ist krank
15K	definition	[defi'niʃn]	Definition; Begriffsbestimmung

Lektion 16

16A	mail-order shopping	['meil-ɔ:də 'ʃɔpiŋ]	Einkauf bei einem Versandhaus
	June	[dʒu:n]	Juni
	limited	['limitid]	mit beschränkter Haftung
	road	[rəud]	(Land-)Straße
	place an order	['pleis ən 'ɔ:də]	einen Auftrag erteilen; eine Bestellung aufgeben
	£57.94 worth of goods	['fifti-'sevn 'paundz 'nainti-'fɔ: 'pens wə:θ əv 'gudz]	Waren im Wert von £57.94
	from your catalogue	[frəm jɔ: 'kætəlɔg]	aus Ihrem Katalog
	spring and summer	['spriŋ ən 'sʌmə]	Frühling / Frühjahr und Sommer
	a Sharp cassette recorder	[ə 'ʃɑ:p kə'set rikɔ:də]	einen Sharp-Kassettenrecorder
	shaver	['ʃeivə]	Rasierapparat; Trockenrasierer
	Ronson battery toothbrush	['rɔnsən 'bætəri 'tu:θbrʌʃ]	Ronson-Batteriezahnbürste
	since it was damaged	['sins it wəz 'dæmidʒd]	da er beschädigt war
	I returned it to you	[ai ri'tə:nd it tə ju]	ich schickte ihn an Sie zurück
	ask for a new one	['ɑ:sk fər ə 'nju: wʌn]	um einen neuen bitten
	I received the toothbrush	[ai ri'si:vd ðə 'tu:θbrʌʃ]	ich erhielt die Zahnbürste
	Deluxe	[di'lʌks]	*(Modellbezeichnung:)* Luxus
	not the right model	['nɔt ðə 'rait 'mɔdl]	nicht das richtige Modell
	send – sent – sent	[send – sent – sent]	schicken – schickte – geschickt
	it seems my note got lost somehow	[it 'si:mz mai 'nəut gɔt 'lɔst sʌmhau]	es scheint, meine Notiz / Mitteilung ging irgendwie verloren
	a bill for £3.50	[ə 'bil fə 'θri: paundz 'fifti]	eine Rechnung über £3.50
	for repairs	[fə ri'pεəz]	für Reparaturen
	under separate cover	[ʌndə 'seprət 'kʌvə]	mit getrennter Post
	and would ask you	[ən wəd 'ɑ:sk ju]	und würde / möchte Sie bitten
	the correct model	[ðə kə'rekt mɔdl]	das richtige Modell
	as soon as possible	[əz 'su:n əz 'pɔsəbl]	so bald wie möglich
	cancel the enclosed bill	['kænsl ði in'kləuzd 'bil]	stornieren Sie die beiliegende Rechnung
	Frank Burton	['fræŋk 'bə:tn]	*(Name)*

16B	the price of each item	[ðə 'prais əv 'i:tʃ 'aitəm]	der Preis für jeden Artikel
	buy things by mail order	['bai θiŋz bai 'meil ɔ:də]	Sachen auf dem Versandweg kaufen
	what's your experience of	[wɔts 'jɔ:r iks'piəriəns əv]	wie sind Ihre Erfahrungen mit
16C	complaint	[kəm'pleint]	Beschwerde; Reklamation
	do you remember selling me this toaster?	[du ju ri'membə 'seliŋ mi ðis 'təustə]	erinnern Sie sich, daß Sie mir diesen Toaster verkauft haben?
	four slices of bread at once	['fɔ: slaisiz əv 'bred ət 'wʌns]	vier Scheiben Brot auf einmal
	six heat settings	['siks 'hi:t setiŋz]	sechs Wärmeeinstellungen
	almost a give-away	['ɔ:lməust ə 'giv-əwei]	fast geschenkt
	it doesn't work	[it dəznt 'wə:k]	er funktioniert nicht
	reliable	[ri'laiəbl]	zuverlässig; verläßlich
	make – made – made	[meik – meid – meid]	machen – machte – gemacht
	good workmanship	['gud 'wə:kmənʃip]	Qualitätsarbeit
	we've never had any complaints	[wiv 'nevə hæd əni kəm'pleints]	wir haben noch nie Reklamationen gehabt
	I've tried this toaster three times	[aiv 'traid ðis 'təustə 'θri: 'taimz]	ich habe diesen Toaster dreimal ausprobiert
	each time I turned it on	['i:tʃ 'taim ai 'tə:nd it 'ɔn]	jedesmal, wenn ich ihn anmachte
	the fuse went	[ðə 'fju:z went]	die Sicherung brannte durch
	bad	[bæd]	schlecht; schlimm
	shall we exchange it for a new one?	[ʃəl wi iks'tʃeinʒ it fər ə 'nju: wʌn]	sollen wir ihn gegen einen neuen umtauschen?
	have confidence in something	[hæv 'kɔnfidəns in sʌmθiŋ]	Vertrauen zu etwas haben
	can you recommend another brand?	[kæn ju rekə'mend ə'nʌðə brænd]	können Sie eine andere Marke empfehlen?
	how about this toaster?	[hau əbaut 'ðis təustə]	wie wäre es mit diesem Toaster?
	good as gold	['gud əz 'gəuld]	(so) gut wie Gold
	auto / automatic	['ɔ:təu / ɔ:tə'mætik]	Automatik- / automatisch
	super	['su:pə]	Super(-)
	colour-selector control	['kʌlə-si'lektə kəntrəul]	Farbwahlregelung, -einstellung
	cut out the sales talk!	['kʌt aut ðə 'seilz tɔ:k]	*(etwa:)* schenken Sie sich Ihre Verkaufsargumente!
	plug the darned thing in!	['plʌg ðə 'dɑ:nd θiŋ 'in]	stecken Sie das verdammte Ding rein (in die Steckdose)!
16D	this time	['ðis taim]	diesmal
16E	it has just arrived	[it əz 'dʒʌst ə'raivd]	er ist gerade angekommen
	it arrived last week	[it ə'raivd 'lɑ:st 'wi:k]	er kam vorige Woche an
	it arrived this morning	[it ə'raivd ðis 'mɔ:niŋ]	er kam heute morgen an
	write – wrote – written	[rait – rəut – 'ritn]	schreiben – schrieb – geschrieben
	sell – sold – sold	[sel – səuld – səuld]	verkaufen – verkaufte – verkauft
16F	how often has she been to Clacton?	['hau 'ɔfn əz ʃi bi:n tə 'klæktən]	wie oft ist sie schon in Clacton gewesen?
16H	meaningful sentences	['mi:niŋful 'sentənsiz]	sinnvolle Sätze

Lektion 17

17A	at the travel agent's	[ət ðə 'trævl eidʒənts]	im Reisebüro
	agent	['eidʒənt]	Agent; Vertreter
	tour	[tuə]	(Rund-)Reise
	leave from Heathrow	['li:v frəm 'hi:θ'rəu]	von Heathrow abfliegen
	at twelve o'clock sharp	[ət 'twelv əklɔk 'ʃɑ:p]	um Punkt zwölf Uhr
	on October the first	[ɔn ɔk'təubə ðə 'fə:st]	am ersten Oktober
	Boston	['bɔstən]	*(Hauptstadt von Massachusetts)*
	travel by rocket	['trævl bai 'rɔkit]	mit der Rakete reisen / fliegen
	it does sound funny	[it 'dʌz saund 'fʌni]	es klingt wirklich komisch
	flying time	['flaiiŋ taim]	Flugzeit
	don't forget	['dəunt fə'get]	vergessen Sie nicht

	is four hours ahead of Boston	[iz 'fɔːr 'auəz ə'hed əv 'bɔstən]	ist Boston vier Stunden voraus
	our actual flying time	[auər 'æktʃuəl 'flaiiŋ taim]	unsere tatsächliche Flugzeit
	quite!	[kwait]	ganz recht!
	six and a quarter hours	['siks ən ə 'kwɔːtər auəz]	sechs und eine Viertelstunde
	if you're dead on time	[if jɔ 'ded ɔn 'taim]	wenn Sie absolut pünktlich sind
	the whole of the second day	[ðə 'həul əv ðə 'sekənd dei]	den ganzen zweiten Tag
	(will there be) any chance of hearing the Boston Symphony Orchestra?	[(wil ðə bi) eni 'tʃɑːns əv hiəriŋ ðə 'bɔstən 'simfəni ɔːkistrə]	wird es eine Möglichkeit geben, das Boston Symphony Orchestra zu hören?
	shall I make a note of it?	[ʃəl ai meik ə 'nəut əv it]	soll ich es mir notieren?
	anyway	['eniwei]	wie dem auch sei; jedenfalls
	travel along the Atlantic coast	['trævl əlɔŋ ði ət'læntik 'kəust]	an der Atlantikküste entlangfahren
	up to Portland	[ʌp tə 'pɔːtlənd]	bis nach Portland
	make an excursion	['meik ən iks'kəːʃn]	einen Ausflug / Abstecher machen
	White Mountains	['wait 'mauntənz]	"weiße Berge"; "weißes Gebirge"
	in northern New Hampshire	[in 'nɔːðən nju 'hæmpʃə]	im nördlichen New Hampshire
	they're very beautiful	[ðεə 'veri 'bjuːtəful]	sie sind sehr schön / wunderschön
	I've been there myself	[aiv biːn ðεə mai'self]	ich bin selbst (schon) da gewesen
	Acadia National Park	[ə'keidjə 'næʃnəl pɑːk]	*(Nationalpark i. US-Staat Maine)*
	is very pretty too	[iz 'veri 'priti 'tuː]	ist auch sehr hübsch
	Mount Desert Island	['maunt 'dezət ailənd]	(island = Insel)
	off the eastern coast of Maine	[ɔf ði 'iːstən 'kəust əv 'mein]	vor der Ostküste von Maine
	go on to Canada	['gəu 'ɔn tə 'kænədə]	nach Kanada weiterreisen
	Quebec	[kwi'bek]	*(Provinz u. Stadt in Kanada)*
	Montreal	[mɔntri'ɔːl]	*(Stadt i. d. kanad. Prov. Quebec)*
	about the same distance	[əbaut ðə 'seim 'distəns]	ungefähr die gleiche Entfernung
	Glasgow	['glɑːzgəu]	*(Stadt i. Schottl., 897 800 Einw.)*
	all the details are on this sheet here	['ɔːl ðə 'diːteilz ər ɔn ðis 'ʃiːt hiə]	alle Einzelheiten sind auf diesem Blatt hier
	Congress Street	['kɔŋgres striːt]	*(Geschäftsstraße in Portland)*
	the heart of downtown Portland	[ðə 'hɑːt əv 'dauntaun 'pɔːtlənd]	das Herz des Geschäftsviertels von Portland
	Northeast Harbour	['nɔːθ'iːst 'hɑːbə]	der Nordosthafen
	St Lawrence River	[snt 'lɔrəns 'rivə]	Sankt-Lorenz-Strom
	street scene	['striːt siːn]	Straßenszene
	downtown Manhattan	['dauntaun mæn'hætən]	unterer Teil von Manhattan
17B	what has he planned?	['wɔt əz i 'plænd]	was hat er geplant?
	will he be travelling alone?	[wil i bi 'trævliŋ ə'ləun]	wird er allein reisen?
	which airline will he fly by?	['witʃ 'εəlain wil i 'flai bai]	mit welcher Fluggesellschaft wird er fliegen?
	in the U.S.	[in ðə 'juː 'es]	in den USA
	the real flying time	[ðə 'riəl flaiiŋ taim]	die wirkliche Flugzeit
	route	[ruːt]	(Reise-, Fahrt-)Route; Strecke
17C	local time	['ləukl taim]	Ortszeit
	Bangor	['bæŋgɔː]	*(Stadt in Maine, 33 168 Einw.)*
	Bar Harbor	['bɑː 'hɑːbə]	*(Stadt in Maine, 2392 Einw.)*
	itinerary	[ai'tinərəri]	Reiseplan; Reiseweg
	explain something to somebody	[iks'plein sʌmθiŋ tə sʌmbədi]	jemandem etwas erklären
	departure and arrival times	[di'pɑːtʃər ən ə'raivl taimz]	Abfahrt- und Ankunftzeiten
	kilometres	['kiləmiːtəz]	Kilometer
17D	location	[ləu'keiʃn]	(geographische) Lage
	15 miles west of London	['fiftiːn mailz 'west əv 'lʌndən]	15 Meilen westlich von London
	east coast	['iːst 'kəust]	Ostküste

	in southwest Maine	[in 'sauθwest 'mein]	in Südwest-Maine
	a popular resort area	[ə 'pɔpjulə ri'zɔːt ɛəriə]	ein beliebtes Erholungsgebiet
	Canada is bounded on the north by the Arctic Ocean	['kænədə iz 'baundid ɔn ðə 'nɔːθ bai ði 'ɑːktik 'əuʃən]	Kanada wird im Norden durch das Nördliche Eismeer begrenzt
	Pacific Ocean	[pə'sifik 'əuʃən]	Pazifischer / Stiller Ozean
	Alaska	[ə'læskə]	*(US-Bundesstaat, 302 173 Einw.)*
	the capital of the province of Quebec	[ðə 'kæpitl əv ðə 'prɔvins əv kwi'bek]	die Hauptstadt der Provinz Quebec
	situated on the north bank	['sitjueitid ɔn ðə 'nɔːθ bæŋk]	am Nordufer gelegen
	southern	['sʌðən]	südlich; Süd-
	New York State is about the size of England	[nju 'jɔːk 'steit iz ə'baut ðə saiz əv 'iŋglənd]	der Staat New York hat ungefähr die Größe von England
	Canton	['kæntɔn]	Kanton *(in der Schweiz)*
	village	['vilidʒ]	Dorf
	the nearest railway station	[ðə 'niərist 'reilwei steiʃn]	der nächste Bahnhof *(d. Eisenbahn)*
17E	a short account of	[ə 'ʃɔːt ə'kaunt əv]	ein kurzer Bericht über
	Wednesdey	['wenzdi]	Mittwoch
	Jumbo jet	['dʒʌmbəu 'dʒet]	Jumbo-Jet *(Großraumdüsenflugzeug)*
	take off – took off – taken off	['teik 'ɔf – 'tuk 'ɔf – 'teikən 'ɔf]	abfliegen – abflog – abgeflogen
	a smooth flight	[ə 'smuːð 'flait]	ein ruhiger Flug
	late	[leit]	spät; verspätet
	sleep – slept – slept	[sliːp – slept – slept]	schlafen – schlief – geschlafen
	though	[ðəu]	obwohl; obgleich
	fairly comfortable	['fɛəli 'kʌmftəbl]	ziemlich / leidlich bequem
	hear – heard – heard	[hiə – həːd – həːd]	hören – hörte – gehört
	a concert given by the Boston Symphony Orchestra	[ə 'kɔnsət 'givn bai ðə 'bɔstən 'simfəni ɔːkistrə]	ein Konzert, das gegeben wurde v. Boston Symphony Orchestra
	which we visited on the sixth day	[witʃ wi 'vizitid ɔn ðə 'siksθ dei]	den wir am sechsten Tag besuchten
	Adirondack Mountains	[ædi'rɔndæk 'mauntənz]	*(Gebirge im US-Staat New York)*
	forest	['fɔrist]	(großer) Wald
	pay a short visit	['pei ə 'ʃɔːt 'vizit]	einen kurzen Besuch abstatten
	John Brown's body lies a-mouldering in the grave	['dʒɔn 'braunz 'bɔdi laiz ə'məuldriŋ in ðə 'greiv]	John Browns Leichnam liegt vermodernd im Grabe (moulder = vermodern; *John Brown = amerik. Freischärler, 1859 gehängt*)
	farm	[fɑːm]	Farm; Bauernhof
	Lake Placid	['leik 'plæsid]	*(Wintersportzentrum, 3500 Ew.)*
17F	Olympic stadium	[ə'limpik 'steidiəm]	Olympiastadion
	the Olympic Games were due to open on . . .	[ði ə'limpik 'geimz wə 'djuː tu 'əupən ɔn]	die Olympischen Spiele sollten am . . . anfangen
	were they well organized?	[wəː ðei 'wel 'ɔːgənaizd]	waren sie gut organisiert?
	the outstanding athletes	[ði aut'stændiŋ 'æθliːts]	die herausragenden Athleten

Lektion 18

18A	living by the motorway	['liviŋ bai ðə 'məutəwei]	Wohnen an der Autobahn
	Henderson	['hendəsn]	*(Familienname)*
	move into a new house	['muːv intu ə 'njuː 'haus]	in ein neues Haus ziehen
	whereabouts is it?	['wɛərəbauts 'iz it]	in welcher Gegend ist es?
	right next to the motorway	['rait 'nekst tə ðə 'məutəwei]	direkt neben der Autobahn
	intersection	[intə'sekʃn]	(Straßen-)Kreuzung
	isn't it very noisy there?	[iznt it veri 'nɔizi ðɛə]	ist es da nicht sehr laut?
	there are lorries going past all the time	[ðər ə 'lɔriz gəuiŋ pɑːst ɔːl ðə 'taim]	es fahren die ganze Zeit Lastwagen vorbei

Substantive auf *-y* haben in der Pluralform *-ies*, wenn dem *-y* nicht ein *a, e, o* oder *u* vorausgeht: balcony – balcon**ies**, country – countr**ies**, emergency – emergenc**ies**, inquiry – inquir**ies**, lorry – lorr**ies**.
Aber natürlich: day – days, key – keys, journey – journeys usw.

	it doesn't get on their nerves	[it 'dʌznt get ɔn ðεə 'nə:vz]	er geht ihnen nicht auf die Nerven
	serious	['siəriəs]	ernst(haft)
	you can't be serious	[ju 'kɑ:nt bi 'siəriəs]	das kann nicht dein Ernst sein
	what it's like at the side of a motorway	[wɔt its 'laik ət ðə 'said əv ə 'məutəwei]	wie es am Rand einer Autobahn ist / zugeht
	the noise drives you out of your mind	[ðə 'nɔiz draivz ju aut əv jɔ: 'maind]	der Lärm bringt einen um den Verstand
	watch the traffic	['wɔtʃ ðə 'træfik]	den Verkehr beobachten
	promenade	[prɔmə'nɑ:d]	Promenade
	how can anyone stand that awful noise?	[hau kən 'eniwʌn 'stænd ðæt 'ɔ:fl 'nɔiz]	wie kann (irgend) jemand diesen gräßlichen Lärm aushalten?
	get ill	['get 'il]	krank werden
	to Mrs Henderson it's a great advantage	[tə misiz 'hendəsn its ə 'greit əd'vɑ:ntidʒ]	für Frau Henderson ist es ein großer Vorteil
	build – built – built	[bild – bilt – bilt]	bauen – baute – gebaut
	look out of the window	['luk aut əv ðə 'windəu]	aus dem Fenster schauen / gucken
	she prefers the motorway	[ʃi pri'fə:z ðə 'məutəwei]	sie zieht die Autobahn vor
	she feels she has more privacy	[ʃi 'fi:lz ʃi hæz mɔ: 'privəsi]	sie hat das Gefühl, daß sie unbeobachteter ist ("mehr Privatheit hat")
	when she's sunbathing	[wen ʃiz 'sʌnbeiðiŋ]	wenn sie sich sonnt
	nobody will notice her	['nəubədi wil 'nəutis hə]	niemand wird sie bemerken
	the cars go much too fast	[ðə 'kɑ:z gəu 'mʌtʃ tu: 'fɑ:st]	die Autos fahren viel zu schnell
18C	apartment house	[ə'pɑ:tmənt haus]	Wohngebäude; Mietshaus
	residential street	[rezi'denʃəl 'stri:t]	Straße in einer Wohngegend
	the way people live	[ðə 'wei 'pi:pl 'liv]	die Art, wie Menschen wohnen
	a rented flat	[ə 'rentid 'flæt]	eine gemietete Wohnung
	high / low rent	['hai / 'ləu 'rent]	hohe / niedrige Miete
	own a flat *(Brit.)* / an apartment *(US)*	['əun ə 'flæt / ən ə'pɑ:tmənt]	eine Wohnung (als Eigentum) besitzen
	furnished – unfurnished	['fə:niʃt – 'ʌn'fə:niʃt]	möbliert – unmöbliert
	landlord – tenant	['lændlɔ:d – 'tenənt]	Vermieter – Mieter
	give someone notice	['giv sʌmwʌn 'nəutis]	jemandem kündigen
	we have to give six months' notice	[wi hæf tə giv 'siks 'mʌnθs 'nəutis]	wir müssen eine Kündigungsfrist von sechs Monaten einhalten
	we have a house of our own	[wi hæv ə 'haus əv auər 'əun]	wir haben ein eigenes Haus
	repairs aren't our business	[ri'pεəz ɑ:nt 'auə biznis]	Reparaturen sind nicht unsere Sache / gehen uns nichts an
	disadvantages	[disəd'vɑ:ntidʒiz]	Nachteile
	pet	[pet]	(zahmes) Haustier
	condominium	[kɔndə'minjəm]	*(US:)* Eigentumswohnung
	owner-occupied flat	['əunər-ɔkjupaid 'flæt]	*(Brit.:)* Eigentumswohnung
	land	[lænd]	Land; Boden
	a detached house	[ə di'tætʃt 'haus]	ein freistehendes Haus
	a semidetached house	[ə 'semidi'tætʃt 'haus]	ein halb freistehendes Haus
	which is cheaper?	['witʃ iz 'tʃi:pə]	welches ist billiger?
	neighbourhood	['neibəhud]	Nachbarschaft; Gegend
	more space	['mɔ: 'speis]	mehr Platz; mehr Raum
	lock the door and go away	['lɔk ðə 'dɔ:r ən 'gəu ə'wei]	die Tür abschließen und wegfahren
	shops and stores	['ʃɔps ən 'stɔ:z]	Läden und Kaufhäuser
	near at hand	['niər ət 'hænd]	nahe dabei; in der Nähe

	the slums	[ðə 'slʌmz]	die Elendsviertel
	ugly houses	['ʌgli 'hauziz]	häßliche Häuser
	in bad repair	[in 'bæd ri'pɛə]	in schlechtem Zustand
	overcrowded	[əuvə'kraudid]	überfüllt
	not enough fresh air	[nɔt inʌf 'freʃ 'ɛə]	nicht genug frische Luft
	backyard	['bæk'jɑːd]	Hinterhof
	cockroaches, mice, and rats are vermin	['kɔkrəutʃiz 'mais ən 'ræts ə 'vəːmin]	(Küchen-)Schaben, Mäuse und Ratten sind Ungeziefer
	mouse – mice	[maus – mais]	Maus – Mäuse
	outside lavatories	['autsaid 'lævətriz]	Außentoiletten
	no bathrooms	['nəu 'bɑːθrumz]	keine Badezimmer
	suburb	['sʌbəːb]	Vorort
18D	a small house	[ə 'smɔːl 'haus]	ein kleines Haus
	storey	['stɔːri]	Stock(werk); Etage, Geschoß
	which floor do you live on?	['witʃ flɔː du ju 'liv ɔn]	in welchem Stockwerk wohnen Sie?
	what rooms are there in your flat?	['wɔt 'rumz ɑ ðər in jɔː 'flæt]	was für Zimmer sind in Ihrer Wohnung?
	what kind of furniture?	['wɔt kaind əv 'fəːnitʃə]	was für Möbel?
	traditional	[trə'diʃnəl]	traditionell; herkömmlich
	heavy – light	['hevi – lait]	schwer – leicht
	cellar	['selə]	Keller
	in your present home	[in jɔː 'preznt 'həum]	in Ihrer jetzigen Wohnung
	I've lived here since 1970	[aiv 'livd hiə sins . . .]	ich wohne hier (schon) seit 1970
	I've lived here for ten years	[aiv 'livd hiə fə 'ten 'jiəz]	ich wohne hier (schon) seit zehn Jahren
	a cosy room	[ə 'kəuzi 'rum]	ein gemütliches Zimmer
	convenient	[kən'viːniənt]	bequem (gelegen); praktisch
	neighbour	['neibə]	Nachbar(in)
	a faraway place in the country	[ə 'fɑːrəwei 'pleis in ðə 'kʌntri]	ein abgelegener Ort auf dem Lande
18E	Kensington	['kenziŋtən]	*(Londoner Stadtbezirk)*
	they are a noisy lot	[ðɛər ə 'nɔizi 'lɔt]	sie sind eine laute Bande
	they themselves	['ðei ðəm'selvz]	sie selbst / selber
	Gerald	['dʒerəld]	*(männlicher Vorname)*
	leave – left – left	[liːv – left – left]	ausziehen – auszog – ausgezogen
18F	translate accordingly	[træns'leit ə'kɔːdiŋli]	übersetzen Sie entsprechend
	best cooking in the British Isles	['best 'kukiŋ in ðə 'britiʃ 'ailz]	beste Küche auf den Britischen Inseln
18G	likes and dislikes	['laiks ən 'dislaiks]	Neigungen und Abneigungen
	study a catalogue	['stʌdi ə 'kætəlɔg]	einen Katalog studieren
	go shopping	['gəu 'ʃɔpiŋ]	einkaufen gehen
	play football	['plei 'futbɔːl]	Fußball spielen

Lektion 19

19A	beer and rolls	['biər ən 'rəulz]	Bier und Brötchen
	at the local	[ət ðə 'ləukl]	im (Orts-)Gasthaus
	Cumbria	['kʌmbriə]	*(Grafschaft i. NW-England)*
	beer flows free	['biə 'fləuz 'friː]	Bier fließt frei / kostenlos
	Charles Northam	['tʃɑːlz 'nɔːðəm]	*(Name)*
	a black dog	[ə 'blæk 'dɔg]	ein schwarzer Hund
	since then	['sins 'ðen]	seitdem
	drink – drank – drunk	[driŋk – dræŋk – drʌŋk]	trinken – trank – getrunken
	40,000 pints of his favourite mild	['fɔːti θauzənd 'paints əv iz 'feivərət 'maild]	40 000 Pint seines Lieblings-Mild *(= leichtes engl. Bier)*
	when the brewery discovered	[wen ðə 'bruəri dis'kʌvəd]	als die Brauerei entdeckte
	how long he had been a customer	[hau lɔŋ i əd biːn ə 'kʌstəmə]	wie lange er (schon) (ein) Kunde gewesen war

	decide	[di'said]	beschließen
	for the rest of his life	[fə ðə 'rest əv iz 'laif]	für den Rest seines Lebens
	in future	[in 'fju:tʃə]	in Zukunft
	yard	[jɑ:d]	*(engl. Elle = 91,4 cm)*
	cottage	['kɔtidʒ]	Häuschen; Hütte
	the beer will be on the brewery	[ðə 'biə wil bi ɔn ðə 'bruəri]	das Bier wird zu Lasten der Brauerei gehen
	this is very generous	[ðis iz veri 'dʒenərəs]	das ist sehr großzügig
	it won't (= will not) make any difference	[it 'wəunt meik eni 'difrəns]	es wird keinen Unterschied machen
	drinking habits	['driŋkiŋ hæbits]	Trinkgewohnheiten
	I'm not going to drink myself to death now	[aim 'nɔt gəuiŋ tə 'driŋk maiself tə 'deθ 'nau]	ich werde mich jetzt nicht zu Tode trinken
	Martha	['mɑ:θə]	*(weiblicher Vorname)*
	a lifelong teetotaller	[ə 'laiflɔŋ ti:'təutlə]	eine "lebenslange" Abstinenzlerin
	I don't mind his drinking	[ai 'dəunt 'maind hiz 'driŋkiŋ]	ich habe nichts ("gegen sein Trinken") dagegen, daß er trinkt
	people might think	[pi:pl mait 'θiŋk]	die Leute könnten denken
	pocket money	['pɔkit mʌni]	Taschengeld
	it's not the beer that has kept him going all these years	[its 'nɔt ðə 'biə ðət əz kept im gəuiŋ ɔ:l ði:z 'jiəz]	es ist nicht das Bier, das ihn alle diese Jahre auf den Beinen gehalten hat
	elderberry wine	['eldəberi 'wain]	Holunder(beer)wein
	he used to come in soaking wet	[hi 'ju:stə 'kʌm 'in 'səukiŋ 'wet]	er pflegte klitschnaß hereinzukommen
	after working in the fields all day	[ɑ:ftə 'wə:kiŋ in ðə 'fi:ldz ɔ:l dei]	nachdem er den ganzen Tag auf den Feldern gearbeitet hatte
	catch – caught – caught	[kætʃ – kɔ:t – kɔ:t]	fangen – fing – gefangen
	he never caught a cold	[hi 'nevə 'kɔ:t ə 'kəuld]	er bekam nie eine Erkältung
19B	at what age	[ət 'wɔt 'eidʒ]	in welchem Alter
	if he continues to drink	[if i kən'tinju:z tə 'driŋk]	wenn er weiterhin trinkt ("fortfährt zu trinken")
	generosity	[dʒenə'rɔsəti]	Großzügigkeit
	bad for his health	['bæd fər iz 'helθ]	schlecht für seine Gesundheit
19C	I can't believe it	[ai 'kɑ:nt bi li:v it]	ich kann es nicht glauben
	England	['iŋglənd]	*(Teil von Großbritannien)*
19D	townspeople move about a great deal	['taunzpi:pl 'mu:v ə'baut ə greit di:l]	Städter ziehen häufig um
	lead a regular life	['li:d ə 'regjulə 'laif]	ein regelmäßiges Leben führen
	what's his job?	[wɔts iz 'dʒɔb]	was ist sein Beruf?
	many different jobs	['meni 'difrənt 'dʒɔbz]	viele verschiedene Berufe
	use your imagination	['ju:z jɔ:r imædʒi'neiʃn]	gebrauchen Sie Ihre Phantasie
	he usually works . . .	[hi 'ju:ʒəli wə:ks]	meistens arbeitet er . . .
	feed the animals	['fi:d ði 'æniməlz]	die Tiere füttern
	milk the cows	['milk ðə 'kauz]	die Kühe melken
	repair the machinery	[ri'pɛə ðə mə'ʃi:nəri]	die Maschinen reparieren
	drive to the market	['draiv tə ðə 'mɑ:kit]	zum Markt fahren
	factory	['fæktəri]	Fabrik
	work in the open air	['wə:k in ði 'əupən 'ɛə]	im Freien arbeiten
	work overtime	['wə:k 'əuvətaim]	Überstunden machen
	in their spare time	[in ðɛə spɛə 'taim]	in ihrer Freizeit
	start all over again	['stɑ:t ɔ:l əuvər ə'gen]	noch einmal ganz von vorn anfangen
	where would you rather live?	['wɛə wud ju 'rɑ:ðə 'liv]	wo würden Sie lieber leben?
19E	he's trying to protect her	[hiz traiiŋ tə prə'tekt hə:]	er versucht, sie zu beschützen
	he enjoyed himself very much	[hi in'dʒɔid imself veri 'mʌtʃ]	er amüsierte sich sehr

	at the party last night	[ət ðə 'pɑ:ti lɑ:st nait]	auf der Party gestern abend
19F	in the past	[in ðə 'pɑ:st]	in der Vergangenheit; früher
	child – children	[tʃaild – 'tʃildrən]	Kind – Kinder
	a little boy	[ə litl 'bɔi]	ein kleiner Junge
	a young girl	[ə jʌŋ 'gə:l]	ein junges Mädchen
19G	a quick one at the bar	[ə 'kwik wʌn ət ðə 'bɑ:]	ein schneller (Drink) an der Bar
	have a quick one	[hæv ə 'kwik wʌn]	noch schnell einen trinken

Lektion 20

20A

Anthony ['æntəni]	Else [els]	Nichols ['niklz]	Una ['ju:nə]
Booth [bu:ð]	Garnett ['gɑ:nit]	Rita ['ri:tə]	Warren ['wɔrən]
Dandy ['dændi]	Mitchell ['mitʃəl]	Stubbs [stʌbz]	

till death us do part	[til 'deθ ʌs du: 'pɑ:t]	*(veraltet:)* bis daß der Tod uns scheidet
television series	['teliviʒn siəriz]	Fernsehserie
comedy	['kɔmədi]	Komödie; Lustspiel
appear on BBC Television	[ə'piər ɔn 'bi:bi:si: 'teliviʒn]	*(etwa:)* im Fernsehprogramm der BBC erscheinen
at intervals	[ət 'intəvəlz]	"in Abständen"; von Zeit zu Zeit
an East End working man	[ən 'i:st end 'wə:kiŋ mæn]	ein Arbeiter aus dem Londoner East End
he's in his mid-fifties	[hi:z in iz 'mid-'fiftiz]	er ist Mitte fünfzig
terraced house	['terəst 'haus]	Reihenhaus
a plump woman	[ə 'plʌmp wumən]	eine pummelige / rundliche Frau
stupid but good-hearted	['stju:pid bət 'gud-'hɑ:tid]	dumm, aber gutmütig
daughter	['dɔ:tə]	Tochter
a lazy, long-haired layabout	[ə 'leizi 'lɔŋ-hɛəd 'leiəbaut]	ein fauler, langhaariger Gammler
half-baked Socialist opinions	['hɑ:f-beikt 'səuʃəlist ə'pinjənz]	unausgegorene sozialistische Meinungen / Ansichten
ignorant	['ignərənt]	unwissend; ungebildet
selfish	['selfiʃ]	selbstsüchtig; egoistisch
bloody-minded	['blʌdi-'maindid]	giftig; widerlich; eklig
character	['kæriktə]	Charakter; Mensch
he hates new ideas	[hi 'heits 'nju: ai'diəz]	er haßt neue Ideen
coloured people	['kʌləd pi:pl]	farbige Menschen; Farbige
foreigners	['fɔrənəz]	Ausländer
trade unions	['treid 'ju:njənz]	Gewerkschaften
viewers react to him in different ways	['vju:əz ri'ækt tə him in 'difrənt 'weiz]	die Zuschauer reagieren auf ihn in unterschiedlicher Weise
some find him offensive	['sʌm faind im ə'fensiv]	manche finden ihn widerwärtig
folk hero	['fəuk hiərəu]	Volksheld
others just think him funny	['ʌðəz dʒʌst θiŋk im 'fʌni]	andere finden ihn einfach komisch
I consider the series good entertainment	[ai kən'sidə ðə siəriz 'gud entə'teinmənt]	ich halte die Serie für gute Unterhaltung
some typical statements	[səm 'tipikl 'steitmənts]	einige typische Äußerungen
Pakistanis and Indians	[pɑ:kis'tɑ:niz ən 'indiənz]	Pakistani(s) und Inder
mixed marriages should not be allowed	['mikst 'mæridʒiz ʃud 'nɔt bi ə'laud]	Mischehen sollten nicht erlaubt sein
workers are trying to destroy the country	['wə:kəz ə traiiŋ tə dis'trɔi ðə 'kʌntri]	die Arbeiter versuchen, den Staat zu zerstören
their bloody strikes and go-slows	[ðɛə 'blʌdi 'straiks ən 'gəu'sləuz]	ihre verfluchten Streiks und Bummelstreiks

	a proper democracy	[ə 'prɔpə di'mɔkrəsi]	eine richtige Demokratie
	shoot – shot – shot	[ʃu:t – ʃɔt – ʃɔt]	erschießen – erschoß – erschossen
	they were asked about the series	[ðei wər 'ɑ:skt əbaut ðə 'siəriz]	sie wurden über die Serie befragt
	about half of them	[əbaut 'hɑ:f əv ðəm]	etwa die Hälfte von ihnen
	express an opinion	[iks'pres ən ə'pinjən]	eine Meinung zum Ausdruck bringen
	he's right more often than he's wrong	[hi:z 'rait mɔ:r ɔfn ðən i:z 'rɔŋ]	er hat öfter recht als unrecht
20B	programme	['prəugræm]	Programm
	who is it about?	['hu:z it ə'baut]	von wem handelt es?
	describe the main characters	[dis'kraib ðə 'mein 'kæriktəz]	beschreiben Sie die Hauptcharaktere
	the series as a whole	[ðə 'siəriz əz ə 'həul]	die Serie als Ganzes
	with similar views	[wið 'similə vju:z]	mit ähnlichen Ansichten
20C	multiracial society	['mʌlti'reiʃl sə'saiəti]	"Vielrassengesellschaft"
	both A and B	['bəuθ 'ei ən 'bi:]	sowohl A als auch B
	(total) population	[('təutl) pɔpju'leiʃn]	(Gesamt-)Bevölkerung
	mainly immigrants	['meinli 'imigrənts]	hauptsächlich Einwanderer
	Commonwealth	['kɔmənwelθ]	*(Staatengemeinschaft d. ehemaligen brit. Weltreichs)*
	the West Indies	[ðə 'west 'indiz]	Westindien
	Asia and Africa	['eiʃə ən 'æfrikə]	Asien und Afrika
	the victims of discrimination	[ðə 'viktimz əv diskrimi'neiʃn]	die Opfer von (Rassen-)Diskriminierung
	difficult	['difikəlt]	schwierig
	a decent place to live	[ə 'di:snt pleis tə 'liv]	ein anständiger Ort zum Wohnen
	workmates	['wə:kmeits]	Arbeitsgefährten, -kameraden
	they are hostile to them	[ðɛə 'hɔstail tə ðəm]	sie sind ihnen gegenüber feindselig eingestellt
	William Edward Burghardt Du Bois	['wiljəm 'edwəd 'bə:ghɑ:t du 'bɔiz]	*(amerik.-ghanaischer Schriftsteller u. Politiker, 1868–1963)*
	the twentieth century	[ðə 'twentiəθ 'sentʃəri]	das zwanzigste Jahrhundert
	colour line	['kʌlə lain]	Rassenschranke
	this is certainly true of the United States	[ðis iz 'sə:tnli 'tru: əv ðə ju:'naitid 'steits]	für die Vereinigten Staaten trifft dies bestimmt / gewiß zu
	what America means to me	[wɔt ə'merikə 'mi:nz tə 'mi:]	was Amerika mir bedeutet
	Pearl S. Buck	['pə:l 'es 'bʌk]	*(amerik. Schriftstell., 1892–1973)*
	it is not healthy	[it iz 'nɔt 'helθi]	es ist nicht gesund
	when a nation lives within a nation	[wen ə 'neiʃn livz wi'ðin ə 'neiʃn]	wenn ein Volk innerhalb eines Volkes lebt
	coloured Americans	['kʌləd əmerikənz]	farbige Amerikaner
	confident of its tomorrow	['kɔnfidənt əv its tə'mɔrəu]	"zuversichtlich hinsichtlich seiner Zukunft"
	refugees	[refju'dʒi:z]	Flüchtlinge
	among its own citizens	[əmʌŋ its 'əun 'sitiznz]	unter seinen eigenen Bürgern
	discuss the problem	[dis'kʌs ðə 'prɔbləm]	diskutieren Sie das Problem
	underprivileged groups	[ʌndə'privilidʒd 'gru:ps]	benachteiligte Gruppen
	they're at a disadvantage	[ðɛər ət ə disəd'vɑ:ntidʒ]	sie sind im Nachteil
	nowadays	['nauədeiz]	heutzutage
	nationality	[næʃə'næləti]	Nationalität; Staatsangehörigkeit
	race	[reis]	Rasse
	customs	['kʌstəmz]	Sitten und Gebräuche
	create problems	[kri'eit 'prɔbləmz]	Probleme schaffen / hervorrufen
20D	stinker Alfred	['stiŋkər 'ælfrid]	(das) Ekel Alfred
	wearing slippers	['wɛəriŋ 'slipəz]	Pantoffeln tragend

	smoking a cigar	['sməukiŋ ə si'gɑ:]	eine Zigarre rauchend
	silly cow!	['sili 'kau]	blöde / dumme Kuh!
	who always wore jeans	[hu 'ɔlwiz wɔ: 'dʒi:nz]	die immer Jeans trug
	a liberal son-in-law	[ə 'libərəl 'sʌn-in-lɔ:]	ein liberaler Schwiegersohn
	he hated long hair	[hi 'heitid 'lɔŋ 'hɛə]	er haßte lange Haare
	beards and miniskirts	['biədz ən 'miniskə:ts]	Bärte und Miniröcke
	foreign workers	['fɔrən 'wə:kəz]	ausländische (Gast-)Arbeiter
	eggheads	['eghedz]	"Eierköpfe"; Intellektuelle
	and above all the left	[ən ə'bʌv 'ɔ:l ðə 'left]	und vor allem die Linke(n)
	they laughed at the stinker	[ðei 'lɑ:ft ət ðə 'stiŋkə]	sie lachten über das Ekel
	some were worried about his popularity	['sʌm wə 'wʌrid əbaut iz pɔpju'lærəti]	manche waren besorgt über seine Popularität
	one heart and one soul	['wʌn 'hɑ:t ən 'wʌn 'səul]	ein Herz und eine Seele
	a vaccine against smallpox	[ə 'væksi:n əgenst 'smɔ:lpɔks]	ein Impfstoff gegen (die) Pocken
	it acts like an infection	[it 'ækts laik ən in'fekʃn]	er wirkt wie eine Infektion
	instead of causing the illness, it prevents it	[insted əv 'kɔ:ziŋ ði ilnəs it pri'vents it]	anstatt die Krankheit zu verursachen, verhütet er sie
20E	the German counterpart	[ðə 'dʒə:mən 'kauntəpɑ:t]	das deutsche Gegenstück
	the series was a success	[ðə 'siəriz wəz ə sək'ses]	die Serie war ein Erfolg
	compare the two	[kəm'pɛə ðə 'tu:]	vergleichen Sie die beiden
	dangerous	['deinʒərəs]	gefährlich
20F	the topics of this lesson	[ðə 'tɔpiks əv ðis 'lesn]	die Themen dieser Lektion
	he's an actor	[hi:z ən 'æktə]	er ist Schauspieler
20G	viewing time	['vju:iŋ taim]	Einschaltzeit ("Sehzeit")
	U.K. (= United Kingdom)	['ju: 'kei / ju'naitid 'kiŋdəm]	Vereinigtes Königreich (= Großbritannien u. Nordirland)
	radio listening times	['reidiəu 'lisniŋ taimz]	Einschaltzeiten ("Radio-Hör-Zeiten")
	in the wrong order	[in ðə 'rɔŋ 'ɔ:də]	in der falschen Reihenfolge
	which figure belongs to which group?	['witʃ 'figə bilɔŋz tə 'witʃ 'gru:p]	welche Zahl gehört zu welcher Gruppe?

Lektion 21

21A	you were a toolmaker	[ju wər ə 'tu:lmeikə]	Sie waren Werkzeugmacher
	before you went into business	[bi'fɔ: ju went intə 'biznis]	bevor Sie Geschäftsmann wurden ("ins Geschäft gingen")
	I gave up my job	[ai 'geiv ʌp mai 'dʒɔb]	ich gab meine Arbeitsstelle auf
	biro	['baiərəu]	Kugelschreiber
	soft drinks	['sɔft 'driŋks]	alkoholfreie Getränke
	two ices, please!	['tu: 'aisiz 'pli:z]	zwei Eis, bitte!
	kiosk	['kiɔsk]	Kiosk; Verkaufsstand
	Russell Hill station	['rʌsl 'hil 'steiʃn]	(hill = Berg; Hügel)
	how do you manage it all?	['hau dju 'mænidʒ it ɔ:l]	wie schaffen Sie das alles?
	my eldest son	[mai 'eldist 'sʌn]	mein ältester Sohn
	I work ninety hours, and so does my wife	[ai wə:k 'nainti 'auəz ən 'səu dəz mai 'waif]	ich arbeite neunzig Stunden und meine Frau auch
	he's working for his exams just now	[hiz wə:kiŋ fər iz ig'zæmz dʒəst nau]	er bereitet sich jetzt gerade auf seine Prüfungen vor
	are you better off now?	[ɑ: ju betər 'ɔf nau]	sind Sie jetzt besser gestellt?
	earn £50 a week	[ə:n 'fifti 'paundz ə 'wi:k]	die Woche 50 Pfund verdienen
	I had no worries / debts	[ai hæd 'nəu 'wʌriz / 'dets]	ich hatte keine Sorgen / Schulden
	we owe the bank . . .	[wi 'əu ðə 'bæŋk]	wir schulden der Bank . . .
	it's nice to be your own master	[its 'nais tə bi jɔ:r 'əun 'mɑ:stə]	es ist schön, wenn man sein eigener Herr ist
	I've never been happier	[aiv 'nevə bi:n 'hæpiə]	ich bin noch nie glücklicher gewesen
21C	a small shopkeeper	[ə 'smɔ:l 'ʃɔpki:pə]	ein kleiner Ladenbesitzer

	I finish at 7 p.m.	[ai 'finiʃ ət 'sevn 'pi:'em]	ich höre um 19 Uhr auf
	he does the deliveries	[hi dʌz ðə di'livəriz]	er macht die Lieferungen
	a turnover of about . . .	[ə 'tə:nəuvər əv əbaut]	ein Umsatz von etwa . . .
	he must be rolling in money	[hi 'mʌst bi 'rəuliŋ in mʌni]	er muß im Geld schwimmen
	mortgage	['mɔ:gidʒ]	Hypothek
	interest payments	['intrəst peimənts]	Zinszahlungen
	loan	[ləun]	Darlehen; Kredit
	overheads	['əuvəhedz]	allgemeine Unkosten; fixe Kosten
	his monthly profit	[hiz 'mʌnθli 'prɔfit]	sein monatlicher Gewinn
	is it profitable?	[iz it 'prɔfitəbl]	rentiert es sich?
	expenses	[iks'pensiz]	Ausgaben; (Un-)Kosten; Aufwand
	920 ÷ 12 (= nine hundred and twenty divided by twelve)	['nain hʌndrəd ən 'twenti di'vaidid bai 'twelv]	neunhundertzwanzig geteilt durch zwölf
	what does he have to pay interest on?	['wɔt dəz i hæf tə pei 'intrəst ɔn]	worauf muß er Zinsen bezahlen?
	is it fair?	[iz it 'fɛə]	ist es fair / gerecht?
21D	he's finishing his breakfast	[hi:z 'finiʃiŋ iz 'brekfəst]	er beendet gerade sein Frühstück
	in the front room	[in ðə 'frʌnt 'rum]	im vorderen Zimmer
	take a short stroll	[teik ə 'ʃɔ:t 'strəul]	einen kleinen Bummel machen
	down the narrow path	[daun ðə 'nærəu 'pɑ:θ]	den schmalen Weg hinunter
	to the bottom of his garden	[tə ðə 'bɔtəm əv iz 'gɑ:dn]	zum untersten Ende seines Gartens
	his back garden	[hiz 'bæk 'gɑ:dn]	der Garten hinter seinem Haus
	marrows and cabbages	['mærəuz ən 'kæbidʒiz]	Kürbisse und Kohlköpfe
	beans and potatoes	['bi:nz ən pə'teitəuz]	Bohnen und Kartoffeln
	on the shop floor	[ɔn ðə 'ʃɔp 'flɔ:]	in der Werkhalle
	on the assembly line	[ɔn ði ə'sembli lain]	am Fließband / Montageband
	the whistle blows	[ðə 'wisl 'bləuz]	die Pfeife ertönt
	he changes into his gardening clothes	[hi 'tʃeindʒiz intu iz 'gɑ:dniŋ kləuðz]	er zieht sich für die Gartenarbeit um ("wechselt in seine Gartenarbeitskleider")
	he goes outside	[hi 'gəuz aut'said]	er geht raus / nach draußen
	potter about in the garden	['pɔtər ə'baut in ðə 'gɑ:dn]	im Garten herumhantieren
21E	Prime Minister	['praim 'ministə]	Premierminister
	I normally wake up about a quarter to eight	[ai 'nɔ:məli weik 'ʌp əbaut ə 'kwɔ:tə tu 'eit]	ich wache normalerweise gegen Viertel vor acht auf
	work on (dispatch) boxes	['wə:k ɔn (dis'pætʃ) 'bɔksiz]	an Depeschen arbeiten
	meeting	['mi:tiŋ]	Sitzung; Konferenz
	which begin at ten	[witʃ bi'gin ət 'ten]	die um zehn beginnen
	Tuesdays and Thursdays	['tju:zdiz ən 'θə:zdiz]	dienstags und donnerstags
	answer questions	['ɑ:nsə 'kwestʃənz]	Fragen beantworten
	the House (of Commons)	[ðə 'haus (əv 'kɔmənz)]	das Unterhaus
	tray	[trei]	Tablett
	the No. (= Number) 10 staff	[ðə 'nʌmbə 'ten 'stɑ:f]	der Mitarbeiterstab im Haus Downing Street Nr. 10
	we go across to the House	[wi 'gəu əkrɔs tə ðə 'haus]	wir gehen rüber ins Unterhaus
	I don't always succeed	[ai 'dəunt ɔ:lwiz sək'si:d]	es gelingt mir nicht immer
	there may be some official function	[ðə mei bi sʌm ə'fiʃl 'fʌŋkʃən]	da ist vielleicht irgendeine offizielle Verpflichtung
	as for television and radio	[æz fə 'teliviʒn ən 'reidiəu]	was Fernsehen und Radio angeht
	the eight o'clock news	[ði 'eit ə klɔk 'nju:z]	die Achtuhrnachrichten
	salary	['sæləri]	Gehalt
21F	the more interesting job	[ðə mɔ:r 'intrəstiŋ 'dʒɔb]	der interessantere Beruf
	his main interest in life	[hiz 'mein 'intrəst in 'laif]	sein Hauptinteresse im Leben

	monotonous and boring	[məˈnɔtənəs ən ˈbɔːriŋ]	monoton/eintönig und langweilig
	boring and tiring	[ˈbɔːriŋ ən ˈtaiəriŋ]	langweilig und ermüdend
	give reasons for your answer	[giv ˈriːznz fə jɔːr ˈɑːnsə]	geben Sie Gründe für Ihre Antwort
21G	read the papers	[ˈriːd ðə ˈpeipəz]	die Zeitungen lesen
	most of the day	[ˈməust əv ðə ˈdei]	den größten Teil des Tages
	behind the counter	[bihaind ðə ˈkauntə]	hinter dem Ladentisch
	P.M.	[ˈpiː ˈem]	(= Prime Minister)
21H	some comparisons	[səm kəmˈpærisnz]	einige Vergleiche
	twice	[twais]	zweimal

Lektion 22

22A	political rights	[pəˈlitikl ˈraits]	staatsbürgerliche Rechte
	and yet	[ən ˈjet]	und doch
	although	[ɔːlˈðəu]	obwohl; obgleich
	members of Parliament	[ˈmembəz əv ˈpɑːləmənt]	Parlamentsabgeordnete
	equal before the law	[ˈiːkwəl bəfɔː ðə ˈlɔː]	gleich vor dem Gesetz
	get credit	[ˈget ˈkredit]	einen Kredit erhalten
	under the Equal Pay Act	[ʌndə ði ˈiːkwəl ˈpei ækt]	gemäß dem "Gleiche-Bezahlung-Gesetz"
	for the same employer	[fə ðə ˈseim imˈplɔiə]	für denselben Arbeitgeber
	at the same place of work	[ət ðə ˈseim ˈpleis əv ˈwəːk]	am selben Arbeitsplatz
	have a right to something	[hæv ə ˈrait tə sʌmθiŋ]	ein Recht auf etwas haben
	the same rate of pay	[ðə ˈseim ˈreit əv ˈpei]	die gleiche Bezahlung(shöhe)
	less well trained	[ˈles ˈwel ˈtreind]	weniger gut ausgebildet
	do the cooking and washing	[du ðə ˈkukiŋ ən ˈwɔʃiŋ]	das Kochen und Waschen erledigen
	the shopping / the cleaning	[ðə ˈʃɔpiŋ / ðə ˈkliːniŋ]	das Einkaufen / das Saubermachen
	in at least one respect	[in ət liːst ˈwʌn rispekt]	in mindestens einer Hinsicht
	they are apparently equal	[ðɛər əˈpærəntli ˈiːkwəl]	sie sind offenbar gleich
	according to a survey	[əkɔːdiŋ tu ə ˈsəːvei]	nach einer Erhebung / Untersuchung
	the most popular pastime	[ðə ˈməust ˈpɔpjulə ˈpɑːstaim]	der beliebteste Zeitvertreib
	for both sexes	[fə ˈbəuθ ˈseksiz]	für beide Geschlechter
	white-collar workers	[ˈwait-ˈkɔlə wəːkəz]	Angestellte ("Weiße-Kragen-Arbeiter")
	average wages	[ævridʒ ˈweidʒiz]	Durchschnittslöhne
	blue-collar workers	[ˈbluː-ˈkɔlə wəːkəz]	Arbeiter ("Blaue-Kragen-Arbeiter")
22B	the situation in this country	[ðə sitjuˈeiʃn in ˈðis kʌntri]	die Situation hierzulande
	why is it that . . .	[ˈwai ˈiz it ðət]	wie kommt es, daß . . .
22C	typical women's occupations	[ˈtipikl ˈwiminz ɔkjupeiʃnz]	typische Frauenberufe
	percentage	[pəˈsentidʒ]	Prozentsatz; (Prozent-)Anteil
	in selected occupations	[in siˈlektid ɔkjuˈpeiʃnz]	in ausgewählten Berufen
	typist	[ˈtaipist]	Stenotypist(in)
	nurse	[nəːs]	Krankenpfleger(in)
	telephone operator	[ˈtelifəun ɔpəreitə]	Telefonist(in)
	schoolteacher	[ˈskuːltiːtʃə]	(Schul-)Lehrer(in)
	butcher	[ˈbutʃə]	Fleischer; Metzger; Schlächter
	postman	[ˈpəustmən]	Briefträger; Postbote
	soldier	[ˈsəuldʒə]	Soldat
	from the start	[frəm ðə ˈstɑːt]	von Anfang an
	the Salvation Army	[ðə sælˈveiʃn ˈɑːmi]	die Heilsarmee
22D	would you mind answering a few questions?	[wud ju maind ˈɑːnsəriŋ ə fjuː ˈkwestʃənz]	würde es Ihnen was ausmachen, einige Fragen zu beantworten?
	look after the home	[ˈluk ɑːftə ðə ˈhəum]	sich um das Heim kümmern

	at the same time	[ət ðə 'seim 'taim]	zur gleichen Zeit; gleichzeitig
	employ somebody	[im'plɔi sʌmbədi]	jemanden anstellen / beschäftigen
	do the housework	[du: ðə 'hauswə:k]	die Arbeit im Haushalt verrichten
	necessary	['nesəsri]	notwendig; nötig
	housewife – housewives	['hauswaif – 'hauswaivz]	Hausfrau – Hausfrauen
	iron handkerchiefs and shirts	['aiən 'hæŋkətʃifs ən 'ʃə:ts]	Taschentücher u. Hemden bügeln
	blouses and dresses	['blauziz ən 'dresiz]	Blusen und Kleider
	underwear	['ʌndəwɛə]	Unterwäsche
	nightdresses and pyjamas	['naitdresiz ən pə'dʒɑ:məz]	Nachthemden und Schlafanzüge
	polish shoes	['pɔliʃ 'ʃu:z]	Schuhe putzen
	waste a lot of time	['weist ə 'lɔt əv 'taim]	viel Zeit verschwenden
	organize the housework	['ɔ:gənaiz ðə 'hauswə:k]	die Hausarbeit organisieren
22E	women drivers	['wimin draivəz]	weibliche Autofahrer
	men drivers	['men draivəz]	männliche Autofahrer
	slow – slower – slowest	[sləu – 'sləuə – 'sləuist]	langsam – langsamer – langsamste
	safe – safer – safest	[seif – 'seifə – 'seifist]	sicher – sicherer – sicherste
	careful / careless	['kɛəful / 'kɛələs]	vorsichtig / unvorsichtig
	a polite driver	[ə pə'lait 'draivə]	ein höflicher (Auto-)Fahrer
	men are less patient	['men ə 'les 'peiʃnt]	Männer sind weniger geduldig
	aggressive	[ə'gresiv]	aggressiv
	drunk at the wheel	['drʌŋk ət ðə 'wi:l]	betrunken am Steuer
22I	possibility	[pɔsə'biliti]	Möglichkeit
	choose – chose – chosen	['tʃu:z – tʃəuz – 'tʃəuzn]	wählen – wählte – gewählt
	four possibilities to choose from	['fɔ: pɔsə'bilitiz tə 'tʃu:z frɔm]	vier Möglichkeiten zur Auswahl
	car park	['kɑ: pɑ:k]	Parkplatz

Lektion 23

23A	records	['rekɔ:dz]	Rekorde
	superlatives	[su'pə:lətivz]	Superlative
	argue about something	['ɑ:gju: əbaut sʌmθiŋ]	sich über etwas streiten
	strong – stronger – strongest	[strɔŋ – 'strɔŋgə – 'strɔŋgist]	stark – stärker – stärkste
	the smallest bird	[ðə 'smɔ:list 'bə:d]	der kleinste Vogel
	Guinness	['ginis]	*(irischer Brauereikonzern)*
	the tallest man	[ðə 'tɔ:list 'mæn]	der größte Mann / Mensch
	inch	[intʃ]	Zoll *(= 2,54 cm)*
	the most intelligent animal	[ðə məust in'telidʒənt 'æniməl]	das intelligenteste Tier
	chimpanzee	[tʃimpæn'zi:]	Schimpanse
	the most common illness	[ðə məust 'kɔmən 'ilnəs]	die am häufigsten vorkommende ("gewöhnlichste") Krankheit
	common cold	['kɔmən 'kəuld]	Schnupfen
	we learn from Guinness	[wi 'lə:n frəm 'ginis]	wir erfahren von Guinness
	the language with the most words	[ðə 'læŋgwidʒ wið ðə 'məust 'wə:dz]	die Sprache mit den meisten Wörtern
	the world's most valuable painting	[ðə 'wə:ldz məust 'væljubl 'peintiŋ]	das wertvollste Gemälde der Welt
	Leonardo (da Vinci)	[li:ə'nɑ:dəu (də 'vintʃi)]	*(ital. Universalgenie, 1452–1519)*
	"Mona Lisa"	['məunə 'li:zə]	*(um 1503 gemalt; Louvre, Paris)*
	department store	[di'pɑ:tmənt stɔ:]	Kaufhaus
	Macy's	['meisiz]	*(at 34th Street and Broadway)*
	the largest bookshop	[ðə 'lɑ:dʒist 'bukʃɔp]	die größte Buchhandlung
	Foyle's	[fɔilz]	*(119–125 Charing Cross Road, W.C.2)*
	so far	['səu 'fɑ:]	bisher
	John Lennon	['dʒɔn 'lenən]	*(geb. 1940 in Liverpool)* † 1980

	Paul McCartney	['pɔ:l mə'kɑ:tni]	*(geb. 1942 in Liverpool)*
	the Beatles	[ðə 'bi:tlz]	*(Beatgruppe aus Liverpool)*
	which sold more than a million records each	[witʃ səuld 'mɔ: ðən ə 'miljən rekɔ:dz 'i:tʃ]	von denen jeweils mehr als eine Million Schallplatten verkauft wurden
	set – set – set	[set – set – set]	setzen – setzte – gesetzt
	it has set up a record itself	[it əz 'set ʌp ə 'rekɔ:d it'self]	es hat selbst einen Rekord aufgestellt
	with sales of	[wið 'seilz əv]	mit einem Absatz von
	commercially sold	[kə'mə:ʃəli 'səuld]	kommerziell verkauft / vertrieben
	congratulations!	[kəngrætju'leiʃnz]	herzlichen Glückwunsch!
	letters were exchanged	['letəz wər iks'tʃeinʒd]	Briefe wurden ausgetauscht
	his publisher	[hiz 'pʌbliʃə]	sein Verleger
	his latest novel	[hiz 'leitist 'nɔvl]	sein neuester Roman
	the reply was . . .	[ðə ri'plai wəz . . .]	die Antwort lautete . . .
23B	publish a book	['pʌbliʃ ə 'buk]	ein Buch herausbringen / verlegen
	everyday conversation	['evridei kɔnvə'seiʃn]	Alltagsgespräch, -unterhaltung
	get better service	[get 'betə 'sə:vis]	besser bedient werden
23C	special exercise	['speʃl 'eksəsaiz]	besondere Übung; Sonderübung
	in full	[in 'ful]	vollständig; ungekürzt
23D	Gothic	['gɔθik]	gotisch; Gotik
	powerful corporations	['pauəful kɔ:pə'reiʃnz]	mächtige Konzerne
	few people know	['fju: pi:pl 'nəu]	wenige Leute wissen
	cathedral	[kə'θi:drəl]	Dom; Kathedrale
	St John the Divine	[snt 'dʒɔn ðə di'vain]	"Sankt Johannes der Göttliche"
	though still unfinished	[ðəu 'stil ʌn'finiʃt]	obwohl immer noch unvollendet
	Europe	['juərəp]	Europa
	at present	[ət 'preznt]	zur Zeit; im Augenblick
	name some corporations	['neim səm kɔ:pə'reiʃnz]	nennen Sie einige Konzerne
23E	Albert Thorogood	['ælbət 'θʌrəgud]	*(Name)*
	he had done something spectacular	[hi əd dʌn sʌmθiŋ spek'tækjulə]	er hatte etwas Aufsehenerregendes getan
	almost nothing at all	[ɔ:lməust 'nʌθiŋ ə'tɔ:l]	fast überhaupt nichts
	able-bodied	['eibl-'bɔdid]	körperlich gesund
	he had been on the dole	[hid bi:n ɔn ðə 'dəul]	er war stempeln gegangen
	collect £12,000	[kə'lekt 'twelv 'θauznd 'paundz]	zwölftausend Pfund (ein)kassieren
	unemployment benefits	['ʌnim'plɔimənt benifits]	Arbeitslosenunterstützung
	"Idle Albert"	['aidl 'ælbət]	"der faule Albert"
	dozens of offers	['dʌznz əv 'ɔfəz]	Dutzende von Angeboten
	accept an offer	[ək'sept ən 'ɔfə]	ein Angebot annehmen
	pass the day	['pɑ:s ðə 'dei]	den Tag verbringen
23F	by October he had collected £12,000	[bai ɔk'təubə hid kə'lektid 'twelv 'θauznd 'paundz]	bis Oktober hatte er zwölftausend Pfund kassiert
	reporter	[ri'pɔ:tə]	Reporter
23H	he's the best actor I know	[hi:z ðə 'best æktər ai 'nəu]	er ist der beste Schauspieler, den ich kenne

Lektion 24

24A	Britain exports dog skins to Belgium	['britn iks'pɔ:ts 'dɔg skinz tə 'beldʒəm]	Großbritannien exportiert Hundefelle nach Belgien
	sell skins abroad	['sel 'skinz ə'brɔ:d]	Felle ins Ausland verkaufen
	yes, exactly that	['jes ig'zæktli 'ðæt]	ja, genau das
	they're made into gloves	[ðɛə meid intə 'glʌvz]	sie werden zu Handschuhen verarbeitet

	breed – bred – bred	['bri:d – bred – 'bred]	züchten – züchtete – gezüchtet
	I'm afraid . . .	[aim ə'freid]	ich fürchte . . .; leider . . .
	they do just that	[ðei du 'dʒʌst 'ðæt]	sie tun genau das
	stray dogs	['strei dɔgz]	streunende / herrenlose Hunde
	the dog had to be destroyed	[ðə dɔg hæd tə bi dis'trɔid]	der Hund mußte getötet werden
	dogs' home	['dɔgz həum]	Hundeasyl; Tierheim
	they might be wearing coats	[ðei mait bi wεəriŋ 'kəuts]	sie könnten Mäntel tragen
	sheep – sheep	[ʃi:p – ʃi:p]	Schaf – Schafe
	nobody ever says	['nəubədi 'evə 'sez]	niemand sagt je(mals)
	people shouldn't (= should not) wear sheepskin	[pi:pl 'ʃudnt wεə 'ʃi:pskin]	die Leute sollten kein Schaf(s)-fell tragen
	he understands us	[hi ʌndə'stændz əs]	er versteht uns
	he's sad	[hiz 'sæd]	er ist traurig
	right now	['rait 'nau]	gerade jetzt
	at the beginning of the holidays	[ət ðə bi'giniŋ əv ðə 'hɔlədiz]	zu Beginn der Ferien
	abandon a dog	[ə'bændən ə dɔg]	einen Hund aussetzen
	their skins will eventually be made into gloves	[ðεə 'skinz wil i'ventʃuəli bi meid intə 'glʌvz]	ihre Felle werden schließlich zu Handschuhen verarbeitet werden
	end up in a dogs' home	[end ʌp in ə 'dɔgz həum]	in einem Hundeasyl landen
	find a new owner	[faind ə 'nju: 'əunə]	einen neuen Besitzer finden
	they may well be sold to the leather trade	[ðei mei 'wel bi 'səuld tə ðə 'leðə treid]	es kann gut sein, daß sie an den Lederhandel verkauft werden
24B	articles of clothing	['ɑ:tiklz əv 'kləuðiŋ]	Kleidungsstücke
	import from a country	[im'pɔ:t frəm ə kʌntri]	aus einem Land importieren
	why are there so many stray dogs around?	['wai ə ðεə səu meni 'strei 'dɔgz əraund]	warum gibt es überall so viele streunende Hunde?
	what can one do with a cat?	[wɔt kən wʌn 'du: wið ə 'kæt]	was kann man mit einer Katze tun?
	what do you think of him?	[wɔt də ju 'θiŋk əv im]	was halten Sie von ihm?
	puppies for sale	['pʌpiz fə seil]	junge Hunde zu verkaufen
	Club Row Market	['klʌb 'rəu 'mɑ:kit]	*(Straßenmarkt in London E.1)*
24C	Alsatian	[æl'seiʃn]	deutscher Schäferhund
	she was taken to hospital	[ʃi wəz teikən tə 'hɔspitl]	sie wurde ins Krankenhaus gebracht
	after a dog had bitten her in the arm	[ɑ:ftər ə 'dɔg əd 'bitn ər in ði 'ɑ:m]	nachdem ein Hund sie in den Arm gebissen hatte
	bite – bit – bitten	[bait – bit – 'bitn]	beißen – biß – gebissen
	she had gone . . .	[ʃi:d 'gɔn]	sie war gegangen . . .
	she had put her arm through the iron grille	[ʃi:d put ər 'ɑ:m θru: ði 'aiən 'gril]	sie hatte den Arm durch das Eisengitter gesteckt
	put – put – put	[put – put – put]	stecken – steckte – gesteckt
	shed	[ʃed]	Schuppen
	keep – kept – kept	[ki:p – kept – kept]	halten – hielt – gehalten
	the dog had gripped her arm	[ðə 'dɔg əd 'gript ər 'ɑ:m]	der Hund hatte ihren Arm gepackt
	her screams were heard by . . .	[hə: 'skri:mz wə 'hə:d bai]	ihre Schreie wurden von . . . gehört
	she rushed out and freed her	[ʃi 'rʌʃt 'aut ən 'fri:d hə]	sie stürzte heraus und befreite sie
	reactions to the incident	[ri'ækʃnz tə ði 'insidənt]	Reaktionen auf den Vorfall
	if a dog attacks a child	[if ə 'dɔg ə'tæks ə 'tʃaild]	wenn ein Hund ein Kind anfällt
	blame the dog	['bleim ðə 'dɔg]	dem Hund die Schuld geben
	in most cases it's the humans who're at fault	[in 'məust keisiz its ðə 'hju:mənz huər ət 'fɔ:lt]	in den meisten Fällen sind die Menschen diejenigen, die Schuld haben
	parents don't control their children properly	['pεərənts dəunt kən'trəul ðεə tʃildrən 'prɔpəli]	die Eltern beaufsichtigen ihre Kinder nicht richtig

	well-behaved dogs	['wel-biheivd 'dɔgz]	wohlerzogene Hunde
	throw stones at somebody	['θrəu 'stəunz ət 'sʌmbədi]	Steine nach jemand werfen
	I would be prepared	[ai wəd bi pri'pεəd]	ich wäre bereit
	put a fine-wire mesh over the grille	[put ə 'fain-'waiə 'meʃ əuvə ðə 'gril]	ein engmaschiges Drahtnetz über das Gitter machen
24D	run – ran – run	[rʌn – ræn – rʌn]	laufen – lief – gelaufen
	she was lucky	[ʃi wəz 'lʌki]	sie hatte Glück
	whose fault is it?	['hu:z 'fɔ:lt iz it]	wessen Schuld ist es?
	he was nasty to the dog	[hi wəz 'nɑ:sti tə ðə 'dɔg]	er war garstig zu dem Hund
	get bitten	['get 'bitn]	gebissen werden
	aggressiveness	[ə'gresivnəs]	Aggressivität; Angriffslust
24F	sentences in the passive	['sentənsiz in ðə 'pæsiv]	Sätze im Passiv / in d. Leideform
24H	add negative tags	['æd 'negətiv 'tægz]	verneinte "Anhängsel" anhängen
24I	she bought it from a trader	[ʃi 'bɔ:t it frəm ə 'treidə]	sie kaufte ihn von einem Händler
	the injured child	[ði 'indʒəd 'tʃaild]	das verletzte Kind
	St Mary's Hospital	[snt 'mεəriz 'hɔspitl]	"St.-Marien-Krankenhaus"

Lektion 25

25A	chewing gum for the eyes	['tʃu:iŋ gʌm fə ði 'aiz]	Kaugummi für die Augen
	how long has he been watching TV?	['hau 'lɔŋ əz i bi:n wɔtʃiŋ 'ti:'vi:]	wie lange sieht er schon fern?
	it says here in the paper	[it 'sez hiər in ðə 'peipə]	hier in der Zeitung heißt es
	watching television can harm the development of young children	['wɔtʃiŋ 'teliviʒn kən 'hɑ:m ðə di'veləpmənt əv 'jʌŋ 'tʃildrən]	Fernsehen kann bei kleinen Kindern der Entwicklung schaden
	TV rays	['ti:'vi: reiz]	Fernsehstrahlen
	brain	[brein]	Gehirn
	a TV fan	[ə 'ti: 'vi: fæn]	ein Fernseh-Fan
	maybe that's why	[meibi 'ðæts wai]	vielleicht ist das der Grund, warum
	let – let – let	[let – let – let]	lassen – ließ – gelassen
	it's just this article here	[its 'dʒʌst ðis 'ɑ:tikl hiə]	es ist nur dieser Artikel hier
	it worries me a bit	[it 'wʌriz mi ə bit]	er macht mir etwas Sorgen
	activities	[æk'tivətiz]	Aktivitäten; Betätigungen
	they're passive	[ðεə 'pæsiv]	sie sind passiv / untätig
25B	the commercials will be on in a minute	[ðə kə'mə:ʃlz wil bi 'ɔn in ə 'minit]	in einer Minute kommt die Reklame
	say grace	['sei 'greis]	das Tischgebet sprechen
25C	effects	[i'fekts]	(Aus-)Wirkungen; Folgen
	documentary	[dɔkju'mentəri]	Dokumentarfilm; Kulturfilm
	educational programme	[edju'keiʃnəl 'prəugræm]	Bildungsprogramm; Kultursendung
	quiz show	['kwiz ʃəu]	Quizveranstaltung
	variety show	[və'raiəti ʃəu]	Unterhaltungssendung
	crime films	['kraim filmz]	Kriminalfilme
	horror films	['hɔrə filmz]	Horrorfilme; Gruselfilme
	go to the opera	[gəu tə ði 'ɔprə]	in die Oper gehen
	the worst show	[ðə 'wə:st ʃəu]	die schlechteste Show
	violence	['vaiələns]	Gewalttätigkeit
	unsuitable for children	['ʌn'su:təbl fə 'tʃildrən]	für Kinder ungeeignet
	ideal for children	[ai'diəl fə 'tʃildrən]	ideal für Kinder
	the products that are advertised	[ðə 'prɔdʌkts ðət ər 'ædvətaizd]	die Erzeugnisse, für die geworben wird
	see – saw – seen	[si: – sɔ: – si:n]	sehen – sah – gesehen
	announcer	[ə'naunsə]	Ansager(in); Sprecher(in)
	entertainer	[entə'teinə]	Unterhaltungskünstler(in)

	political programmes	[pə'litikl prəugræmz]	politische Sendungen
	bloody war scenes	['blʌdi 'wɔ: si:nz]	blutige Kriegsszenen
	living room	['liviŋ rum]	Wohnzimmer
	American-made programmes	[ə'merikən-meid 'prəugræmz]	Sendungen amerikanischen Ursprungs
	show – showed – shown	[ʃəu – ʃəud – ʃəun]	zeigen – zeigte – gezeigt
	network	['netwə:k]	Sendergruppe; Fernsehanstalt
	homemade programmes	['həummeid 'prəugræmz]	im Inland produzierte Sendungen
	cater for some people's tastes	['keitə fə 'sʌm pi:plz teists]	dem Geschmack einiger Menschen gerecht werden
25E	the present perfect simple	[ðə 'preznt 'pə:fikt 'simpl]	die einfache Form des Perfekts
25F	the present perfect progressive	[ðə 'preznt 'pə:fikt prə'gresiv]	die Verlaufsform des Perfekts
	several years ago	['sevrəl 'jiəz əgəu]	vor mehreren Jahren
	go on asking each other questions	['gəu 'ɔn ɑ:skiŋ i:tʃ ʌðə 'kwestʃənz]	fahren Sie fort, einander Fragen zu stellen

Lektion 26

26A	poetry	['pəuətri]	Poesie; Dichtung(en); Gedichte
	I rather like reading poetry, don't you?	[ai 'rɑ:ðə 'laik ri:diŋ pəuətri 'dəunt 'ju:]	ich lese ziemlich / recht gern Gedichte, du nicht?
	A. E. Housman	['ei 'i: 'hausmən]	*(engl. Dichter, 1859–1936)*
	Carl Sandburg	['kɑ:l 'sændbə:g]	*(amerik. Dichter, 1878–1967)*
	a wise man	[ə 'waiz 'mæn]	ein kluger / weiser Mann
	crown	[kraun]	*(frühere engl. Münze)*
	guinea	['gini]	*(alte engl. Goldmünze)*
	give pearls away and rubies	[giv 'pə:lz əwei ən 'ru:biz]	verschenke Perlen und Rubine
	fancy	['fænsi]	Phantasie
	no use to talk to me	['nəu 'ju:s tə tɔ:k tə 'mi:]	zwecklos, mit mir zu sprechen
	tender and full of wisdom	['tendər ən 'ful əv 'wizdəm]	zart und voller Weisheit
	I wonder if . . .	[ai 'wʌndər if]	ich möchte wissen, ob . . .
	old things are in	['əuld θiŋz ər 'in]	alte Sachen sind in Mode
	they call it nostalgia	[ðei kɔ:l it nɔ'stældʒə]	man nennt es Nostalgie
	typically American	['tipikli ə'merikən]	typisch amerikanisch
	I can almost smell it	[ai kən 'ɔ:lməust 'smel it]	ich kann es fast / beinahe riechen
	he collected folk songs	[hi kəlektid 'fəuk sɔŋz]	er sammelte Volkslieder
	biography	[bai'ɔgrəfi]	Biographie; Lebensbeschreibung
	Abraham Lincoln	['eibrəhæm 'liŋkən]	*(16. Präsid. d. USA, 1809–1865)*
	which do you like best?	['witʃ də ju laik 'best]	welches gefällt dir am besten?
	that's hard to say	[ðæts 'hɑ:d tə 'sei]	das ist schwer zu sagen
	there's one short one	[ðəz 'wʌn 'ʃɔ:t wʌn]	es gibt ein kurzes (Gedicht)
	the fog comes on little cat feet	[ðə 'fɔg 'kʌmz ɔn 'litl 'kæt fi:t]	der Nebel kommt auf kleinen Katzenfüßen
	it sits looking	[it 'sits lukiŋ]	er sitzt und schaut
	silent	['sailənt]	still; ruhig; schweigsam
	haunches	['hɔ:ntʃiz]	Lenden; Gesäß
	and then, moves on	[ən 'ðen 'mu:vz 'ɔn]	und zieht dann weiter
26B	silently closing her bedroom door	['sailəntli 'kləuziŋ hə 'bedrum 'dɔ:]	leise ihre Schlafzimmertür schließend
	leaving a note	['li:viŋ ə 'nəut]	ein Briefchen zurücklassend
	she goes downstairs to the kitchen	[ʃi 'gəuz 'daun'stɛəz tə ðə 'kitʃən]	sie geht nach unten in die Küche
	clutch something	['klʌtʃ sʌmθiŋ]	etwas umklammern
	quietly turning the backdoor key	['kwaiətli 'tə:niŋ ðə 'bækdɔ: 'ki:]	leise den Hintertürschlüssel umdrehend
	step outside	['step aut'said]	nach draußen treten

	we sacrificed most of our lives	[wi 'sækrifaist 'məust əv ɑ: 'laivz]	wir opferten den größten Teil unseres Lebens
	Father snores	['fɑ:ðə 'snɔ:z]	Vater schnarcht
	she gets into her dressing gown	[ʃi gets intə hə 'dresiŋ gaun]	sie zieht ihren Morgenrock an
	she picks up the letter that's lying there	[ʃi 'piks ʌp ðə 'letə ðəts 'laiiŋ ðɛə]	sie nimmt den Brief auf, der dort liegt
	stand – stood – stood	[stænd – stud – stud]	stehen – stand – gestanden
	at the top of the stairs	[ət ðə 'tɔp əv ðə 'stɛəz]	oben auf der Treppe
	she breaks down	[ʃi 'breiks 'daun]	sie bricht zusammen
	cry	[krai]	schreien; weinen; (laut) rufen
	daddy, our baby is gone	['dædi ɑ: 'beibi iz 'gɔn]	Papi, unser Kleines ist weg
	treat someone thoughtlessly	['tri:t sʌmwʌn 'θɔ:tləsli]	jemanden rücksichtslos behandeln
	how could she do this to me	[hau kud ʃi 'du: ðis tə mi:]	wie konnte sie mir das antun
	we never thought of ourselves	[wi 'nevə θɔ:t əv ɑ:'selvz]	wir haben nie an uns gedacht
	never a thought for ourselves	['nevər ə 'θɔ:t fər ɑ:'selvz]	nie ein Gedanke an uns selbst
	we struggled hard	[wi 'strʌgld 'hɑ:d]	wir quälten uns schwer
	to get by	[tə 'get 'bai]	um zurechtzukommen
	keep an appointment	['ki:p ən ə'pɔintmənt]	eine Verabredung einhalten
	a man from the motor trade	[ə 'mæn frəm ðə 'məutə treid]	ein Mann aus der Autobranche
	something inside that was always denied	['sʌmθiŋ in'said ðət wəz 'ɔ:lwiz di'naid]	etwas im Innern, das immer verweigert / vorenthalten wurde
26C	the sentences in brackets	[ðə 'sentənsiz in 'brækits]	die Sätze in Klammern
	in the context of the song	[in ðə 'kɔntekst əv ðə 'sɔŋ]	im Zusammenhang des Liedes
26D	message	['mesidʒ]	Botschaft; Mitteilung; Aussage
	what similarities are there?	['wɔt simi'lærətiz ɑ: ðə]	was für Ähnlichkeiten bestehen?
	in the sixties	[in ðə 'sikstiz]	in den sechziger Jahren
	well-known	['wel-'nəun]	(gut) bekannt; wohlbekannt
	do you have any favourites?	[du ju hæv əni 'feivərəts]	haben Sie irgendwelche "Lieblinge"?
26E	March	[mɑ:tʃ]	März
	Fockbury, Worcestershire	['fɔkbəri 'wustəʃə]	*(Dorf u. Grafschaft in Westengl.)*
	after studying at Oxford	[ɑ:ftə 'stʌdiiŋ ət 'ɔksfəd]	nachdem er in Oxford studiert hatte
	a clerk in the Patent Office	[ə 'klɑ:k in ðə 'peitnt ɔfis]	Angestellter beim Patentamt
	professor of Latin	[prə'fesər əv 'lætin]	Professor für Latein
	their language was simple	[ðɛə 'læŋgwidʒ wəz 'simpl]	ihre Sprache war einfach
	their verse was melodious	[ðɛə 'və:s wəz mə'ləudiəs]	ihre Verse waren melodisch
	he died on April 30	[hi 'daid ɔn . . .]	er starb am 30. April
26F	January	['dʒænjuəri]	Januar
	Galesburg, Illinois	['geilzbə:g ili'nɔi]	*(Stadt u. Bundesstaat d. USA)*
	he began earning his living	[hi bi'gæn ə:niŋ iz 'liviŋ]	er begann, seinen Lebensunterhalt zu verdienen
	all sorts of odd jobs	[ɔ:l sɔ:ts əv 'ɔd 'dʒɔbz]	alle möglichen Gelegenheitsarbeiten
	fight – fought – fought	[fait – fɔ:t – fɔ:t]	kämpfen – kämpfte – gekämpft
	Spanish-American War	['spæniʃ-ə'merikən 'wɔ:]	Spanisch-amerikan. Krieg *(1898)*
	college	['kɔlidʒ]	*(höhere Lehranstalt)*
	he finally became a journalist and writer	[hi 'fainəli bikeim ə 'dʒə:nəlist ən 'raitə]	er wurde schließlich Journalist und Schriftsteller
	singer	['siŋə]	Sänger(in)
26G	have you ever met her?	[hæv ju evə 'met ə]	hast du sie je getroffen?
	he's going to marry her	[hiz gəuiŋ tə 'mæri hə]	er wird sie heiraten
26H	when she understood	[wen ʃi ʌndə'stud]	als sie verstand / begriff
	a smart young car salesman	[ə 'smɑ:t jʌŋ 'kɑ: seilzmən]	ein fescher junger Autoverkäufer

27A	the ideal secretary	[ði ai'diəl 'sekrətri]	die ideale Sekretärin
	Mr Green	[mistə 'gri:n]	(green = grün)
	win – won – won	[win – wʌn – wʌn]	gewinnen – gewann – gewonnen
	competition	[kɔmpə'tiʃn]	Wettbewerb
	I encouraged her	[ai in'kʌridʒd hə]	ich ermutigte sie
	enter a competition	['entər ə kɔmpə'tiʃn]	sich zu einem Wettbewerb anmelden
	reasonable shorthand and typing speeds	['ri:znəbl 'ʃɔ:thænd ən 'taipiŋ spi:dz]	angemessenes Tempo in Kurzschrift und Maschineschreiben
	familiar with office routine	[fə'miljə wið 'ɔfis ru:ti:n]	mit der Büroroutine / den üblichen Büroarbeiten vertraut
	loyal and reliable	['lɔiəl ən ri'laiəbl]	treu und zuverlässig / verläßlich
	have a pleasant personality	[hæv ə 'pleznt pə:sə'næləti]	ein angenehmes Wesen haben
	positive	['pɔzətiv]	positiv
	he doesn't give a damn about his work	[hi 'dʌznt giv ə 'dæm əbaut iz wə:k]	seine Arbeit ist ihm völlig schnuppe
	what about looks?	[wɔt əbaut 'luks]	wie ist es mit dem Aussehen?
	it's a matter of taste	[its ə mætər əv 'teist]	es ist Geschmackssache
	she ought to be neat	[ʃi ɔ:tə bi 'ni:t]	sie sollte ordentlich / gepflegt / adrett sein
	neatness is another matter	['ni:tnəs iz ə'nʌðə 'mætə]	Ordentlichkeit / Gepflegtheit ist eine andere Sache / etw. anderes
	untidy	[ʌn'taidi]	unordentlich
	Bermuda	[bə'mju:də]	*(Inselgruppe im Westatlantik)*
	Nassau	['næsɔ:]	*(Hauptst. d. Bahama-Inseln)*
	the organizers	[ði 'ɔ:gənaizəz]	die Organisatoren / Veranstalter
	temporary secretary	['tempərəri 'sekrətri]	"vorübergehende" Sekretärin
27B	the two bricklayers	[ðə 'tu: 'brikleiəz]	die beiden Maurer
	I'm laying bricks	[aim 'leiiŋ 'briks]	ich lege Backsteine; ich mauere
	replied the second	[riplaid ðə 'sekənd]	antwortete der zweite
27C	interview somebody	['intəvju: sʌmbədi]	jemanden interviewen
	main qualities	['mein 'kwɔlitiz]	Haupteigenschaften
	the girl's appearance	[ðə gə:lz ə'piərəns]	das Aussehen des Mädchens
	agree with a statement	[ə'gri: wið ə steitmənt]	einer Äußerung zustimmen
	do without a secretary	['du: wi'ðaut ə sekrətri]	ohne Sekretärin auskommen
27D	plus an extra ticket	['plʌs ən 'ekstrə tikit]	und einen zusätzlichen Flugschein
	a relation	[ə ri'leiʃn]	ein Verwandter; eine Verwandte
	spend a lot of money	['spend ə lɔt əv 'mʌni]	viel Geld ausgeben
	spending money	['spendiŋ mʌni]	Taschengeld
	luxury accommodation	['lʌkʃəri əkɔmə'deiʃn]	Luxusunterkunft
	above-average speed	[ə'bʌv-'ævridʒ 'spi:d]	überdurchschnittliches Tempo
	a pleasant speaking voice	[ə 'pleznt 'spi:kiŋ vɔis]	eine angenehme (Sprech-)Stimme
	a thorough knowledge	[ə 'θʌrə 'nɔlidʒ]	gründliche Kenntnisse
	get on well with somebody	['get 'ɔn 'wel wið sʌmbədi]	gut mit jemand zurechtkommen
	she must be hard-working	[ʃi məst bi 'ha:d-'wə:kiŋ]	sie muß fleißig sein
	efficient and tactful	[i'fiʃnt ən 'tæktful]	tüchtig und taktvoll
	grammar and spelling	['græmər ən 'speliŋ]	Grammatik und Rechtschreibung
	her boss got a case of finest Scotch whisky	[hə: 'bɔs gɔt ə 'keis əv 'fainist 'skɔtʃ 'wiski]	ihr Chef bekam einen Kasten mit bestem schottischen Whisky
	based on the newspaper cutting	['beist ɔn ðə 'nju:speipə kʌtiŋ]	auf der Grundlage des Zeitungsausschnitts
	once again	['wʌns ə'gen]	noch einmal
	use *should* throughout	['ju:z 'ʃud θru:aut]	gebrauchen Sie durchweg *should*
	entrant	['entrənt]	Teilnehmer(in)

27E	the first prize included ...	[ðə 'fəːst 'praiz inkluːdid]	zum ersten Preis gehörten ...
27F	straight from the horse's mouth	['streit frəm ðə 'hɔːsiz 'mauθ]	aus erster Hand ("direkt aus dem Maul des Pferdes")
27G	medium-sized firm	['miːdiəm-saizd 'fəːm]	mittelgroße Firma
	lunch hour	['lʌntʃ auə]	Mittagspause
	a full-time job	[ə 'ful-taim 'dʒɔb]	eine Ganztagsbeschäftigung
	a part-time job	[ə 'pɑːt-taim 'dʒɔb]	eine Teilzeitbeschäftigung
	desk	[desk]	Schreibtisch
	nature of work	['neitʃər əv 'wəːk]	Art der Arbeit
	satisfying work	['sætisfaiiŋ 'wəːk]	befriedigende Arbeit
	a responsible job	[ə ris'pɔnsəbl 'dʒɔb]	eine verantwortungsvolle Arbeit
	amount of work	[ə'maunt əv 'wəːk]	Arbeitsmenge
	boss's behaviour	['bɔsiz bi'heivjə]	Verhalten des Chefs
	he's very fussy	[hiːz 'veri 'fʌsi]	er ist sehr pingelig
	he's hard to please	[hiːz 'hɑːd tə 'pliːz]	er ist schwer zu befriedigen
	colleague	['kɔliːg]	Kollege; Kollegin
	ready to help	['redi tə 'help]	hilfsbereit
	fringe benefits	['frindʒ benifits]	freiwillige Sozialleistungen
	luncheon vouchers	['lʌntʃən vautʃəz]	Essenmarken
	canteen	[kæn'tiːn]	Kantine
	paid holidays	['peid 'hɔlədiz]	bezahlter Urlaub
	Christmas bonus	['krisməs 'bəunəs]	Weihnachtsgratifikation
	promotion prospects	[prə'məuʃn prɔspekts]	Aussichten auf Beförderung
27H	you will succeed	[jul sək'siːd]	du wirst Erfolg haben
	there is so little competition	[ðəz 'səu litl kɔmpə'tiʃn]	es ist so wenig Konkurrenz da
	Elbert Hubbard	['elbət 'hʌbəd]	*(amerik. Schriftst. u. Verleger)*
27I	he's very good-looking	[hiz veri 'gud-'lukiŋ]	er sieht sehr gut aus
	she's married	[ʃiz 'mærid]	sie ist verheiratet
	he's rather impatient	[hiz 'rɑːðər im'peiʃnt]	er ist ziemlich ungeduldig
	self-confident	['self-'kɔnfidənt]	selbstbewußt; selbstsicher
	an exciting job	[ən ik'saitiŋ 'dʒɔb]	eine aufregende Tätigkeit
	hectic	['hektik]	hektisch; aufgeregt
27J	attractive fringe benefits	[ə'træktiv 'frindʒ benifits]	attraktive Sozialleistungen

Lektion 28

28A	mug somebody	['mʌg sʌmbədi]	jemanden überfallen u. ausrauben
	give evidence	[giv 'evidəns]	(als Zeuge) aussagen
	get into a train	[get intu ə 'trein]	in einen Zug einsteigen
	fairly empty	['fɛəli 'empti]	ziemlich leer
	subway	['sʌbwei]	*(US:)* Untergrundbahn, U-Bahn
	they surrounded me	[ðei sə'raundid mi]	sie umringten mich
	stood in front of me	[stud in 'frʌnt əv mi]	standen vor mir
	push somebody	['puʃ sʌmbədi]	jemanden schubsen / schieben
	went for my breast pocket	[went fə mai 'brest pɔkit]	griff nach meiner Brusttasche
	and snatched my wallet	[ən 'snætʃt mai 'wɔlit]	und riß meine Brieftasche an sich
	briefcase	['briːfkeis]	Aktentasche
	within a few seconds	[wiðin ə fjuː 'sekəndz]	innerhalb v. ein paar Sekunden
	the doors were still open	[ðə 'dɔːz wə 'stil 'əupən]	die Türen waren noch geöffnet
	carriage	['kæridʒ]	Wagen (eines Zuges)
	they didn't take any notice	[ðei 'didnt teik əni 'nəutis]	sie nahmen keine Notiz (davon)
	I was not hurt	[ai wəz 'nɔt 'həːt]	ich wurde / war nicht verletzt
	I was so surprised that ...	[ai wəz 'səu sə'praizd ðət]	ich war so überrascht, daß ...
	I didn't resist	[ai 'didnt ri'zist]	ich leistete keinen Widerstand
	call for help	['kɔːl fə 'help]	um Hilfe rufen
28B	mugger	['mʌgə]	(meist jugendl. Straßen-)Räuber
	attack somebody	[ə'tæk sʌmbədi]	jemanden angreifen / überfallen

	steal – stole – stolen	[stiːl – stəul – ˈstəulən]	stehlen – stahl – gestohlen
	draw conclusions from a fact	[ˈdrɔː kənˈkluːʒnz frəm ə fækt]	aus einer Tatsache Schlüsse ziehen
	prevent muggings	[priˈvent ˈmʌgiŋz]	Raubüberfälle verhindern
	make suggestions	[meik səˈdʒestʃənz]	Vorschläge machen
28C	a temporary occupation	[ə ˈtempərəri ɔkjuˈpeiʃn]	eine vorübergehende Beschäftigung
	our correspondent reports . . .	[ɑː kɔrisˈpɔndənt riˈpɔːts]	unser Korrespondent berichtet . . .
	grow up – grew up – grown up	[ˈgrəu ˈʌp – ˈgruː ˈʌp – ˈgrəun ˈʌp]	aufwachsen – aufwuchs – aufgewachsen
	Harlem	[ˈhɑːləm]	*(Negerstadtteil v. New York)*
	brothers and sisters	[ˈbrʌðəz ən ˈsistəz]	Brüder und Schwestern; Geschwister
	clothes	[kləuðz]	Kleider; Kleidung
	either . . . or	[ˈaiðə . . . ɔː]	entweder . . . oder
	work was impossible	[ˈwəːk wəz imˈpɔsəbl]	Arbeiten war unmöglich
	besides	[biˈsaidz]	außerdem
	a total of about $400 (= four hundred dollars)	[ə ˈtəutl əv əbaut ˈfɔː hʌndrəd ˈdɔləz]	eine (Gesamt-)Summe von etwa 400 Dollar
	beat – beat – beaten	[biːt – biːt – ˈbiːtn]	schlagen – schlug – geschlagen
	the dog may bark so loudly	[ðə ˈdɔg mei bɑːk səu ˈlaudli]	vielleicht bellt der Hund so laut
	that all hell breaks loose	[ðət ˈɔːl ˈhel breiks luːs]	daß der Teufel los ist ("daß die ganze Hölle losbricht")
	take up a job	[teik ʌp ə ˈdʒɔb]	einen Beruf ergreifen
	get married	[ˈget ˈmærid]	heiraten
	social worker	[ˈsəuʃl wəːkə]	Sozialarbeiter
28D	the average amount	[ði ˈævridʒ əˈmaunt]	der Durchschnittsbetrag
	is it in order if . . .	[iz it in ˈɔːdər if]	ist es in Ordnung, wenn . . .
	robber	[ˈrɔbə]	Räuber
	New York's black ghetto	[nju ˈjɔːks ˈblæk ˈgetəu]	New Yorks schwarzes Getto
28E	the problems facing us today	[ðə ˈprɔbləmz ˈfeisiŋ əs təˈdei]	die Probleme, denen wir heute gegenüberstehen
	the rate has tripled	[ðə ˈreit əz ˈtripld]	die Quote hat sich verdreifacht
	official estimates	[əˈfiʃl ˈestimətsl]	offizielle / amtliche Schätzungen
	an adult burglar	[ən ˈædʌlt ˈbəːglə]	ein erwachsener Einbrecher
	go to jail	[gəu tə ˈdʒeil]	ins Gefängnis kommen
	for any single burglary	[fər eni ˈsiŋgl ˈbəːgləri]	für irgendeinen einzelnen Einbruch
	people are not in agreement	[piːpl ə nɔt in əˈgriːmənt]	die Leute sind sich nicht einig
	the causes of crime	[ðə ˈkɔːziz əv kraim]	die Ursachen der Kriminalität
	cure	[kjuə]	Heilmittel
	poverty	[ˈpɔvəti]	Armut; Not
	poor education	[ˈpuər edjuˈkeiʃn]	mangelhafte Schulbildung
	unemployment	[ˈʌnimˈplɔimənt]	Arbeitslosigkeit
	natural causes	[ˈnætʃərəl ˈkɔːziz]	natürliche Ursachen
	conservatives argue	[kənˈsəːvətivz ɑːgjuː]	die Konservativen behaupten
	he's the master of his fate	[hiːz ðə ˈmɑːstər əv iz ˈfeit]	er ist der Herr seines Schicksals
	moral code	[ˈmɔrəl ˈkəud]	Moralkodex
	respect for law and order	[risˈpekt fə lɔː ən ˈɔːdə]	Respekt vor Recht und Ordnung
	harsh penalties	[ˈhɑːʃ ˈpenltiz]	strenge Strafen
	the best means to reduce crime	[ðə ˈbest ˈmiːnz tə riˈdjuːs ˈkraim]	die besten Mittel, um die Kriminalität zu verringern
	they're fed up with it	[ðɛə fed ˈʌp wið it]	sie haben davon die Nase voll
	many a liberal	[ˈmeni ə ˈlibərəl]	so mancher Liberaler
	as one mayor put it	[əz wʌn ˈmɛə put it]	wie ein Bürgermeister es ausdrückte
	the night before	[ðə ˈnait bəˈfɔː]	am Abend / in der Nacht vorher

	the courts are understaffed	[ðə 'kɔ:ts ər 'ʌndə'stɑ:ft]	die Gerichte haben Personalmangel
	they're overworked and in need of reform	[ðɛər 'əuvə'wə:kt ən in ni:d əv ri'fɔ:m]	sie sind überlastet und reformbedürftig
	more and more private citizens	['mɔ:r ən 'mɔ: 'praivət 'sitiznz]	immer mehr Privatleute ("private Bürger")
	take personal action	[teik 'pə:snl 'ækʃən]	selber Maßnahmen ergreifen
	patrol a neighbourhood	[pə'trəul ə 'neibəhud]	eine Gegend abpatrouillieren
	suspicious activities	[səs'piʃəs æk'tivətiz]	verdächtige Vorgänge
	testify against somebody	['testifai əgenst sʌmbədi]	gegen jemanden aussagen
	seek action against someone	['si:k 'ækʃən əgenst sʌmwʌn]	gegen jemanden vorgehen
	judges who are "soft"	['dʒʌdʒiz hu ə 'sɔft]	Richter, die "weich" sind
28F	per 1,000 inhabitants	[pə: 'wʌn 'θauznd in'hæbitənts]	pro 1000 Einwohner
	violent crime	['vaiələnt kraim]	Gewaltverbrechen, -kriminalität
	property crime	['prɔpəti kraim]	Eigentumsdelikte, -vergehen
28G	rise – rose – risen	[raiz – rəuz – 'rizn]	steigen – stieg – gestiegen
	0.3 (= nought point three)	['nɔ:t pɔint 'θri:]	0,3 (= null Komma drei)
28H	the leader of a party	[ðə 'li:dər əv ə 'pɑ:ti]	der Führer einer Partei
	win an election	['win ən i'lekʃn]	eine Wahl gewinnen
	a speech on television	[ə 'spi:tʃ ɔn 'teliviʒn]	eine Rede im Fernsehen
	abolish something	[ə'bɔliʃ sʌmθiŋ]	etwas abschaffen
	fight something	['fait sʌmθiŋ]	etwas bekämpfen
	put an end to something	[put ən 'end tə sʌmθiŋ]	mit etwas Schluß machen
	we're going to raise wages	[wiə gəuiŋ tə 'reiz 'weidʒiz]	wir werden die Löhne erhöhen
28I	steal from a rich man	['sti:l frəm ə 'ritʃ mæn]	einem reichen Mann etw. stehlen
	evidence	['evidəns]	Beweis(material); Beweise

Lektion 29

29A	globe-trotter	['gləub-trɔtə]	Globetrotter; Weltenbummler
	Jesse Hart Rosdail	['dʒesi 'hɑ:t 'rɔzdeil]	*(aus Elmhurst i. US-Staat Illinois)*
	elementary school	[eli'mentəri sku:l]	*(etwa:)* Grund- und Hauptschule
	the Midwest / Middle West	[ðə 'mid'west / 'midl 'west]	der Mittlere Westen (der USA)
	territory	['teritri]	Territorium; Gebiet
	recently	['ri:sntli]	kürzlich; vor kurzem
	Newsweek	['nju:zwi:k]	*(amerikan. Nachrichtenmagazin)*
	scenery nut	['si:nəri nʌt]	*(etwa:)* Landschaftsfanatiker
	I love glaciers and waterfalls	[ai 'lʌv 'glæsiəz ən 'wɔ:təfɔ:lz]	ich liebe Gletscher und Wasserfälle
	New Zealand	[nju: 'zi:lənd]	Neuseeland
	a combination of	[ə kɔmbi'neiʃn əv]	eine Kombination / Verbindung von
	Norway	['nɔ:wei]	Norwegen
	certain high areas	[sə:tn 'hai 'ɛəriəz]	bestimmte hochgelegene Gebiete
	in the Himalayas	[in ðə himə'leiəz]	im Himalaja
	Angola and the Congo	[æŋ'gəulə ən ðə 'kɔŋgəu]	Angola und der Kongo
	they're all pretty much alike	[ðɛər ɔ:l 'priti mʌtʃ ə'laik]	sie sind alle ziemlich ähnlich
	art gallery	['ɑ:t gæləri]	Kunstgalerie; Gemäldegalerie
	the wide open spaces	[ðə 'waid 'əupən 'speisiz]	die weiten offenen Flächen
	walk	[wɔ:k]	zu Fuß gehen
	I recommend a bicycle	[ai 'rekəmend ə 'baisikl]	ich empfehle ein Fahrrad
	invite somebody	[in'vait sʌmbədi]	jemanden einladen
	an overnight stay	[ən 'əuvənait 'stei]	eine Übernachtung
	take unusual holidays	[teik ʌn'ju:ʒuəl 'hɔlədiz]	"außergewöhnliche Ferien machen"
	travel light	['trævl 'lait]	reisen Sie mit leichtem Gepäck

	expect something	[iks'pekt sʌmθiŋ]	etwas erwarten
	be sure to read up on every place	[bi 'ʃuə tə 'ri:d 'ʌp ɔn 'evri 'pleis]	vergessen Sie nicht, über jeden Ort nachzulesen
	then you may still decide	[ðen ju mei 'stil disaid]	dann können Sie immer noch entscheiden
	after the trip is over	['ɑ:ftə ðə trip iz 'əuvə]	nachdem die Reise vorbei ist
	there was something you shouldn't have missed	[ðə wəz 'sʌmθiŋ ju 'ʃudnt əv 'mist]	da war etwas, das Sie nicht hätten auslassen dürfen
29B	a handful of countries	[ə 'hændful əv 'kʌntriz]	eine Handvoll Länder
	North Korea	['nɔ:θ kə'riə]	Nordkorea
	North Vietnam and China	['nɔ:θ viət'næm ən 'tʃainə]	Nordvietnam und China
29C	travel by ship	['trævl bai 'ʃip]	mit dem Schiff fahren
29D	the absolute minimum	[ði 'æbsəlu:t 'miniməm]	das absolute Minimum
	transport	['trɑ:nspɔ:t]	Beförderung
	Rotel Tours	[rəu'tel 'tuəz]	*(bayerisches Reiseunternehmen)*
	consist of	[kən'sist əv]	bestehen aus
	a specially constructed trailer	[ə 'speʃəli kənstrʌktid 'treilə]	ein besonders konstruierter Anhänger
	combine	[kəm'bain]	kombinieren; in sich vereinigen
	function	['fʌŋkʃən]	Funktion
	dining area	['dainiŋ ɛəriə]	Eßbereich
	dressing room	['dresiŋ rum]	Um-, Ankleideraum
	dormitory	['dɔ:mitri]	*(an sich:)* Gebäude mit Schlafräumen
	the traveller	[ðə 'trævlə]	der / die Reisende
	the comforts of life	[ðə 'kʌmfəts əv 'laif]	die Annehmlichkeiten des Lebens
	washing and toilet facilities	['wɔʃiŋ ən 'tɔilit fəsilətiz]	Waschgelegenheiten und Toiletten
	depend on something	[di'pend ɔn sʌmθiŋ]	von etwas abhängig sein
	camping ground	['kæmpiŋ graund]	Campingplatz
	butter	['bʌtə]	Butter
	supper	['sʌpə]	Abendessen; Abendbrot
	tinned ready-cooked dishes	['tind 'redi-'kukt diʃiz]	"Büchsen-Fertiggerichte"
	its low cost	[its 'ləu 'kɔst]	seine / ihre niedrigen Kosten
	get to remote places	[get tə ri'məut 'pleisiz]	an entlegene Orte gelangen
	have the means	[hæv ðə 'mi:nz]	die (Geld-)Mittel haben
	courage	['kʌridʒ]	Mut
	travel right across the Sahara	[trævl 'rait əkrɔs ðə sə'hɑ:rə]	quer durch die Sahara reisen
	from Tunis to Accra	[frəm 'tju:nis tu ə'krɑ:]	von Tunis nach Accra *(in Ghana)*
	for ... marks	[fə ... 'mɑ:ks]	für ... Mark
	including the flight	[in'klu:diŋ ðə 'flait]	einschließlich des Fluges
	Tunisia	[tju'niziə]	Tunesien
29E	how many can it accommodate?	['hau meni kən it ə'kɔmədeit]	wie viele kann es unterbringen?
	take a shower	['teik ə 'ʃauə]	duschen
	an additional meal	[ən ə'diʃnəl 'mi:l]	eine zusätzliche Mahlzeit
	tinned food	['tind 'fu:d]	Büchsennahrung; Konserven
	what do you personally think of this form of travel?	[wɔt də ju 'pə:snəli θiŋk əv ðis fɔ:m əv 'trævl]	was halten Sie persönlich von dieser Art des Reisens?
	would it appeal to you?	[wud it ə'pi:l tə ju]	würde es Ihnen zusagen?

29F

France [frɑ:ns] Frankreich **Greece** [gri:s] Griechenland **Italy** ['itəli] Italien	**Netherlands** ['neðələndz] Niederlande **Scandinavia** [skændi'neivjə] Skandinavien **Spain** [spein] Spanien	**Yugoslavia** [ju:gə'slɑ:viə] Jugoslawien

get along in a country	['get ə'lɔŋ in ə kʌntri]	in einem Land zurechtkommen
popularity	[pɔpju'læriti]	Beliebtheit; Popularität

speak – spoke – spoken	[spi:k – spəuk – 'spəukən]	sprechen – sprach – gesprochen
the twelve countries listed	[ðə 'twelv kʌntriz 'listid]	die zwölf aufgeführten Länder

29G

being in company [bi:iŋ in 'kʌmpəni] Geselligkeit
ball games ['bɔ:l geimz] Ballspiele
boating ['bəutiŋ] Bootfahren
cycling ['saikliŋ] Radfahren
dancing ['dɑ:nsiŋ] Tanzen
filming ['filmiŋ] Filmen
fishing ['fiʃiŋ] Angeln
flirting ['flə:tiŋ] Flirten
hiking ['haikiŋ] Wandern
mountain climbing ['mauntən klaimiŋ] Bergsteigen
riding ['raidiŋ] Reiten
sailing ['seiliŋ] Segeln
skiing ['ski:iŋ] Skifahren; Skilaufen
skin diving ['skin daiviŋ] (Sport-)Tauchen
walking ['wɔ:kiŋ] Spazierengehen
waterskiing ['wɔ:təski:iŋ] Wasserski(laufen)

engage in an activity	[in'geidʒ in ən æk'tiviti]	"sich einer Aktivität widmen"
a short winter holiday	[ə 'ʃɔ:t 'wintə hɔlədi]	ein kurzer Winterurlaub

Lektion 30

30A	a sleepless night	[ə 'sli:pləs 'nait]	eine schlaflose Nacht
	hot and tired	['hɔt ən 'taiəd]	erhitzt und müde
	destination	[desti'neiʃn]	Reiseziel
	too much sitting around	['tu: mʌtʃ 'sitiŋ ə'raund]	"zuviel Herumsitzen"
	too little exercise	['tu: litl 'eksəsaiz]	zu wenig (körperliche) Bewegung
	I was to spend the night	[ai wəz tə 'spend ðə 'nait]	ich sollte die Nacht verbringen
	a huge building	[ə 'hju:dʒ 'bildiŋ]	ein riesiges Gebäude
	the ultimate in luxury and convenience	[ði 'ʌltimət in 'lʌkʃəri ən kən'vi:njəns]	das Äußerste an Luxus und Bequemlichkeit
	prospectus	[prəs'pektəs]	Prospekt
	promise	['prɔmis]	versprechen; verheißen
	everything one can possibly want	['evriθiŋ wʌn kən 'pɔsəbli 'wɔnt]	alles, was man sich nur wünschen kann
	an up-to-the-minute hotel	[ən 'ʌp-tə-ðə-'minit həu'tel]	ein supermodernes Hotel
	the usual functional box	[ðə 'ju:ʒuəl 'fʌŋkʃənəl 'bɔks]	der übliche funktionale Kasten
	one large double blanket	['wʌn 'lɑ:dʒ 'dʌbl 'blæŋkit]	eine große Doppel(bett)decke
	tucked in on three sides	['tʌkt 'in ɔn 'θri: 'saidz]	auf drei Seiten eingesteckt
	a bedside table	[ə 'bedsaid 'teibl]	ein Nachttisch
	some chairs	[səm 'tʃɛəz]	einige Stühle / Sessel
	a folded cardboard sign	[ə 'fəuldid 'kɑ:dbɔ:d 'sain]	ein gefaltetes Pappschild
	who cares?	['hu: 'kɛəz]	wer kümmert sich darum?
	open a letter	['əupən ə 'letə]	einen Brief öffnen
	there followed one of those guest questionnaires	[ðə 'fɔləud wʌn əv ðəuz 'gest kwestʃə'nɛəz]	es folgte einer jener Gastfragebogen
	spotlessly clean	['spɔtləsli 'kli:n]	blitzsauber ("fleckenlos sauber")
	prompt service	['prɔmt 'sə:vis]	schnelle / prompte Bedienung
	and so on	[ən 'səu ɔn]	und so weiter
	the room was clean enough	[ðə 'rum wəz 'kli:n i'nʌf]	das Zimmer war durchaus sauber
	the trouble was	[ðə 'trʌbl wɔz]	das Problem war
	it had an unpleasant smell	[it hæd ən 'ʌn'pleznt 'smel]	es hatte einen unangenehmen Geruch
	the reason was obvious	[ðə 'ri:zn wəz 'ɔbviəs]	der Grund lag auf der Hand
	and there had been none for a long time	[ən ðər əd 'bi:n nʌn fər ə 'lɔŋ 'taim]	und da war lange keine gewesen
	the room was smelly	[ðə rum wəz 'smeli]	das Zimmer war muffig
	the window was sealed	[ðə 'windəu wəz 'si:ld]	d. Fenster war fest verschlossen
	I pressed a button	[ai 'prest ə 'bʌtn]	ich drückte (auf) einen Knopf
	I phoned the front desk	[ai 'fəund ðə 'frʌnt 'desk]	ich rief bei der Rezeption an
	a voice with a smile	[ə 'vɔis wið ə 'smail]	eine Stimme mit einem Lächeln
	can I have it opened?	[kæn ai hæv it 'əupənd]	läßt es sich öffnen?
	temperature	['temprətʃə]	Temperatur

	maximum comfort	['mæksiməm 'kʌmfət]	höchster Komfort
	I'm dying of heat	[aim 'daiiŋ əv 'hi:t]	ich sterbe vor Hitze
	the room stinks	[ðə 'rum 'stiŋks]	das Zimmer stinkt
	the smile was gone	[ðə 'smail wəz 'gɔn]	das Lächeln war verschwunden
	a fan to stir the air up a bit	[ə 'fæn tə 'stə: ði εər 'ʌp ə bit]	ein Ventilator, um die Luft ein bißchen in Bewegung zu bringen
	no requirement for fans	[nəu ri'kwaiəmənt fə 'fænz]	kein Bedarf an Ventilatoren
	the telephone clicked	[ðə 'telifəun 'klikt]	das Telefon klickte
	a vast hotel	[ə 'vɑ:st həu'tel]	ein riesiges Hotel
	an efficient hotel	[ən i'fiʃnt həu'tel]	ein leistungsfähiges Hotel
	computer-run	[kəm'pju:tə-rʌn]	computergesteuert, -gelenkt
	there was something missing	[ðə wəz 'sʌmθiŋ 'misiŋ]	es fehlte etwas
	perfectly organized	['pə:fiktli 'ɔ:gənaizd]	perfekt organisiert
30B	the writer	[ðə 'raitə]	der Verfasser / Autor
	come – came – come	[kʌm – keim – kʌm]	kommen – kam – gekommen
	was he looking forward to the meetings?	[wɔz i lukiŋ 'fɔ:wəd tə ðə 'mi:tiŋz]	freute er sich auf die Sitzungen / Verhandlungen?
30C	what purposes are they good for?	[wɔt 'pə:pəsiz ə ðei 'gud fɔ:]	für welche Zwecke sind sie gut / eignen sie sich?
	honeymoon	['hʌnimu:n]	Flitterwochen; Hochzeitsreise
30E	isn't she smart, darling?	[iznt ʃi 'smɑ:t 'dɑ:liŋ]	ist sie nicht clever, Liebling?
	she picks the things	[ʃi piks ðə θiŋz]	sie wählt die Sachen (aus)
30F	shorten the sentences	['ʃɔ:tn ðə 'sentənsiz]	verkürzen Sie die Sätze
30G	talk about yourself	['tɔ:k əbaut jɔ:'self]	sprechen Sie über sich selbst
	I served my apprenticeship	[ai 'sə:vd mai ə'prentisʃip]	ich war in der Lehre ("absolvierte meine Lehre / Lehrzeit")
	children aged . . .	['tʃildrən 'eidʒd]	Kinder im Alter von . . .
	hobby	['hɔbi]	Hobby; Steckenpferd
	Mildgyth	['mildgiθ]	*(weiblicher Vorname)*
	Gwendolen	['gwendəlin]	*(weiblicher Vorname)*
	Buccleuch	[bə'klu:]	*(Familienname)*

WORTSCHATZREGISTER

Die Zahlen und Buchstaben verweisen auf die Lektionsabschnitte, in denen ein Wort oder Ausdruck in einer bestimmten Bedeutung bzw. Anwendung zum erstenmal vorkommt.
Die "Hochleistungswörter" *about, at, by, do (does, doesn't, done, don't), for, from, get, in, of, on, to, up* wurden nicht in dieses Wortschatzregister aufgenommen, weil sie in sehr vielen Lektionen in immer neuen Bedeutungen und Anwendungen vorkommen. Für diese Wörter sei auf die zusammenfassenden Übersichten und Übungen des Arbeitsbuches verwiesen (→ Register des Arbeitsbuches).

Abkürzungen:
E = Eigenschaftswort (Adjektiv)
F = Fürwort (Pronomen)
H = Hauptwort (Substantiv)
P = Präposition
U = Umstandswort (Adverb)
V = Verb

GRAMMATIKREGISTER